I REMEMBER

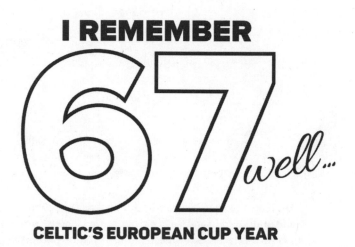

CELTIC'S EUROPEAN CUP YEAR

DAVID POTTER

First published by Pitch Publishing, 2016

Pitch Publishing
A2 Yeoman Gate
Yeoman Way
Worthing
Sussex
BN13 3QZ
www.pitchpublishing.co.uk

ISBN 978-1-78531-158-1

Typesetting and origination by
Printed by TJ International Ltd, Padstow, Cornwall

CONTENTS

JANUARY

• • • • • • •

As the bells tolled to usher in 1967, Celtic supporters were just a tad muted. The match at Dundee had seen the first reverse of the season when the team, at one point 2-1 up, had gone down 3-2 to Dundee United at Tannadice Park. It was generally agreed that Ronnie Simpson had had one of his less happy games, but it was also true that a defeat had been long overdue. Indeed it might have happened the previous week at Pittodrie in a disappointing 1-1 draw. A few weeks before that, on a hard pitch at Kilmarnock, the team had not looked too great either. So a defeat had been coming. But there was still such a lot to savour in 1966 and so much to look forward to in 1967. Shoulders were shrugged and folk said: "It won't do them any harm." A defeat can become a success very quickly – if one learns from it.

The Scottish League Cup and the Glasgow Cup were already on the sideboard. The Scottish League Cup Final at the end of October 1966 had been one long, tense occasion as Celtic, having scored through Bobby Lennox in the first half, held out against a desperate Rangers onslaught for the rest of the game. It was the day of Willie O'Neill's famous clearance off the line. Newspapers thought that Rangers had deserved at least a draw. Maybe, but Celtic were the winners, and the old order had changed. So often before, particularly in the calendar year of 1964, Celtic had been the better team, but Rangers had won. We were the masters now.

Progress had been made in Europe and we were now in the quarter-finals of the European Cup, following wins over Zurich and Nantes, the champions of Switzerland and France respectively. Liverpool, the champions of England, had blown up in Amsterdam and Celtic were now getting some reluctant (but no less sincere) praise from down south. Joe McBride had injured himself the previous week at Pittodrie, but Celtic had already strengthened their squad by signing Willie Wallace from Hearts and he had already shown signs of fitting in very well with Stein's attacking philosophy, alongside Steve Chalmers, Jimmy Johnstone, Bobby Lennox and others, with Bertie Auld and Bobby Murdoch orchestrating things in the midfield.

The atmosphere at Parkhead remained upbeat and positive, with optimistic messages flooding out in the weekly *The Celtic View.* The future seemed to offer a great deal. Indeed in comparison to where the team had been two years earlier, it was barely believable. There was even talk that Celtic could win that European Cup, something that no British team had done previously. Such talk had been confined for a spell to drunken men in pubs a few minutes before "chucking out" time on a Saturday night (rigidly 10pm in Scotland in 1966), but lately, more respectable sources, like Sam Leitch of *The Sunday Mirror,* had uttered similar sentiments.

But there was even more to it than that. For the first time since the days of Willie Maley in his prime before the First World War, Celtic were the first team talked about when football was mentioned. Briefly, the Empire Exhibition Trophy team of 1938 had enjoyed this status, but they did not last long at the top. Jock Stein had now shown not the least of his many talents by manipulating the media. Rangers were also doing reasonably well – they were still in Europe as well as maintaining a challenge in the league championship – but their exploits invariably came second even in newspapers like *The Scottish Daily Express,* which had hitherto been unashamedly pro-Rangers.

Events on the east side of the city were now far more interesting and thrilling. Rangers fans were quieter, more cowed and less confident as more and more people in the swinging sixties, with its emphasis on freedom and tolerance, were beginning to ask embarrassing questions about the perceived lack of Roman Catholics at Ibrox. The Scottish press, which had hitherto been quite happy to pretend that no religious discrimination existed at Ibrox, now began to give the problem a reluctant acknowledgement, with even a comparison made with apartheid in South Africa.

In short, Celtic had captured the moral high ground. They were now the leading team in Scotland. Even the Hogmanay defeat at Tannadice, which was the main talking point at New Year first footing parties, showed how far Celtic had come as the team was dissected, analysed and examined in an effort to find out what had gone wrong. Ronnie Simpson had had one of his rare poor games, Jim Craig would need to be brought back and we should have scored more in the first half. All these things were worked into the conversations, whisky in hand, so far had Celtic progressed. A few years ago, we had dreaded the New Year with a likely beating by Rangers.

There was little doubt that, in Jock Stein, Celtic had a mastermind at the helm. The signing of Willie Wallace in December was little short of brilliant. Wallace, a talented player for Hearts, was clearly becoming frustrated with their lack of success and their apparent lack of ambition. Their devastating loss of the Scottish League to Kilmarnock 18 months earlier, by serendipity the very same day that Celtic won the Scottish Cup of 1965, would affect them for decades. Yet Wallace was a great player and a prolific goalscorer, with one standout game for Hearts against Celtic at Tynecastle in January 1966 making Celtic sit up and take notice. Celtic had, more than once, expressed interest in Wallace, but so too had Rangers.

Stein was aware that Rangers might yet come in for Wallace. Their interest had to be taken seriously for Wallace was of a non-Catholic background. Had he been a Catholic, Stein could have bided his time, knowing that the player would come to Celtic anyway for Rangers would never have touched him. But in the case of Wallace, there was genuine competition. Having issued a few smokescreens about some bogus interest in another player, Stein waited until Rangers were in Germany in the early days of December, distracted on European business, before making his move. Rangers returned from Germany to discover that Wallace was a Celtic player. Stein also got the considerable additional benefit of being able to knock Rangers off the back pages yet again, his capturing of Willie Wallace even upstaging Rangers' impressive defeat of Borussia Dortmund.

It was also astonishingly perspicacious. Stein could not possibly have known just how bad Joe McBride's injury would be on Christmas Eve at Pittodrie, but he did know that there was some sort of problem with Joe's knee and that it might, sooner or later, become an issue. Celtic would thus be deprived of their star goalscorer. There were those who might have queried the necessity to buy another forward when McBride was Scotland's leading goalscorer (and he would stay that way, incidentally, all season, although he never kicked a ball after Hogmanay), but Jock, as always, knew best.

Stein had turned 44 in September. He was therefore at the height of his powers. He combined football knowledge, man-management and a magisterial air of dominating all conversation while knowing exactly what he was talking about. He was also passionate about the game and the club that, as he frequently said himself, were by no means his first love but were certainly his greatest and longest lasting. He loved the fans, and he loved communicating with them, never being afraid to travel to supporters' functions nor to talk to the people whom he recognised as the lifeblood of the game. "Football without fans is nothing," Stein once said. Bertie Auld frequently told how Jock would open the dressing room window just a little so that the players could see and hear the fans outside.

Slowly, Stein's campaign against hooliganism began to have an effect. Supporters occasionally let themselves down, but such occurrences were becoming less common. To a certain extent, it was because it was easier to support a winning team, but it was also because of Stein's constant appeals in *The Celtic View,* whether written by himself or ghosted by John McPhail or someone else. He made Celtic fans feel pride in their team, and if you are proud of your team and indeed yourself, there is no reason to act like a thug.

Football in Scotland was actually doing well, by some distance the most common topic of conversation in pub, workplace and school playground, clearly outstripping horse racing and sex.

England winning the World Cup the previous summer was, however, sitting uneasily on Scottish shoulders, particularly as Scotland felt that, potentially at least, they could do better than their arch-rivals. But Scotland had failed to qualify – a blow to the prestige of Jock Stein, who had been given temporary control of the team – and the nation had been obliged to watch the success of their neighbours.

Scotland had beaten England three years in a row, in 1962, 1963 and 1964, drawn in 1965 and lost very narrowly, 3-4, at Hampden in April 1966. They were not far behind, it was felt, but England were not going to let anyone forget for a very long time that they had won the World Cup. Domestic football in England was also going through a boom, although every successful English team did have a fair smattering of Scottish players and indeed the bigger teams tended to have Scottish managers like Matt Busby, Bill Shankly and Tommy Docherty.

The domestic game in Scotland was also on the up. There was, of course, the perpetual Glasgow tension, with the pendulum now showing unmistakable signs of turning green and white, but there were other strong teams as well. The third force in Scotland at the time were Dunfermline Athletic, a team which had, of course, been built by Jock Stein in 1961 and, under Willie Cunningham, carried on the tradition. They perhaps lacked flair, but were determinedly and ruthlessly efficient, with a defence which showed a distinct reluctance to take any prisoners.

Kilmarnock, the league winners of 1965, were a team of similar character to Dunfermline. For a provincial team, they punched consistently above their weight, and would seldom give in without a fight. When managed by Willie Waddell, they were not always liked by Celtic supporters for their robust approach – with one particular game in August 1964 springing to mind – but now that ex-Celt Malky MacDonald had returned to manage them, they played football that was at least as successful, although not necessarily any more attractive, and they would have a good run in Europe this year.

The city of Dundee, with its two clubs in such close proximity, was an enigma. Dundee were capable of good performances – and it was the opinion of Bob Crampsey that Dundee's league-winning team of 1962 was the best team for sheer football that Scotland ever produced – but their directors had the fatal and self-destructive tendency to sell their best players for short-term gain at a time when they did not really have to do so. Ian Ure, Alan Gilzean and, this year, Charlie Cooke had all gone south with fatal long-term consequences for the Dens Park side. Dundee would still have their occasional good performances, but the club's transfer policy consistently disappointed fans, who began to stay away.

Their neighbours, Hogmanay's winners over Celtic, Dundee United, were more of a force to be reckoned with. They were the *parvenus*, the *nouveaux riches*, the *arrivistes* of Scottish football. They had only been promoted in 1960, thereby unleashing the power of a large but dormant support to achieve respectability in Scottish football. It was, of course, no accident that their rise coincided with a time when Celtic were in comparative decline. In the 1950s and previously, the massive Irish population of Dundee had uncompromisingly supported Celtic, and indeed the city of Dundee had generally been looked upon as a Celtic-supporting area. But with the rise from obscurity of Dundee United (of undeniable Irish origins and who had, until 1923, been called the Dundee Hibs), the Dundee Irish now had a strong local team to identify with.

Wisely managed by Jerry Kerr and prudently stewarded by an enthusiastic board of directors who had been shrewd enough to run their own lottery, called Taypools, long before anyone else realised the money-making potential of such things, Dundee United consolidated their position, on one occasion in 1962 beating Rangers at Ibrox to help their neighbours Dundee win the league a month later. In recent years, they had invested in Scandinavia, bringing players like Finn Dossing, Mogens Berg, Lennart Wing and Orjan Persson to Tannadice. Always a difficult team to beat at home, their away form was less impressive but they were clearly here to stay. And, of course, on the last day of 1966, they had beaten Celtic.

A revival was at last forthcoming from Aberdeen, now that the grimly determined Eddie Turnbull was in charge. A good team in the mid-1950s, the Dons had subsequently slipped badly because of what some saw as complacent and unambitious management, and they had been more often in the bottom half of the league than the top. As if that were not bad enough, they had (rare in the developed world) suffered an outbreak of typhoid in 1964. Never an obsessive footballing city in the sense that Glasgow was, Aberdeen, a city which now had its own TV station, the enthusiastic but somewhat amateurish Grampian TV, had lost interest in football until the arrival of Turnbull. But there were clear signs now that the fishermen and farmers of the fertile North East were beginning to return. The game on Christmas Eve – a disappointing 1-1 draw with Celtic – had seen a huge crowd.

Edinburgh's moment seemed to have passed, at least temporarily. Hearts' failure to win the league in April 1965 had left supporters bitter and disappointed, and Hibs, whose brief spell when Jock Stein was manager in 1964/65 had raised temporary hopes of a return to the glories of the Famous Five of the early 1950s, had failed to build on what Stein had done. Hibs, like Hearts, were certainly capable of hurting the Glasgow teams, but did not seem capable of winning anything themselves.

It would be nice to record that, in 1967, the nation of Scotland, in general terms, was at the crossroads of something dramatic. Most writers do say this sort of thing, but in fact this was not the case. Scotland was on a slow upward climb to prosperity. Everyone complained about their standard of living – everyone always does – but in fact things that had been slowly improving during the previous 15 years were continuing to get better. University education for those from a working-class background, like myself, was hardly the norm. On the other hand, it was now far from unusual. It was gentle and genteel progress under the benign, albeit scarcely charismatic guidance of Labour Prime Minister Harold Wilson.

Slowly, perhaps painfully slowly, the Glasgow slums, many of which were not all that far from Celtic Park, were starting to be demolished. These monstrous remains of the Industrial Revolution should, of course, have been removed many decades earlier – and it is to the eternal shame of the Labour Party in Glasgow that this did not happen a lot sooner. But now, at last, men like Sam Allison were beginning to knock down these breeding grounds of disease and filth. It would take a long time to happen, and in some cases the replacements were not a great deal better, but at least everyone now had some sort of living space, and, glory of glories, an indoor toilet! Amazingly in 1967, there were still a few houses without such a luxury or even running water. But change was happening.

Politically, Scotland stayed Labour. The Scottish National Party was now beginning to make itself heard, although still in its infancy, and Glasgow in particular returned Labour MPs by the barrow load, and with majorities that needed to be weighed rather than counted – unless, of course, you lived in the north-west of the city and read *The Glasgow Herald*. Most of Scotland read the Dundee-based *Sunday Post*. It was as good as any for the football, it was couthy and undeniably Scottish, and contained, of course, The Broons and Oor Wullie. Where it failed and failed totally, however, was in its politics. It tried to persuade people to vote Conservative. Its failure was astonishing in its scale.

We were, of course, in the middle of the "swinging sixties". We baby boomers (those born immediately after the war when the soldiers returned) were now in our 20s or getting close to it. The National Health Service had guaranteed our survival, and there was now in place a generation that was not going to do what it was told. It was a well-educated generation as well – Scottish education was at its best in the late 1950s and early 1960s – and questions now began to be asked about why some people had more money than others, about why black people in South Africa and the United States were looked upon as second-class citizens, and closer to home, about why no Roman Catholics ever seemed to play for Rangers.

The new generation seemed to be symbolised with its music. Although at New Year in particular, Andy Stewart and others fought a gallant rearguard action to protect traditional Scottish music, music had gone, for the past ten years, "pop". You could call it rock 'n' roll, you could call it what you wanted, but it was noisy, here to stay and subversive. Men started wearing their hair longer, something that shocked the older people, who would raise their hands in horror and moan – until someone would point out that men like Jesus Christ and Robert Burns actually had long hair, as well as the four men from Liverpool called The Beatles, who were changing the world. "Aye, but the good Lord and the national bard kept their hair tidy" was the reply.

The churches, both Church of Scotland and Roman Catholic, began to lose members. Reasons were hard to analyse, but to a certain extent at least, it was a rebellion by the young. Churches usually, of course, have a dismal propensity to side with the rich against the poor, however much there may be some patronising regard for the "little black boys and girls" in vaguely distant lands. The Christian message had, for centuries, deliberately eschewed and ignored texts like "it is easier for a camel to pass through the eye of a needle than it is for a rich man to enter the Kingdom of Heaven", and although Jesus did a certain amount to provide loaves and fishes for the needy, nevertheless, according to the church, he seemed to expect his followers to do what they were told by the bourgeoisie, and in particular to stay away from such people as wanted governments to ban the bomb and feed people instead.

There was also the matter of sex. In recent years, there had appeared something called "the pill", which women could take, allowing them to have as much sex as they wanted without being trapped by pregnancy. The Roman Catholic Church immediately saw the obvious threat to their membership if this happened, and the Church of Scotland became even more worried in that it raised the uncomfortable spectre of their members having fun and enjoying themselves!

Religion in Glasgow, of course, often meant nothing other than the dismal sectarianism that befouled the city. Yet even that was being attacked, not least because Celtic's manager was a non-Catholic and was bringing obvious success. But there were also plays beginning to appear on television, satirising such divisions, particularly on the theme of a young girl bringing home an eligible and charming young man. Everything went well over the tea table. The fellow was good looking, had a job with prospects, his parents seemed to be decent people, a wedding the following June was being hinted at – until he mentioned the school that he had gone to, something that in the west of Scotland automatically "gave away" his religion. Immediately we got tears, tantrums and: "How could she do this to us? We brought her up right, then she wants to marry one of *them!*"

And where was your humble servant in the middle of all this? I was a first-year student doing Latin, Greek and Ancient History at St Andrews University in Fife. Bright enough to cope with anything they could throw at me academically, but totally overwhelmed and outgunned by the raucous English and American voices that assailed one's ears constantly, I struggled. Now, of course, experience of life will tell one that empty vessels do indeed make the most noise and that the loud voices concealed the same sort of anxieties that I suffered from, but I was only 18. I came from a good working-class background. My mother was couthy, canny, frugal and even a little parsimonious, whereas my father, a World War II veteran who now worked in a jute factory and talked constantly about Jimmy McGrory and Patsy Gallacher, was more prone to the romantic approach to life. His almost perpetual good humour often concealed the desire to be a rebel, but he was an armchair rebel.

I had been always well looked after and, as an only child and a late child, much loved and doted upon. I was also unashamedly parochial from the small town of Forfar. I was thus, when I went to St Andrews University, rather sheltered from some things, notably people who actually did say things like "yah!" and "sooper" and talked about "daddy's yacht" without apparently having me on. In later years, taking the advice of Robert Burns, I would be able to "look and laugh at a' that", and on one occasion I got a piece of bitter revenge over the jet-set. It was after my father got a job as an oiler of factory equipment and I was able to say with a straight face "Oh, daddy dabbles in oil!" In your first year, totally naïve, disorientated and homesick, it was terrifying, intimidating and isolating. But in the same way as Maoist Chinese said that one could always be "protected by the thoughts of Chairman Mao" and his little red book of utterances, I felt that I had the thoughts of chairman Jock in *The Celtic View* every Wednesday to protect me.

In the case of the Americans, there was a certain affinity which could eventually be reached once you broke down the barriers of how rich America was, the almost inevitable tears late at night when discussing the break-up of "momma" and "papa's" marriage in unhappy circumstances some time previously and the patronising descriptions of Scotland being "quaint" and "cute". The reason why so many Americans were here in Scotland was because it was one way of avoiding Vietnam. It is often said that there is no criticism by foreigners of America that is not also made in America itself, and this was true here. "Hey, hey LBJ, how many kids did you kill today?" was chanted as loudly by Americans as it was by Scottish students, with the added dimension, of course, that the American students after their year in St Andrews might well be invited to join the conflict, whereas we, under the Labour government of the admirable Harold Wilson, were free from that.

Americans, as a rule, did not follow football, or soccer as they called it. Those whose families were of Irish or Scottish origin tended to sympathise with Celtic, however, and I recall one night persuading one American on an exchange year from the College of William and Mary in Virginia to try to get the name changed. The English, however, were a totally different matter.

Words and phrases like "uppity" and "in your face" did not quite cover it. You see, they had, as they kept telling us, won the World Cup in summer 1966. It was painful for us, and I recall telling a German student shortly after my arrival in St Andrews that I had thought that England were lucky to beat Germany. His look was one of puzzlement and even hurt before I added that I was talking about the World Cup Final rather than events of 20 years before that. He immediately laughed and joined in the condemnation of the Soviet linesman and the ball that was never over the line. "Und why did they get to play all zeir games at Vembley?" he shouted with the same sort of passion and venom that his father talked about the Treaty of Versailles.

The English students, of whom there were a great number, of all social classes, were, when football was mentioned, quite unbearable. Yet I soon discovered that they were by no means monolithic. The north-south divide was quite pronounced and Arsenal supporters hated Liverpool, while Manchester United were almost universally despised. But they did not hate Scotland with anything like the venom that Scots hated England. In such circumstances, a certain admiration began to grow for Celtic, particularly after the demise of Liverpool from Europe, and the feeling was even expressed that it would be nice to see a Scottish team win the European Cup.

Rangers supporters struggled at St Andrews University. Although the town of St Andrews has a dismal tradition of religious intolerance, with chaps getting burned for their faith and bishops getting murdered and thrown out of windows for reasons that were hard to understand, nevertheless, by 1966, the stress was very much on racial and religious acceptance. The abolition of apartheid in South Africa was looked upon as a necessity (apart from one or two people of entrenched views in the Conservative Society) and in that climate, it was difficult to defend Rangers' religious policy. Indeed I can honestly say that in the same way I never encountered a single American who defended his country's policy in Vietnam, I similarly never met a single Rangers supporter who uncompromisingly defended the Struth and Lawrence policy of religious discrimination.

And girls? The necessity to get oneself a woman is a basic, biological and social one. Yet it was not easy. Churches were united in telling you "hands off", yet advice was forthcoming from students' organisations and enlightened doctors and nurses about how to set about it. For me, there was a particular problem. Intimidated, as I say, by the raucous voices of know-it-all people, and from my limited background with little general conversation except how Celtic were doing, conversation and chatting up were difficult. Yet there was a girl who entered my life, from the north of England, who had spent most of her life in Fife and had a soft spot for Dunfermline Athletic. But two or three weeks of involvement frankly scared me, and I drifted away from her, mainly in the direction of the real and constant love of my life – those who wore the green and white jerseys. I have often regretted this abandonment of that little girl, with so many parallels to the way in which Aeneas abandoned Dido in Virgil's *Aeneid*, and maybe I should have made more of a go of it.

Such was the state of my life when the bells tolled to bring in 1967. The rest of the world was OK. I had loads of friends with whom I had grown up. They supported various teams and discussion was often animated but basically good-natured. My parents were in good health, proud of their son who had now survived his first difficult term and, in the case of my father, the constant hope that "Jock might do it this year". Everyone moaned about the Labour government, but in fact they were far better off than they had ever been. A few people (some who should have known a great deal better) listened to the baleful talk of Enoch Powell – who wanted to repatriate black people to wherever they came from – but you could easily subject them to ridicule and, generally speaking, life was good.

New Year's Day 1967 was a Sunday. A frost came down on New Year's night and effectively knocked out three Celtic games. The January 2 game against Clyde at

Parkhead was off, as indeed was an attempt to play it again on Wednesday, January 4, but the big disappointment was the postponement of the game at Ibrox on January 3, particularly as the weather was nice, crisp and bright and many fans had arrived in Glasgow in full expectation of the game being on. Other games were played at places like Kilmarnock and St Johnstone that day, but significantly perhaps, there was no great protest from either Rangers or Celtic over Mr Syme's decision at Ibrox. I had travelled to Glasgow by car with some friends, and on the way back saw the second half of St Johnstone v Aberdeen, a surprise win for the Saints.

Celtic felt that the trip to Ibrox would have been a good day to bounce back from their Tannadice disappointment and to emphasise the superiority that had already been shown in three Old Firm games this season already in the Glasgow Cup, the league game at Parkhead and the League Cup Final. But possibly there was a silver lining as well to the postponement in that it gave players an extra few days to recover from knocks inevitably sustained at this time of year. The players had been told to meet at Celtic Park at 11am prior to travelling to Ibrox. On hearing that the game was off, Stein immediately organised a practice game and made sure that cameras were there as well. He was never one to miss a propaganda opportunity.

The first game of the momentous year of 1967 therefore was the visit of Dundee to Celtic Park on January 7. That the game was on at all said a great deal for the determination and commitment of the Celtic backroom staff. Rangers' game at Pittodrie was off, so Celtic knew that a win would give them an advantage. The pitch was playable but tricky, but 37,000 saw Celtic off to a good start in 1967 with a 5-1 win, with two goals from Willie Wallace, and one each from Bobby Murdoch, Jimmy Johnstone and Charlie Gallagher. But the most significant change was the return of Jim Craig and the playing of Tommy Gemmell on his more natural side on the left of the park.

Charlie Gallagher's goal was a particularly good one, and *The Celtic View* carried a story of how Jock Stein broke the news to Bertie Auld that Charlie was to take his place. Bertie's reply was a surprising one, namely that he thought that Charlie was better on the hard ground. Bertie may have had tongue in cheek, or maybe was secretly glad not to play on hard pitches, but it allowed Stein to state that "that is typical of the team spirit that leads to success".

If things were booming at one Glasgow club, the same could hardly be said at another, for the impoverished Third Lanark had major unrest among their players. The poor chaps could not get a hot shower after one of their games, and had to make do with cold water. This seemed to have something to do with Thirds' inability to pay their bills, and the writing was now on the wall with ever more clarity for the Cathkin side. They would not see the year out.

The weather eased to become a little milder in midweek and Celtic, with commendable speed, arranged their game against Clyde for Wednesday, January 11 at Celtic Park. *The Evening Times* used the word "dazzling" to describe Celtic's 5-1 win and went into overdrive to talk about one of the goals, scored by Tommy Gemmell. The paper described it as "one of the finest goals notched at Celtic Park" – an ambitious claim when one recalls Sandy McMahon, Jimmy Quinn and Jimmy McGrory – after he met a ball in mid-air with his right foot and "bulleted home" from 30 yards. Once again, the crowd was large and appreciative – over

38,000 for a Wednesday night – and they positively erupted at such brilliance. They departed joyously into that cold January night singing their anthem "We Shall Not Be Moved" and also a new song from an American group called The Monkees, which ran

"I thought love was only found in fairytales,
All right for someone else but not for me.
But love was out to get me, that's the way it seemed.
Disappointment haunted all my dreams.
And then I saw her face. Now I'm a believer…"

There were indeed many people who believed that there was something special going on at Celtic Park.

Charlie Gallagher played superbly that night, but his absence for the following game, though not noticed or commented on at the time, was nevertheless hugely significant in the history of the club. It was the first time that Simpson, Craig and Gemmell; Murdoch, McNeill and Clark; Johnstone, Wallace, Chalmers, Auld and Lennox – the future Lisbon Lions – played together as a team. It was a decision taken by Jock Stein once he tested the Muirton Park pitch, feeling perhaps that the slightly softer nature of the pitch might not suit the silky play of Charlie as much as it would do the slightly more gritty approach of Bertie Auld.

Unaware of the significance of all this, over 21,000 made their way to Muirton Park, Perth to see Celtic take on St Johnstone. It was also one of the very few times that TV cameras had ever been at Muirton to record highlights for the evening's programme. St Johnstone were a team who had given Celtic a great deal of trouble in the recent past – in 1964/65, for example, they had beaten Celtic both home and away – and on this mild January afternoon, such were the crowds outside the small provincial ground (sadly no longer with us – a supermarket now, since the move to McDiarmid Park in 1989) that the kick-off had to be delayed by ten minutes. Even at that, the first half was well advanced before most of the stragglers made their way inside the ground.

They saw a tense first half, with the Perth men, whose cup final this was, giving as good as they got – as they always did when Celtic arrived. On at least two occasions, Ronnie Simpson was called into action before half-time, once seeming to stave his hand. At the other end, the St Johnstone defence, well marshalled by Benny Rooney (son of the Celtic trainer Bob), was holding out, although the pairing of Bobby Murdoch and Jimmy Johnstone, on more than one occasion, gave them a little bother.

We were well into the second half before a piece of brilliance by Jimmy Johnstone put Celtic ahead. Having done it once, Jimmy then did it again, and late in the game Chalmers and Lennox finished the job to give Celtic a 4-0 scoreline, which was perhaps a little hard on the industrious and by no means talentless Saints. Bobby Murdoch would always say that, apart from Rangers, the side that gave Celtic the most trouble in the Stein era was St Johnstone. The fact the goals were scored late in the game – a frequent occurrence in 1967 – said a great deal about Celtic's training methods under Neil Mochan.

What gave Bob Kelly and Jock Stein as much satisfaction as anything was a letter received from Bobby Brown, the manager of St Johnstone. Bobby Brown had been Rangers' goalkeeper in the late 40s and early 50s and had been anything other than the Hun that Celtic supporters loved to hate. Indeed he had been famous for his gentlemanly demeanour and sporting behaviour, occasionally even being known to apologise to ball boys behind his goal when Sammy Cox and Willie Woodburn used foul language. Here, he went out of his way to praise Celtic and their fans for their good-natured support. When one recalled several previous horrific displays of Celtic hooliganism in the past at Perth – one particularly awful Wednesday night in August 1961 came to mind – we realised just how far Celtic had progressed.

The following midweek saw Stein busy giving interviews and keeping the pot boiling as much as he could for the tests to come. The European Cup quarter-final draw had been made and dates for Vojvodina Novi Sad (Wednesdays March 1 and 8) had been arranged, and Celtic had also arranged to play a friendly against similar opposition on February 7, when Dinamo Zagreb were coming to Parkhead. Much was the talk about a new formation that Celtic were going to deploy that night – possibly an attempt to get a large crowd to see a friendly – but the real purpose, he said, was to see how Yugoslav football was played and to find out more about Vojvodina Novi Sad.

The game against Hibs at Parkhead on Saturday, January 21 was in doubt because of the heavy rain that had fallen. That did not, however, deter 41,000 fans from turning up at Celtic Park to see another superb Celtic performance. The heavy conditions persuaded Stein that John Hughes should get the nod over Bobby Lennox, for Hughes had the reputation of being one of the best "bad weather" players in the business, such was his strength and determination to charge through the mud, whereas the slightly more fragile Lennox preferred dry conditions.

The team won comfortably 2-0 and the game was characterised by a brilliant Willie Wallace goal, showing that Celtic had been right to go for him the previous December. It was in the 13th minute when he picked up a pass from John Clark, beat a man, sidestepped a crunching tackle from another and then crashed home from outside the box with a shot that beat the goalkeeper and at least three other defenders. Parkhead simply erupted at such brilliance. Little wonder that the Celtic fans had a banner which said simply "Oor Wullie", after the famous *Sunday Post* character. The second goal was a little more fortuitous. A Jimmy Johnstone corner kick found the head of Bertie Auld, who steered the ball for goal – and it was speeding there when the ball hit Steve Chalmers on the head and was diverted into the net. But a goal is a goal, and this one, along with that of Willie Wallace, was enough to beat a determined Hibs side. This was just before half-time and although Celtic pressed, there was no further scoring. Elsewhere, Rangers edged home against Falkirk and the league table stayed the same, with Celtic five points ahead of Rangers, although Rangers had a game in hand. (Only two points for a win in 1967).

Meanwhile, Celtic and Stein retained the diplomatic initiative with a very crafty piece of thinking. The New Year fixture between Rangers and Celtic still had to be played. It was generally agreed in 1967 that, if possible, playing Old Firm games in the dark nights of January and February was a bad idea given the hooligan problem and the necessity for tight policing. This was probably nonsense. Behaviour at evening games is usually a great deal better, for there is less opportunity to get tanked up on alcohol. But "darkened terracing" was a fine bargaining counter, as we will see.

Celtic now suggested the Monday Spring Holiday of March 27. On the surface, this seemed a great idea. There was a long tradition of playing football matches on that day, the daylight would be better, the game could even kick off in the afternoon and a big crowd could be guaranteed. It seemed ideal. But Celtic offered this date, knowing that Rangers would refuse. For one thing, Rangers would be heavily involved in Europe, playing Real Zaragoza the previous Wednesday, and they also had Hibs on the Saturday. But Celtic also knew, although they pretended that they didn't, that John Greig, the captain of Rangers, was due to be married that day.

Thus Celtic offered that date, knowing what the reply would be. Rangers would thus give the impression that they were putting off the evil hour when they had to play Celtic. They would be accused of cowardice, and as it happened, the game eventually had to be played after the official end of the season. Rangers, of course, might have suggested another date, but failed to do so at this point (they would eventually offer something but in less happy circumstances, and thus lost a certain credibility in the eyes of their supporters).

To what extent this psychological battle affected them in the run-up to the Scottish Cup games, we can never be sure, but there can be little doubt that the events of Saturday, January 28 rocked Scottish football in a way that had never happened before. This day is still talked about in hushed or gleeful tones, depending on what side of the divide one lives. The East Coast Line from Aberdeen to London travels through Berwick. Shielfield Park is just visible from the train. People have still been known to stand up for a quick glimpse of where it all happened.

The midweek before this day was abnormally quiet. Indeed it would have been a fine week for the Old Firm game had it not been for the spurious fear of "darkened terracings". Newspapers showed pictures of Celtic players playing golf at Seamill ahead of the visit of Arbroath to Parkhead in the Scottish Cup and told how Jock Wallace, the goalkeeper and player-manager of Berwick Rangers, was going to take his men to the cinema the night before the game against Glasgow Rangers on Saturday. Rangers were worried about the injury sustained by Ron McKinnon, but hoped to have him fit for the game.

The town of Berwick is technically in England, but in football terms Berwick Rangers are very much part of the Scottish League, even though a few years previously the "Ibrox gangsters" (as the Celtic fanzine *The Shamrock* put it) had tried to remove them and a few others from the league. Berwick made a special effort to be nice to their visitors, who had shamelessly wrecked the place on their last visit in 1960. There would, for example, be a special programme and the lucky number would be a trip to Zaragoza to see Rangers in the Cup Winners' Cup in March. The Rangers team were going to stay in Dunbar (where the Hannoverian general Sir John Cope had also stayed the night before his disaster at Prestonpans in 1745), and the town of Berwick, although hoping to do a good trade before the 2.45pm kick-off, made a wise decision not to allow the opening of pubs at 5pm. In England, pubs normally did not open until 6pm, by which time the undesirables would be heading north.

All this stuff was in the press, who were clearly looking for something to get excited about. Celtic v Arbroath, Berwick v Rangers were generally not good newspaper copy. The previous year, Rangers had been drawn at Ross County, then a poor Highland League team, and similar campaigns had been deployed to whip up interest. Generally speaking, cup "giant-killing" did not really happen in Scotland very often, in direct contrast to what happened in England. Dundee had blown up in Fraserburgh in 1959, but that was the only time that anyone could remember any great humbling of the mighty.

Celtic at home to Arbroath was even more difficult to write about. Arbroath, where Glaswegians still went for their holidays, were by nature a Second Division team. They had been in the First Division once or twice, but the top of the Second Division was their natural habitat. Celtic had a few injuries – Jimmy Johnstone, Bobby Lennox and Joe McBride – but that was hardly a problem in the projected beating of Arbroath. By the morning of the game, Ronnie McKinnon of Rangers had recovered. In fact, there were many exciting ties on that day – Dundee v Aberdeen, Kilmarnock v Dunfermline, Hearts v Dundee United, Morton v Clyde, Motherwell v East Fife, but that night, there was only one game that was talked about as *The Evening Times, The Evening Citizen, The Edinburgh Evening News* and *The Sporting Post* all sold copies far in excess of what they would have expected. The Sunday papers even ordered extra print runs.

The day was very mild for late January. There were even a few moments of sunshine, although mainly cloud cover was the order of the day. A crowd of about 40,000 appeared at Celtic Park, quite clearly the largest crowd that Arbroath had played before for some time, and they were rewarded with some good football played by Celtic. Indeed until they tired in the second half, the men from Angus (Scottish Cup record holders for their 36-0 defeat of Aberdeen Bon Accord in 1885) were by no means disgraced. They were given a generous reception as they appeared, something that was appreciated by the team, which contained quite a few Celtic supporters.

Murdoch, Gemmell and Chalmers all scored good goals before half-time on a soft pitch, and half-time was spent in the thought of more to come. Someone even said that Berwick were 1-0 up on Rangers at half-time (they had kicked off a quarter of an hour before Celtic), but we knew that that couldn't be true. For one thing, how would we know? The Scottish Home Service on the radio was traditionally poor, with one grudging game broadcast at 4.10pm, although the English BBC did make some sort of effort to give score flashes. The Parkhead tannoy system, notoriously slow and inefficient, did seem to say something about Berwick, though, and it was greeted with a loud cheer.

But there was the Parkhead half-time scoreboard. If you bought a programme, it gave you a letter for each game, and the letter would appear on the scoreboard with the half-time score beside it. You didn't really need to buy a programme in fact, for a knowledge of the alphabet would give you an indication of the game you were looking for. Alphabetically that day, Berwick came first (Aberdeen, Airdrie and Ayr were not playing at home) and the score did undeniably read 1-0. The trouble was that the scoreboard operators often got it wrong, and were, as far as Rangers were concerned, not above "having us on" now and again. Sometimes they made it 5-0 or 0-5 just for a laugh. So, "aye, aye", we all said, and treated the affair with a certain amount of scepticism. In any case, even if it were true, Rangers would equalise and then win in the second half.

The second half began at Parkhead. Charlie Gallagher headed the ball over the bar, but it didn't really matter as

Celtic were so far ahead. The Parkhead crowd began to get a little bored and, as often happens in such circumstances, began to cheer on the good play of Arbroath, particularly those players who had said in the newspapers earlier in the week that they were Celtic supporters. The game was fizzling out a little, although the angry figure of Stein was seen gesticulating and demanding more effort.

But then, with only about a quarter of the game left, there seemed to be some disturbance in the Main Stand, all centring around a man with a transistor radio (by no means as common in 1967 as they would become in later years). Even the police, fearing some disorder or indeed that some luckless spectator had taken ill, looked up, but then arms began to be waved, the air began to be punched, people jumped up and down, promiscuous hugs were given to whoever was sitting or standing near you.

Tommy Gemmell suddenly looked pleased with himself and told the players, even the Arbroath ones. Some were stunned, others smiled while Billy McNeill, ultra-professional as always, was seen to be calming everyone while Jock Stein looked even angrier. The news spread all round Celtic Park, along the Rangers End, through the Jungle but even before it reached the Celtic End, everyone guessed what it was all about. "The Huns are f***ed" was the cry, and very soon "The Huns are out of the cup, The Huns are out of the cup, High oh, my daddie oh, the Huns are out of the cup" was sung with gusto round the ground. Bertie Auld's fourth goal a few minutes later was greeted with an almighty cheer, and the game finished with everyone ecstatic, singing, dancing and hugging with even the more douce denizens of the stand smiling and shaking hands with each other.

But was it all true? Cruel deceptions had been practised before – in fact it had been common practice at every Celtic game in the past for someone to start a rumour about the defeat of Rangers, and as there is no limit to what people will believe if they want to believe it, it would always gain credence – but this time, everyone seemed to be convinced it was true. Yet we were still aware of Joseph Goebbels, who had said the bigger the lie, the more people are likely to believe it, and that it was far easier to kid on a crowd than it was an individual. It was only when we reached a chip shop, now long demolished in London Road, which had a television on the wall, that we were entirely convinced.

It is a shame that this result overshadowed everything in Scottish football, nay in Scottish cultural life, for many weeks, for there was other football played that day. Aberdeen, for example, had crushed Dundee 5-0 at Dens Park, Dundee United had eliminated Hearts at Tynecastle and in what TV would show that night to have been an excellent game of football, Kilmarnock and Dunfermline drew 2-2 at Rugby Park. And, of course, poor East Fife had even more cause to be unhappy. They too had "giant-killed" that day, beating Motherwell at Fir Park, but their efforts were to be marginalised.

But Berwick was the word. In truth, however, this had been coming to Rangers for some time. They had only beaten Falkirk 1-0 the previous week because a Falkirk player had missed a sitter in the last minute, and their defeat to Dunfermline before the New Year had been a comprehensive one. But everyone knew who had really beaten them at Berwick that day. It was, of course, Celtic, their obsession, their nemesis, their Waterloo. The early sixties of seeming impregnability (apart from the occasional fall from grace to Dundee or Kilmarnock) had now gone. They were now up against a club of their own financial status, a new, redefined, resurrected, revanchist club and, for the next 20 years, the hegemony of Scottish football would pass quite clearly and unarguably, apart from one or two isolated seasons, from Ibrox to Celtic Park.

Glynn Edwards of *The Glasgow Herald* sounded like Winston Churchill when he intoned portentously: "Never in the history of Scottish football has there been a result to match this one, and because Rangers are Rangers, it will inevitably lead to serious repercussions." Rangers had sustained one piece of bad luck in the serious injury to Willie Johnston, but he had been replaced by Davie Wilson, a man of whom it had once been said that the word "Rangers" was engraved on his heart. Maybe, but the door would soon be shown to Davie, as a career at Dundee United and Dumbarton beckoned. The shockwaves were widespread and long lasting, but somehow in keeping with the Rangers tradition. Rangers were already famous for their knee-jerk reaction to a defeat with their "somebody must carry the can" philosophy. In this case, the support, almost to a man, demanded the heads of forwards Jim Forrest and George McLean. These players would go on and continue to forge good careers for themselves with Aberdeen and Dundee respectively, when slightly more enlightened management at Ibrox would have kept them for at least a spell, even after this particularly bad game. But Scot Symon now said loudly and publicly: "I can no longer defend this team."

Another tradition is that the Ibrox defence must be sacrosanct. There were one or two poor performances at Berwick in the defence as well, but no massive changes were forthcoming there and, of course, the other tradition was that if the team were ever defeated by a smaller side, Rangers would buy their star man. On this occasion they even went one better, for the hero of Berwick, goalkeeper and player-manager Jock Wallace eventually became the Ibrox manager. Poor Sammy Reid, the scorer of the goal, must have wondered why he never got the call. Andy Penman of Dundee, who could often score an opportunistic goal, revealed that opportunism and generally being a "chancer" was part of his make-up when he submitted to the Dundee management his third transfer request of the season a few days after Berwick's victory. Now where, one wondered, would he fancy going to?

For Celtic, this was all a major bonus to their own team's good performance. It was, of course, played down and only hinted at in *The Celtic View*, which had Jock Stein saying, without mentioning any names, that there were surprises in the Scottish Cup and that "one came from a totally unexpected source". Everyone knew who he meant, for it was the main and indeed the only topic of conversation among Celtic fans. It meant basically that the major obstacle to Celtic winning the Scottish Cup had now been removed. Granted, there were still Aberdeen, Hibs, Dundee United and the winner of the Kilmarnock v Dunfermline replay, but Rangers were out. Celtic could now relax at least for a spell after the draw was made, for it paired them at Celtic Park against the winners of Elgin City and Ayr United (it would be Elgin City who won through in another minor piece of giant-killing), and how *The Evening Times* of Monday, January 30, 1967 must have hurt Rangers supporters. It tactlessly said that the Scottish Cup should now be called the "Glasgow" Cup, for all remaining Glasgow teams had been drawn at home –

Celtic, Partick Thistle, Clyde and Queen's Park. The fallers were, of course, Rangers and Third Lanark, a club now heading inexorably towards liquidation.

In the meantime, the shadow boxing continued about the New Year fixture. After March 27 was rejected by Rangers, the Ibrox side now offered February 15. It might have made sense for Celtic to accept this on the grounds that Rangers would be on their knees and a sitting duck for Celtic, but Stein thought it was perhaps better to prolong the agony and knocked back the suggestion. He cited the need to prepare for the European games, the fear of "darkened terracings" and a possible resurgence of crowd violence, and the distinctly specious and unconvincing claim that the bad weather hadn't entirely gone away, and that we would therefore have to rearrange the game yet again if it were to be postponed.

In truth, Celtic were indeed playing games. It is often stated that in cricket, for example, when a captain has a decision to make about whether to bat or bowl, or to declare or to enforce a follow-on, he should always put himself in the position of the opposition, decide what they would really hate to have to do – then make them do it. Stein realised that Rangers, after their humiliation in Berwick, would really want to come back strongly against Celtic at their home ground in order to win back their supporters' credibility. He decided to deny them that opportunity.

And thus ended the month of January 1967. It had been a good month for Celtic with four good wins. Indeed December, with its two draws and one defeat, had in some ways been atoned for. The bad news, of course, was the injury of Joe McBride, which was indeed long term. But goalscoring did not seem to be a huge problem with Willie

Wallace and Steve Chalmers around, and Stein's decision to bring back Jim Craig and put Tommy Gemmell to his more natural side seemed to have been the correct one, for only two goals had been conceded in January.

But there was more than that to be happy about. Billy McNeill was still imperious, Ronnie Simpson, or "faither" as he was called because of his age (he was now 36), was more than capable in the goal. He was possibly a little on the weak side facing shots from a distance, but he was a great reader of a game, with an astonishing ability to be in the right place at the right time. Jimmy Johnstone had had a bad spell with injuries and a loss of form, but was now clearly on the way back, but by some distance, as discerning spectators noticed, the star man of that team, of all the stars, was right-half Bobby Murdoch.

We recalled his early days as a mediocre inside-right, and how he had been moved all over the forward line, where he had often looked like a fish out of water. He had had more than his fair share of abuse from impatient and frustrated supporters until the footballing brain of Jock Stein had spotted that he was simply in the wrong position, and that he was far better pushing the ball forward rather than waiting for it to come to him. The fanzine *The Shamrock* had spotted that too as early as 1964. Why didn't Bob Kelly?

Words like "world class" were freely applied to Murdoch when he took over that position. He could take a grip of a game, distribute the ball, read the wiles of Johnstone and the speed of Lennox, and he also retained the ability to burst through himself and sometimes score. In a club which had always been rich in right-halves – Sunny Jim Young, Johnny Gilchrist, Peter Wilson, Chick Geatons, Bobby Evans, Pat Macauley and Pat Crerand – Bobby Murdoch was now looked upon as the best. It had been a slow process, but he was now a complete player. Years later, in his memoirs, Jimmy McGrory would say that Bobby Murdoch was better than Peter Wilson, and there could be no greater accolade than that.

As the mild month of January 1967 gave way to the rainier but still mild month of February, Celtic had little reason to fear the future. Stern tests awaited, but the resources to deal with them seemed to be there. This was also true, to a certain extent, of my own life as I slowly came to terms with my first year in the august demesne of St Andrews University. Gone was the homesickness and terror of the loudmouth English and American students. They were still there, but I had developed strategies to deal with them, which included retaliation by talking in a loud voice about Celtic, but there was also the better one of ignoring them, and not letting them upset me, or know that I was cowed by them. In time, we became tolerant of each other's culture, and, in many cases, friends.

Study continued, and I began to enjoy life. I had the sense to stay away, to a large extent, from alcohol (God knows, I had seen enough of that in my family when I was young) and not to get too involved with women. The one that I had been seeing before Christmas was now not so much dumped as forgotten about (maybe, indeed certainly, a mistake and without doubt something that I am now ashamed of) and a romance briefly flickered with a girl in the Greek class, but neither of us had the social ability to cope with what was required. We never really got going and maybe, at that stage of my life, it was no bad thing.

You see, I had the other great obsession.

FEBRUARY

•••••••

Celtic's first game in February was on the fourth at Broomfield in Airdrie. Airdrie, never exactly a Celtic-sympathising part of the world, were always tough opponents. As recently as 1962, Celtic had lost there in a game which finally ended any league aspirations that their young and inconsistent side might have had, and Stein was at pains to stress that under no circumstances were they to be taken lightly. Managed by a crusty character called Archie Wright, Airdrie had in previous weeks been showing signs of improvement, emerging from the pack in their annual struggle against relegation, and they were still in the Scottish Cup. They possessed a genuinely good goalkeeper called Roddy McKenzie, who was aspiring to Northern Ireland recognition, one or two bruisers of defenders, often euphemistically described as "rugged", and a few midfielders and forwards capable of producing the goods on their day.

The ground, situated in a hollow in one of Scotland's least salubrious or picturesque areas, was, paradoxically, old and quaint. It had a pavilion in the corner, one that looked a bit like the old Victorian Celtic Park pavilion which had been burnt in 1929. Indeed it would not have looked all that out of place on a cricket field, and it was now unusual to see players run out of a pavilion in the corner of a ground. The pitch was traditionally narrower than most, something that did not necessarily suit teams like Celtic, who enjoyed the long-passing switch of play from one side to the other, and the surface was never one of the better ones in Scotland.

The game was all-ticket, and they had gone by the Wednesday, although there was, as always, a black market outside the ground. On this day, such was the interest in the game and the prowess of Celtic, the usual ploy of waiting until one minute to three, then offering cost price or lower hoping the tout would cut his losses, did not work. Very few tickets were in circulation outside the ground, and the noise from within indicating the arrival of the teams running out came with ground tickets at four shillings (20 pence) changing hands for £1. The ground was packed, in some areas uncomfortably so.

Stein had decided to play Jimmy Johnstone but basically to allow him to do as he wanted and not to be restricted to the right wing. This was often pompously referred to as "a roving commission", but it was rather a realistic acceptance by the big man that Johnstone's talent simply defied analysis and tactics. Auld and Hughes could similarly be loose cannons on occasions, whereas men like Chalmers and Wallace responded better to instructions.

Sometimes the emotionally insecure wee Jimmy, who may have been the best player on the planet but was no confident city slicker, worried about his lack of instructions from the big man. He listened patiently one day, it was said, but when no instructions were forthcoming, he piped up and said: "Whit aboot me, boss?" Jock looked him up and down and said: "You? The rest can get the ba' tae you, and you can dae whit the hell ye want wi' it!" Jimmy, for his part, would then go around telling everyone else: "Ye'se a' heard whit the big man said. Gie me the ba'!"

It would be fair to say that this particular game took second place to the match at Ibrox that afternoon. Berwick were still dominating everyone's conversation and the visit of Hearts to Glasgow was looked upon with the same sort of sadistic enthusiasm and general nosiness that makes people watch road accidents to see if the victim will recover. Rangers' much-changed team did indeed win that day – the scapegoats having been dropped to appease the mob in the tradition of Pontius Pilate of old – but Berwick were still the talk of the day. Berwick's 3-1 half-time scoreline against Clydebank was cheered to the echo at most grounds and Billy Reid, the substitute of Airdrie, must have wondered why he was given a cheer from some Celtic fans as he took his seat on the bench. The Glasgow grapevine, that creature of a thousand ears, a thousand eyes and a million mouths, had discovered that his brother was no less a person than Sammy Reid, who had scored the crucial goal last week at Shielfield Park.

The weather was coldish but dry in Airdrie. That Celtic were in for an uncompromising struggle that day was clear from an early stage, when John Hughes received a knock that did not look like an accident. Fortunately, he returned soon after, and soon after that, Celtic went ahead. It was an unusual error from the normally excellent Roddy McKenzie in the Airdrie goal. Murdoch put in a fine ball, Wallace flicked it on, and then McKenzie, after appearing to have both hands on the ball, dropped it at the grateful feet of Jimmy Johnstone, who opened the scoring.

This settled Celtic but they still had a great deal of work to do. Airdrie nearly scored from what looked like an offside position, a Tommy Gemmell error almost gave a goal away, then virtually on half-time Airdrie headed against the bar. Celtic, on the other hand, attacked well and had several near misses themselves, so it was a minor surprise that half-time was reached and the team were only 1-0 up. It was also a minor surprise that no-one had been booked or sent off by the tolerant referee, Mr Wilson of Glasgow.

Tackles continued to be bruising and tough in the second half – this was, after all, the heyday of Scottish football, in which there was never any place for "softies" – but soon after half-time the game took a decided turn towards Celtic when Steve Chalmers scored a great goal, beating two defenders before shooting home past McKenzie. Twenty minutes later, Bertie Auld scored a third with a second attempt at a penalty after Johnstone had been fouled spectacularly in the box, and the game was all over.

Stein and the Celtic fans were happy about this win at a traditionally tough venue. The players had not risen to the sometimes blatant provocation of the opposition, had concentrated on the game, and although Roddy McKenzie had been responsible for one goal and failed to save the penalty properly, the same man had prevented Celtic from reaching a higher score. The play was fast, impressive and universally admired by all journalists in the following day's papers. Rangers had beaten Hearts, so there was no real gain, but it was nevertheless another step along the way towards the league championship as "we nightly pitched our moving tent a day's march nearer home", in the words of my father, who had on several occasions been on the receiving end of Churchillian rhetoric in 1943.

Another example of Stein's psychological warfare became obvious when he casually allowed himself to be quoted to the effect that he would like the league to be over and done with "by the end of March". This was not really likely to happen unless Rangers suffered a total collapse, but it did give the impression that Stein himself thought that it might just come about, and if it did, it would allow Celtic more time to concentrate on other things, notably the European Cup.

It was with the European Cup in mind that Stein had organised a friendly match on Tuesday, February 7 at Celtic Park against Dinamo Zagreb of Yugoslavia. Dinamo Zagreb had, of course, met Celtic in December 1963 in the European Cup Winners' Cup and friendly relationships had been established. Dinamo, on their midwinter break and ready to resume their season, were only too keen to come to Glasgow, a city in western Europe with good restaurants and hotels, and to play a game in front of a big crowd. They did, of course, have first-hand knowledge of Vojvodina Novi Sad and would be duly asked about them through Stein's interpreters, who were employed for the purpose. Dinamo Zagreb, Stein twigged, would be very happy to co-operate in the downfall of Vojvodina Novi Sad.

It was a friendly occasion in every sense of the word, and 46,000 turned up, enticed by Stein's apparently revolutionary style of football, which he talked about incessantly. It seemed to have some resemblance to the "total football" style of play practised by Holland some years later in the 1974 World Cup, in that players were instructed not to stroll gently to take a throw-in, nor were they allowed to wait for the regular corner kick taker to appear. The man closest to the action must take it. The formation seemed to be 3-4-3 or perhaps more accurately 3-2-2-3, and the players all wore different numbers on their pants from what they were used to. John Hughes, for example, wore number five and Tommy Gemmell number eight.

Unfortunately, it did not work or, more accurately, the system may have worked, but Celtic's forwards all had an off day, missing a barrow load of chances, which reminded supporters of the bad old lacking-in-confidence, insecure, neurotic days of the pre-Stein era. Dinamo Zagreb then scored a late goal and won 1-0. In spite of all that, both teams received an ovation from the crowd for what had been perceived as a good game of football, in spite of the somewhat blatant gimmickry and artificiality of the occasion.

"A failure, therefore a success" was the way it was para-doxically put in one newspaper, but whether that was true or not, we certainly did not hear any more about any new system, at least not directly and not immediately, even though Stein said that they would try again. There were, of course, pluses in this adventure. A crowd of 46,000 was a tidy little earner in February for a friendly, even allowing for what had to be paid to the Yugoslavs. Fringe players like David Cattenach were given a run-out and the Yugoslav media went home to tell Vojvodina Novi Sad's players and supporters that Celtic's forward play was not very good. Some people thought that Stein was sufficiently Machiavellian to tell his players to miss chances deliberately, and at least one member of the playing staff described the whole exercise as a fraud. It was, however, a useful work-out for some of the players. Someone within *The Celtic View* treated himself to a little cynicism on this one, for there was a cartoon of 11 goalkeepers running out and a fan saying that they were trying out a new defensive plan!

At least as important a consideration was that it kept Celtic in the public eye in a week in mid-February when there was not very much going on. It may even have been little more than an attempt to divert attention from Rangers, who played Clyde in a league game at Shawfield the following night. Rangers, in fact, won that game 5-1 to reduce the gap to three points, underlining the fact that, Berwick or no Berwick, they were by no means a bad team in 1967. Indeed events would prove it, for one does not reach the final of a major European trophy, even the less prestigious and now defunct European Cup Winners' Cup, with a poor team, and the very fact that they almost kept pace with Celtic for so long in that season surely says something about their quality.

Saturday, February 11 saw the attention switch to Ayrshire. Both Celtic and Rangers were in the county of Robert Burns, with Celtic at Somerset Park, Ayr and Rangers at Rugby Park, Kilmarnock. This state of affairs was brought about because Celtic had been scheduled to play Ayr United at Somerset on October 22, 1966. But as that game was on the same day as the Wales v Scotland international, it had to be postponed, and would have been played the following midweek. The snag was that Somerset Park did not, as yet, have floodlights and the game would have had to be played in the afternoon. But Celtic then suggested a swapping of fixtures, so that Celtic played Ayr at Parkhead in October and at Somerset Park in February. But Rangers were at Kilmarnock.

With a rare stroke of common sense (Celtic themselves suggested it), it was agreed to stagger the kick-offs to minimise the chance of both sets of supporters meeting at a railway station or somewhere where trouble could start. Celtic's game at Ayr was brought forward to a 1pm kick-off, (so that there would, in any case, be no problem with the lack of floodlights), while Rangers' game went ahead at the normal time of 3pm.

But there was a little more to it than that, because Rangers were being watched by a VIP. It is often said that managers "spy" on other teams. This might not have been good imagery to employ in this case, for the VIP was no less a person that Alexei Kosygin, Prime Minister of the Soviet Union, one of the most influential people in the world and a man who had his finger on a nuclear trigger.

The true purpose of his mission to Great Britain has never been disclosed, but the Cold War had been thawing for some time, and possibly there was no reason other than the making of friends and trying to persuade the British to prevail upon the Americans to stop what they were doing in Vietnam. Mr Kosygin had already met with the Prime Minister, Harold Wilson, and the Queen before he came to Scotland and when he arrived as a genuine football fan, he was invited to attend the game at Rugby Park between Kilmarnock and Rangers.

This was a rare propaganda coup for Killie and Rangers, and Celtic fans were left muttering and wondering why Mr Kosygin was not coming to see the league champions of the previous year and the leading aspirants this year. Fanciful suggestions included the Queen putting her foot down and the fact that Sean Connery (then James Bond, who regularly ate KGB agents for breakfast!) was a Celtic supporter. In truth, Kilmarnock and Rangers was a better game, won narrowly by Rangers and thoroughly enjoyed by the Soviet guest.

By the time that game kicked off, Celtic had already won. It was a curious game. In the first place, the idea of the early start did not attract the fans for there were visible spaces on the terracing when the game kicked off (although most were filled up by half-time), and the other thing was that Ayr's manager, a bouncy, jovial character called Ally MacLeod, who had played for Third Lanark and Blackburn Rovers, sent his team out in their reserve strip, which just happened to be orange. Two weeks later, Sammy Baird would do the same with Stirling Albion – in Baird's case quite deliberately – and those of the paranoid tendencies saw some sort of conspiracy here as well. Ally's managerial career was in its infancy at Somerset Park. In retrospect, it might have been better if he had stayed with the Honest Men.

Stein gave Charlie Gallagher an outing for this game. There were perhaps reasons for this, as we will discover. In the event, the game turned out to be rather typical of many games played by Celtic at this time. A slow start – in this case not helped by the early kick-off and the slow trickling in of fans who had shown a distinct reluctance to leave the cosy pub – and a poor first half preceded the breakthrough and then a devastating performance in the second half, which produced a 5-0 victory.

Jimmy Johnstone opened the scoring towards the end of the first half with a header from a Gemmell cross (for a small man, Jimmy scored a remarkable amount of goals with his head), then in the second half, Stevie Chalmers scored a hat-trick and John Hughes the other goal with a fierce drive. The good bit about the early start is that you can head home knowing the job has been done and await the other results in a relaxed frame of mind. Rangers, as we have said, beat Kilmarnock, so the gap remained at three points. Mr Kosygin was indeed impressed. If Rangers thought, however, that their victory was in any way responsible for an improvement in the prospects for world peace, they were sadly mistaken. Eighteen months later, Mr Kosygin's Soviet Union nearly provoked World War III by invading Czechoslovakia. Perhaps he was upset at Rangers fans apparently singing "The Red Flag" to welcome him, but altering the word "red" to "blue".

The burning world issue in 1967 was, however, Vietnam. It was a war which had sneaked up on the world, as it were, in that there had never been any formal declaration of war. It had all been put in motion years previously by President John F Kennedy, whose picture one could still buy from the street vendors outside Celtic Park on match day. In the eyes of most people, he could still do no wrong three and a half years after his assassination in November 1963 – and that was in spite of his now obvious and acknowledged sexual transgressions with several ladies, including, it was said, the luscious Hollywood actress Marilyn Monroe. But JFK it was who had started the whole business by committing American troops to prop up a corrupt and illegal regime in South Vietnam. South Vietnam was, of course, not Communist, as distinct from North Vietnam, which was.

Following the death of Kennedy, the whole thing gradually intensified throughout 1964, 1965 and 1966 until, by early 1967, words like "genocide" were freely used to describe what the Americans were doing. Newspapers like *The Daily Mirror* in Great Britain showed pictures of the after-effects of bombing on innocent children and asked why the world was allowing this thing to happen. Mercifully, Britain never joined in, but, to its detriment, Australia did, falling for the line peddled by the Americans that the "domino theory" of states collapsing one by one to the Communist menace would eventually plunge Australia into Communism.

It was incredibly naïve of the Australians to believe that, but no more so than the things one heard from the US itself. Mercifully in the US Presidential Election of 1964, the Americans rejected a man called Barry Goldwater, who gave every indication of wanting to "nuke" North Vietnam, but even the winning candidate, Lyndon B Johnson, showed no signs of wanting to "de-escalate" this conflict, which was rapidly getting out of hand.

America itself was struggling to cope with all this. On the one hand, there were the Yankee Doodle Dandies, who wanted to go "all the way with LBJ" and not to stop until North Vietnam was utterly defeated. Words like "patriotism" and "freedom" (words always used by the American right wing when it is under pressure) were bandied about, along with the Stars and Stripes. They were terrifying, reminding us in Scotland about the extreme elements of the Orange Order, but one of the strong things about the USA (which, basically, has more good points than it does bad) is that the media and TV stations are not afraid to criticise their government's policies. The bad points about this awful war simply could not be hidden.

There thus grew up a very strong peace movement, which grew in strength when the US government began to introduce the "draft", a form of conscription, to replace the clear and obvious deaths and maimings that were being sustained on the battlefield. The peace movement, which included the lunatic fringe of hippies and "flower power", as well as the more sensible, reasoned approach of all those who linked peace in Vietnam with human rights for black people, attracted numbers that embarrassed the US government, and occasionally violent measures were taken against them, thus raising further questions about the US in the 1960s.

But, of course, there was also the third group in the US, and this was the most numerous and the most significant. They, in time, would be called "the silent majority" and were what would be known in other societies as "the middle classes" or "the bourgeoisie". They were affluent, comfortable and church-going. They enjoyed a good standard of living, and were usually quite self-assured and self-confident. They were, unfortunately, very "patriotic" and tended to believe that the US President (whether one liked him or not, whether one voted for him or not), being the head of state as well as the leader of the government, or the "administration" as the Americans liked to call it, must be supported. This reminded historians of "the Divine Right of Kings" in 17th-century England. For this reason, while the father of a "silent majority" family would stereotypically tell his son about his own exploits on D Day or at Guadalcanal, he would also, with a degree of reluctance perhaps, take a deep sigh and tell his son that it was his "patriotic duty" to "do his bit" in Vietnam. And, of course, young women always loved men in uniforms.

The "silent majority" would, in fact, change their mind eventually once the losses became too intolerable and once it became obvious that America could not win this war, but in 1967 the war continued to intensify. In Great Britain, we watched in horror. Students like myself would go on protest marches about this war, and indeed against apartheid in South Africa (curiously not yet about the similar second-class citizen status of Roman Catholics in Northern Ireland), but the Vietnam war was something far away, and mercifully did not affect us as much as it might have. We had a Prime Minister called Harold Wilson who was not seduced by American arguments into committing British troops. Had Margaret Thatcher or Tony Blair been Prime Minister, it might have been a totally different story. As it was, we were spectators at a particularly brutal spectacle.

The affairs of Scottish football, equally passionate but less violent and bloody, still reigned in our hearts. Supporters stood in a long queue for their tickets for the Vojvodina game, where the tickets cost six shillings (30 pence) and there were no "boys'" tickets. Celtic tried to defend this by using the specious argument that they were worried about the welfare of youngsters in the big crowd, but it fooled no-one. We would have thought more of them if they had just come clean and said they wanted the money.

Celtic did Elgin City, their opponents in the next round of the Scottish Cup on Saturday, February 18, the honour of treating them with the utmost respect. Stein took his players away for a few days to the Seamill Hydro, where the press were allowed to take pictures of them playing golf in the cold but dry weather, and snooker and table tennis in the evenings. The Seamill Hydro was popular with Celtic (it had been used since Maley's time in 1902) and Stein, with his obsessive paranoia about drink, was particularly fond of it, since it was a "hydro" hotel where there was no alcohol.

While there, Stein stressed that Elgin City of the Highland League had already beaten Ayr United, a top-division club and indeed Celtic's most recent opponents, and that as the last round had proved, there were no pushovers in the Scottish Cup. He refrained, at least in public, from mentioning Berwick or Rangers, but everyone knew exactly what he meant. It was also at Seamill where Stein overheard one of his players talking about Saturday's game and saying that it was "just Elgin". The player concerned was given a severe talking to about the folly of underestimating opponents.

Then the team came back to Celtic Park for a workout and a practice match on the Friday. Stein was clearly taking no chances with Elgin, but it was also true that he was thinking of other things as well, notably the European games coming against Vojvodina Novi Sad. Rangers, in the meantime, were paying the price for their Berwick catastrophe by being ignored by the press, although they did manage to lose a friendly in midweek at Stoke City, with Forrest and McLean, the men who were being blamed for Berwick, in sulky resentment at their treatment by Rangers, and angling for a transfer by trying to persuade other teams to take them.

Cup tie Saturday was cold but fair. It was a feature of the 1966/67 Scottish season, incidentally, that very few games were called off and 34,000 appeared at Celtic Park to see Elgin City, with a fair sprinkling of away supporters in the crowd. Celtic made them welcome – the great Jimmy Delaney had, of course, played a few games for Elgin at the end of his career a decade previously – and an Elgin party had already been at Parkhead to see the Zagreb game ten days before. Their supporters, a huge amount of them wearing huge "lum" hats in the club colours of black and white, and containing a large amount of women and open-eyed children whose first trip to a big game in Glasgow this was, made a lot of noise and held up a banner bearing the slogan "Elgin will berrick Celtic", something that made no sense whatsoever other than in the immediate context of February 1967.

It was also a special occasion for one particular Celtic player, the ever-popular Charlie Gallagher. By no means a regular in the team, Charlie was nevertheless widely respected and loved for his ball-playing ability, his visionary passing and his cannonball shot, and had it not been for the fact that he was playing in a great Celtic squad, he would surely have been a first-team regular. He was especially unfortunate in that he and Bertie Auld played the same kind of game. Charlie was possibly the superior of Auld in passing ability, but he lacked the aggression of Bertie. But now Charlie had been given the great honour of being invited to play for Eire against Turkey on February 22 in Ankara.

He was thus the first-ever Scottish-born player to play for Ireland, the rules having recently been changed to that effect. Some club managers have been known to be unhappy about their players being taken away for what could be seen as an irrelevant fixture in a faraway country, where injuries could be sustained. Not so, in the case of Jock Stein or his assistant, Sean Fallon. Fallon had, it was believed, done more than a little lobbying on Charlie's behalf, and Jock devoted a lot of column inches in *The Celtic View* to show his delight at this turn of events. Not only that, but he chose him for the Elgin City game and allowed Charlie to lead the team out. Billy McNeill was, of course, still the captain, for the self-effacing Charlie simply lacked the temperament for that job, but it was still a sign of the respect in which Charlie was held.

It was, of course, a great feather in the cap of the club and for the team's supporters – very many were of Irish extraction albeit, like Gallagher, not exactly born in the Emerald Isle – it meant a great deal. Celtic had had a few Irish caps before, notably Patsy Gallacher, Charlie Tully and Bertie Peacock, but these men had been born in Ireland. Here, we had a Scotsman playing for Ireland. Many men of Irish descent had played for Scotland in the past. Now here it was happening in reverse. Charlie was really only a fringe player of this great XI, and delight was expressed in the particularly passionate rendering of "The Soldiers' Song" from the eager denizens of the Jungle, and the loud cheers every time Gallagher touched the ball.

International football had long been a conundrum for Celtic supporters. It was often a sneer from supporters of other teams that Celtic fans' love of Scotland was somewhat half-hearted. The charge was not entirely without foundation, but there were reasons for it. It was often felt, for example, that men like Jimmy McGrory had been ludicrously under-capped, and it is certainly difficult to explain why he never played at Wembley against England, particularly when he scored at Hampden in 1931 and 1933, his goal in 1933 often credited with the birth of "the Hampden Roar".

In addition, there was the undeniable fact that, in 1967, Rangers supporters had identified with Scotland far more than they do now in 2016. In the 2014 referendum, they had been the ones who had said "No", preferring the Union Jack and the British connection, whereas Celtic fans had tended to link themselves with the "Yes" campaign for Scottish independence. But Celtic fans in 1967 could still recall how Rangers fans in the 1920s and 1930s would sing lovely Scottish songs like "The Wells O' Wearie" and "Loch Lomond", with the occasional addition of words or verses of religious intolerance and hatred, as if they, and they only, were the real Scotsmen. In this, of course, they would find support in some of the tracts put out by the Church of Scotland in the 1920s, which worried about the "Scottish race" being defiled and polluted by the "Irish menace".

It was also undeniably true that Celtic players playing for Scotland would find themselves booed by the ignorant in the crowd. It must be stressed that this was the behaviour of the minority, but the majority were not always as vocal as they could have been in drowning them out, nor did the press always condemn such partisan, sectarian behaviour. Some Celtic players were notoriously reluctant to play for Scotland, but on the other hand, in recent years, men like Willie Fernie, Bobby Collins, Bobby Evans, Billy McNeill, Pat Crerand and Tommy Gemmell had served Scotland with distinction.

So Celtic supporters were often ambivalent and unsure about Scotland. Yet the tradition of the club was very much towards the inclusion of both Scotland and Ireland in their make-up. That is indeed what the word "Celtic", whether pronounced "Keltic" or "Seltic", actually means. The present ground at Celtic Park had, of course, been built with no other purpose in mind than to host Scotland v England internationals, and the old-timers of long ago could still talk nostalgically of how Jimmy Quinn destroyed England in 1910 and how Jimmy McMenemy did likewise in 1914. But this was different. Here we had a Celtic player, born in Scotland of Irish parents, playing for Ireland. There was a great deal to be happy about there.

Elgin City did themselves proud and until almost half-time only a real fool would have written off their chances of a "Berwick" result, or, more credibly, earning themselves a replay at Borough Briggs the following Wednesday afternoon. But Celtic, playing with the confidence that comes from a run of success, and giving young David Cattenach a game at right-back, did not panic and just before half-time a header by Chalmers from a Hughes cross put Celtic ahead. That was in the 43rd minute and those who decided to go to the toilet, or stand in the long queue for the inadequate and not particularly hygienic refreshment bars that were available at Parkhead, missed another two goals before half-time, both scored by Bobby Lennox, who picked up a ball from Gallagher and then another from Chalmers to give Celtic a 3-0 lead.

Hughes scored in the second half, Lennox again and as the gallant Highlanders tired, Wallace got another two. As often happens, the Celtic crowd magnanimously supported Elgin, willing them to get a goal which would have produced the magical 7-1 scoreline (Celtic beat Rangers 7-1 in October 1957), but Billy McNeill and company refused to co-operate and 7-0 it finished. Elgin received the consolation of a very large cheque and a great ovation from the Parkhead crowd, something that visibly affected the many Celtic supporters in the Elgin side.

The build-up in the press and media to this particular Saturday had not featured Celtic too much. The main focus had been very much on whether Berwick Rangers could do it again. They had been drawn against Hibs at Easter Road – as close to a derby match as the isolated Englishmen could get – and it seemed that all of Berwick, from their civic dignitaries downwards, were going to Edinburgh that day.

A bumper crowd of 27,000 appeared – about three times the average home attendance of Hibs – but Hibs refused to co-operate with those who believed that lightning could strike twice. Berwick put up a good performance in the first half, but Jim Scott scored for Hibs just before the interval. Hibs then stayed well on top in the second, although they could not add to their tally. Berwick's goalkeeper, Jock Wallace, even saved a penalty kick. Meanwhile, those whom Berwick had vanquished in the previous round went to Leicester City to play a friendly, lost 0-1 and were disgraced by their supporters, who found English beer a little too difficult to handle.

The surprise of the day was Hamilton beating St Mirren at Love Street, but the ominous result for Celtic was Aberdeen's 5-0 demolition of St Johnstone, all the goals coming in the second half. Aberdeen, with ex-Hib Eddie Turnbull now at the helm, were slowly building up a good side, as had been apparent when Celtic were there on Christmas Eve. Consistency was not yet there, but flair and determination certainly were. They had, of course, made life difficult for themselves and had broken the hearts of their support by selling midfielder Dave Smith to Rangers the previous summer, but now they had another Smith, Jimmy Smith, in their forward line, a man good enough to share the same "Jinky" nickname as Jimmy Johnstone. At least Aberdeen supporters knew that Jimmy Smith would not be sold to Rangers, for reasons that shall be made clear later.

Dundee United and Clyde also won, but Dunfermline were held to a draw at Firhill by Partick Thistle. A draw was also the result between Queen's Park and Airdrie. This last result was of significance to Celtic, for Celtic were drawn at home in the Scottish Cup quarter-finals against the winner of this tie. The quarter-finals would be played on March 11, three days after the second leg of the European Cup quarter-final against Vojvodina. The draw was made on Monday, February 20 during the day, thus allowing Sean Fallon to attend the replay that very night at Broomfield, which was duly and impressively won by Queen's Park. But other commitments, notably the looming quarter-final against Vojvodina, were approaching, and this meant that Queen's Park would have to be put on the back burner for a spell. Tickets for the European Cup second leg, to be played on March 8 at Parkhead, were selling briskly, in spite of the moans about pricing and the queues, and it was already beginning to look as if there might be a 70,000 sell-out.

Charlie Gallagher duly went to Turkey with the Republic of Ireland. The team was managed by ex-Manchester United star Johnny Carey, although the team, like the Scottish one until just before that time, was picked by a committee. Charlie, used to the tight discipline of Jock Stein, was amazed at the slackness and amateurishness of the organisation – apparently they met in a bar of a hotel – but he played well enough by all accounts, although the team didn't. They lost 1-2 to Turkey, an uncompromising team, in the qualifying competition for the 1968 European Championship. Noel Cantwell scored for Ireland, but it was a disappointment, considering that Ireland had won 2-1 against Turkey in December in Ireland. Gallagher, however, now entered the history books as the first-ever Scottish-born player to play for Ireland.

The Celtic View of the following Wednesday appeared as normal. It was usually a good read, with a column by Jock Stein, a few good photographs of the most recent game and a serialisation of James Handley's *The Celtic Story*. There was something very comforting about it, but on this occasion it annoyed me a little and my father a great deal when it carried a headline "How Good Was Paddy Gallacher?" My father's irate phone call to me that night demanded to know who on earth was *Paddy* Gallacher, when everyone without fail called him Patsy. In any case, he ranted, the question "How good was he?" was redundant and otiose. There was no-one better than Patsy Gallacher. "Kerrydale" (whoever he was – John McPhail?) then turned sycophantic in the extreme by saying that "No one is better qualified to answer this question than Mr Robert Kelly, the Celtic chairman." Really? He may have been a director for 36 years, but he hadn't always given the impression of being able to judge a football player when he was in sole charge of the team.

But, give the chairman his due, he did in the same issue sing the praises of "Paddy", whom he sometimes called Patsy, relaying what a great a trickster he was, recalling the 1925 Scottish Cup Final and the goal Patsy scored against Hibs, when he dribbled the ball into the net and out again, as well as a less well-known game when he played against Morton as centre-half. Perhaps typically, Bob Kelly said that Patsy's one failing was occasional indiscipline. By the time I had read that encomium, my feelings towards Mr Kelly had softened a little. I had a reasonably high opinion of Bob as an administrator, statesman and diplomat, as long as he allowed Jock Stein to run the playing side. The greatest thing Bob did was admit in early 1965 that he was wrong, stop hiding behind the loveable McGrory and invite the dynamic Jock Stein to awaken the sleeping giant that was Celtic.

By now, however, what was exercising the mind of Celtic was the quarter-final in distant Yugoslavia. Yugoslavia, of course, does not exist any more, torn apart by an appalling series of genocidal wars in the 1990s, with issues at stake that were frankly incomprehensible to most Western observers. We asked what seemed to be the reasonable question of "Why can't they just get on?" Similar questions have been asked, of course, about the seemingly pointless Arab–Israeli conflicts, or the one that would soon kick off a lot closer to home – Protestants v Catholics in Northern Ireland. Yes, "getting on" or "peaceful co-existence" often strikes one as being not too bad an option.

In 1967, Yugoslavia was held together by Marshall Tito. As dictators go, he was by no means the worst. He had done very well for his country in the Second World War and now laudably refused to toe any Soviet line. He was his own man and it might have been better for them if they had all stuck with him and his appointed successors. Free speech and prosperity, however, were hardly notable concepts in Yugoslavia in 1967, and for Westerners going there, it could be a frightening prospect. Celtic had chartered their own aircraft for February 27, such were the complications of trying to get there otherwise.

Before that, however, they had a slightly shorter trip to make to Stirling on Saturday, February 25 to play Stirling Albion at their ground, called Annfield (as distinct from Anfield, where Liverpool played and still do). Stirling Albion had only existed since the Second World War, replacing a Stirling team called King's Park, and they were happy to be described as Scotland's "yo-yo" team in that they were perpetually battling against relegation from Division One or striving for promotion from Division Two.

They had been managed for a few years by a man called Sammy Baird, who had played at inside-left and left-half for Rangers in the 1950s. He was a tough man, not well liked in Scottish football even, it was whispered, within Ibrox itself, for his overtly tough and abrasive approach and his less-than-welcoming approach to young players who could be considered his rivals. He could, however, be charming and pleasant, and even his sternest critics had to admit that he was doing a good job for Stirling Albion. They had won the Division Two championship in 1965 and had stayed in Division One in 1965/66. In the town of Stirling, not really a hotbed of Scottish football, this was considered success.

Celtic's record at Stirling was not encouraging. In 1962, for example, even though Albion had finished bottom of Division One, they still managed to beat Celtic on February 10 through a goal scored by a chap called Johnny Lawlor, who thus rescued his career from obscurity. Celtic fans had turned nasty that day, as they frequently did in 1962 when things went against them.

We had thought that this sort of sloppy performance on the field, with the concomitant, cretinous behaviour on the terracings, the pubs and the streets, had been eliminated with the arrival of Jock Stein, but then, in 1966, exactly a year earlier, Celtic had gone down 0-1 again with one of the worst performances of that otherwise excellent season. Sammy Baird had playfully put out his team in orange jerseys – and Celtic fans, of course, knew exactly why he did that, but could do little other than hurl abuse in impotent rage as their team let them down.

Now, a year later, we approached this stadium, which could be a beautiful one on a good day with views of the surrounding hills, but the stadium had clearly not been built with the visit of Celtic in mind. There were painfully long queues for the turnstiles and a danger of being crushed when someone got impatient. There was also one vital difference on this day compared with the previous year, and that was rain. Heavy, incessant, depressing rain, which hammered down on us as we waited in the queues for admission to the uncovered terracings. It was a disheartening, depressing experience, and there was something ominous about it all. Sometimes Celtic play well in the rain. They didn't on this occasion.

The team who normally wore red were wearing orange again, something which did at least, in the gloom of a rainy Scottish February afternoon, add a touch of colour. A couple of weeks previously, as we have seen, Ayr United had similarly worn orange. Ally MacLeod, with his background of Third Lanark and Blackburn Rovers, was sufficiently on the periphery of the Neanderthal and primeval religious war of Glasgow to be given the benefit of the doubt. With Sammy Baird, there was no such dubiety. It was quite deliberate, provocative and sadly it seemed to work. The Celtic crowd were nasty and unforgiving, to such an extent as to almost appear to unsettle their own players.

There were other things which unsettled the Celtic team as well. The rain, the pitch openly described as a "quagmire" in various newspapers, the ferocious tackling, the small ground with the crowd almost on top of them in places and the imminent trip to the Balkans all played their part in disturbing the Celtic team out of their normally composed, grimly professional and committed approach. The game being slightly delayed to allow more of the crowd in did not help very much either.

The mood was set when John Hughes was downed shortly after his first touch of the ball within the first minute. The referee, Mr Foote of Glasgow, had a Herculean task and although Stirling were clearly over-motivated, it would be wrong to portray Celtic as injured innocents. Indeed they gave as good as they got, with the slippery surface allowing a tremendous amount of sliding tackles. Quite a few players on either side were lucky not to be sent off (indeed, had this game happened in 2016, they would have been) and quite a lot were equally lucky not to have had their legs broken.

Yet there was some good football as well. Indeed the radio commentators and the press used words like "passionate" as if this were Scottish football at its best. Celtic pressed and pressed but simply could not score in the mud and then, as often happens in such circumstances, Stirling scored in one of their first forays upfield. They forced a corner kick and from it, George Peebles smashed home a hard shot to put Stirling 1-0 up at half-time. George Peebles, of course, had met Celtic before, not least in that awful Scottish Cup Final of 1961, when he had starred for Jock Stein's Dunfermline as they defeated Celtic 2-0.

Half-time came and went, but Stirling goalkeeper Willie Murray continued his inspired form with a fair ladling of luck. He did lose a goal to a John Hughes header early in the second half, but Celtic were unable to force the victory that their outfield play deserved. A Stirling player was carried off, another was sent off for a vicious foul on Willie Wallace, Bobby Murdoch was booked, but after a frantic last ten minutes Celtic were unable to breach the Stirling defence and had to settle for a draw. At the very death, Billy McNeill headed home what looked like a late winner, only to have it mysteriously chalked off. The picture on the front page of *The Celtic View* the following Wednesday shows McNeill rising in splendid isolation (so it couldn't have been a foul) and a defender standing on the goal line (so it couldn't have been offside) and no-one seems to have had a clue why this goal was not allowed.

Jock Stein himself was philosophical, saying: "This, of course, is football." Without mentioning the referee by name, Stein added: "Nor are we at our best when the control of a game is not first class." He went on to say that "there were actions by players of both sides which should be no part of football and were not punished quickly enough". So he was also magnanimous enough to imply that some Celtic players were guilty of the occasional indiscretion as well. Those of us who were at the game knew who he meant – and they were the likely suspects.

Annfield thus continued its melancholy tradition of being a Celtic bogey ground. Stirling Albion seldom caused any problems at Parkhead – their last two visits had seen 7-3 and 6-1 victories for Celtic – but they were difficult on their own ground. Dens Park, Dundee had been considered a bogey ground in the early sixties, but there were reasons for this phenomenon. Dundee, with men like Ure and Gilzean around, were a good side. It was more difficult to explain why Annfield was so difficult, but Billy McNeill would admit years later (after another defeat there in the League Cup in 1980, when he was manager) that Annfield was his least favourite ground in Scotland.

Unfortunately, Rangers beat St Mirren that afternoon and thus the gap at the top was reduced to only two points. It also meant that Rangers could now win the league off their own bat. It would presuppose Rangers winning all their games but that was now possible, for there was still the game at Ibrox postponed at the New Year to be played. It was now beginning to look, given the European commitments of both sides, that this game would have to be played after the scheduled end of the season.

Leaving such domestic concerns to one side, Celtic flew off to Yugoslavia on Monday, February 27, their ultimate destination being the part that is now known as Serbia. The weather, in spite of a few pessimistic forecasts as they left Glasgow, was pleasantly warm when they arrived. Yugoslavia generally had a pleasant Mediterranean climate and, in recent years, had begun to attract quite a few Western holidaymakers, although not yet on the same scale as Spain, for example, had done. Like many countries it was a place where spring arrives suddenly – unlike Scotland, where spring is slow and unpredictable – but Stein had been sufficiently concerned about the possibility of a postponement through bad weather to make enquiries about what would happen in that event.

The one bad piece of news was one that everyone was slowly beginning to guess and it was that Joe McBride, who might have hoped to have recovered sufficiently to allow him to travel at least, had had a relapse. He had had an outing or two in training and in a reserve match at Dundee, but his recovery was to take a great deal longer than had first been thought. Stein made the surprising decision to take Willie Wallace with the party. Wallace was ineligible because he had not been signed in time for this particular round, but Stein thought it would be good to give him experience for future occasions. "Wispy" got on well with the rest of the team, and it was good to have him there in any case for morale reasons. It was also a subtle indication to the Vojvodina manager, a tough-looking and voluble character called Vujadin Boskov, that Stein fully envisaged some future European nights for Willie Wallace this season.

There were a few injury niggles, not least to Jimmy Johnstone, but then again with Jimmy, one never knew how much he exaggerated injuries in the hope of being excused a foreign trip, for he hated flying. Stein agreed that he had had a rough time from the coarse Stirling Albion players, being targeted from the start, but Jimmy was on the plane on Monday. The team took off from Glasgow Airport with the maximum of publicity from BBC, STV and newspapers. Confidence was there, but it was difficult to be too sanguine, or indeed too pessimistic, about what was awaiting. No-one really knew what to expect against this team, who had gone to the trouble of installing new floodlights for the occasion of the arrival of the mighty men from north-west Europe.

Meanwhile, back in Scotland, winter was petering out. February had been a month with both cold and rain, but there had been remarkably little disruption, even in the Highlands. My own life was improving as well. Now, as term progressed at St Andrews, I had settled. The homesickness, that miserable, debilitating, all-encompassing condition, had passed and I was slowly beginning to find more confidence, not least after I had been invited to a residence ball by that girl at the end of January. Nothing lasted – maybe I wanted it to, but didn't really try hard enough – and I was perhaps all the better for not having the complicated involvement of a relationship.

Natural urges remained, but I was now enjoying my studies. I always knew I could do well, and I was focused. I found new friends, this time people with my own interests

– namely the ever-present one of the football team that occupied my thoughts all the time. I couldn't really afford to go and see them that often, but did so now and again, watched them on TV, read voraciously about them and talked about little else. My friends were not necessarily all Celtic supporters but they were able to discuss things rationally, and more of them agreed that this was as likely a year as any for a Scottish team to win the European Cup.

My mother occasionally worried about this obsession, but my father didn't – he, after all, was a fellow sufferer, but sometimes I said to myself that it was as well that it was Celtic I obsessed about. If I didn't have them, I might have started to obsess about myself – and oneself is always a very bad person to think about all the time. At least with Celtic, one is never alone, and with things going as well as they were at that point, the joys were frequent. Even the pain was never a lonely pain. Thousands were suffering with you as well.

My father also once made the valid point that all humans need to love, and conversely, need to hate. Given this basic point, it is as well that "hatred" can be directed at something like Rangers or the Tories – things that you hate strongly, but only in a competitive sense. Some of my best friends were Rangers supporters, and although you wanted to see them defeated, demoralised and, most importantly, quietened, you also wanted them back next year so that you could do it again. It was similar with one's feelings about the British upper class and the royal family. It was just as well that nobody hated them like the French disliked their royals in 1789 and the Russians theirs in 1917. No-one in Britain in 1967 really wanted them to be guillotined – merely to be sentenced to a life on a working-class housing estate or maybe a suburban Edinburgh bungalow, and having to do an honest job of work.

I often wondered about the royal who was my own age – Prince Charles. In time, his son would come to St Andrews University. How would Charlie have coped with life at St Andrews University with me? We might have become friends…

But, leaving such trivialities aside, how were Celtic going to do in Vojvodina Novi Sad?

MARCH

· · · · · · ·

Vojvodina Novi Sad, a little-known outfit before 1967, had surprised even their own supporters by beating Atletico Madrid in the previous round. They had needed a play-off, and extra time, to do it a few days before Christmas 1966. In that game, they had had a couple of players sent off and these two were suspended for the tie against Celtic but, even without these men, Novi Sad were undeniably a good side. Stein, having gathered information from Dinamo Zagreb and his own spies, had studied them.

Stein was right in his assessment that they would be comfortable on the ball, would play together as a unit, would have loads of big, strong defenders and would be extremely difficult to break down. They were emphatically not a "Scottish" side, whose supporters would simply not stand for their negative approach and lack of flair. What they lacked was a Jimmy Johnstone or a John Hughes, men of undeniable ability who could turn a game in the space of a second but also, on occasion, be infuriatingly inconsistent or non-productive. All the Yugoslav players tended to be solid, hard-working, very fit, professional and not prone to making mistakes. Stein was also correct in his prediction that they would use body-checking tactics to thwart Celtic rather than outright kicking or hacking.

There was no away-goals rule in 1967. Already in the event of a draw, a play-off had been scheduled in neutral Rotterdam, something that would have been a distinct anti-climax. It was to be avoided, if possible, and Stein was determined that the game would be won in the second leg at Celtic Park in front of 70,000 fans, who would be a passionate and frenzied asset.

But before that could happen, Celtic had to get a respectable result in Novi Sad. A narrow defeat would not be a disaster, and a draw would be a perfect springboard for a triumph at Parkhead. The ground capacity in Novi Sad was a great deal smaller than Celtic Park – in the event, 25,000 turned up – but to the Celtic team's surprise and delight, the surface was quite acceptable. Doubts and fears had been expressed about the recently installed floodlights, but they were very good indeed.

Novi Sad itself was an underdeveloped city in comparison with Western standards, but there were no complaints about hotel accommodation. Vojvodina's manager predicted a 2-0 victory for his side – although it's never a good idea to be so precise.

Stein kept his mouth shut about what the score would be but, after a long period of coyness, decided to play Bobby Lennox in the forward line with orders to do a lot of running. Lennox tended to be used quite a lot on away legs and for that very reason – namely that he was fast and fit. The ground was likely to be heavy following a great deal of rain, which had prevented Celtic having a training session on the pitch itself.

The game kicked off at 5.30pm Scottish time – not that that made much difference, for neither the BBC nor the STV provided any TV coverage and, very disappointingly, the game was not even on the radio. This was par for the course at the time, but it did not make for an easy tea time, knowing that the team were in action. Often, the further away one is from a game, the worse the tension becomes, for one's mind does play tricks. The TV news programmes gave us a half-time score at about 6.15pm (0-0), and then the BBC Light Programme, as it was then called, gave us the full-time score at about 7.30pm.

It was a result greeted with joy among the Rangers supporters at Ibrox, where their game against Real Zaragoza in the European Cup Winners' Cup was just starting. Their joy was misplaced, for the 0-1 scoreline, only Celtic's second competitive defeat of the season, was by no means a bad result. The loss of the goal was extremely unfortunate, but the look on the face of Vojvodina's manager, Mr Boskov, after the game showed that he felt Celtic had done well. Stein, on the other hand, did not say very much, but expressed a moderate satisfaction that things had not turned out worse.

The first half had, apparently, been typical European first leg material. It was very cat and mouse, with neither team wanting to give very much away. Celtic apologists will say that the semi-final second leg game against Dukla Prague was the first time that Celtic had set out to defend, rather than adopt the traditional gung-ho, cavalier Celtic style of attacking play.

This is not quite true, for the team set-up in Novi Sad was also very defensive in nature, with Celtic absorbing pressure and relying on the occasional breakaway from the tricky Johnstone, the fast-running Lennox or the burly and unpredictable Hughes.

The first half was, frankly, a bit of a bore, as the early stages of European games can be, but Celtic went in at half-time having coped well with all that the Yugoslavs had thrown at them. Vojvodina had proved to be tough opponents, but they were not rough or dirty. Indeed they were very disciplined. A slight concern had been an injury to Bobby Murdoch. The referee, thinking that Murdoch was trying to con him, had been reluctant to stop the game. Bobby duly recovered but it slowed him down for the rest of the match. He would have more problems with injuries a few weeks later, and the trouble was that Murdoch was such a good player – indeed we were all beginning to feel that he was the central character – that if he was off form, we noticed it.

Bobby had come far, we reflected, in the two years since Stein had put him in the right-half position. As a forward, he had been mediocre and we had often wondered whether he would ever make it. But now words like "world class" were applied to him. He had the particular ability to chest a ball down, burst forward and release someone like Johnstone or Hughes with an inch-perfect pass. He was also hardworking and committed, and enjoyed the confidence and support of Jock Stein.

In Novi Sad, Celtic continued, gaining in confidence, until about halfway through the second half, when they lost the only goal of the game. It was not a goal brought about by constant pressure. It was a mistake by Tommy Gemmell, a man visibly tiring after all his forays up and down the field. He passed the ball across the field to John Clark, as he had done many times during the game, but he mishit it.

Clark, himself having grown a little complacent because of all the inch-perfect passes he had given and received, was not quite ready and Stanic ran in and scored easily. When Ronnie Simpson picked the ball out of the net, it was one of the few times that he had actually touched the ball.

It was at moments like this that the captaincy skills of Billy McNeill came to the fore. This was no time for the blame game, for finger-pointing or anger, for knee-jerk reactions or any ill-thought-out response. The important thing was not to allow the situation to get any worse. Damage limitation was the name of the game. Often, a sign of a good team is that they can sustain a reverse and then fight back without letting the mind dwell on the mistake, which might then lead to another. As long as no more goals were lost, Celtic were still very much in the tie. McNeill realised this, gave quiet words of encouragement to his two defenders who had conceded the goal, then rallied the defence and the rest of the team to see the game out. The 0-1 score was slightly disappointing, but not a disastrous or irrecoverable result.

The general opinion, then, in both Scotland and Yugoslavia, was that the game was very open. On the same night, Inter Milan made themselves the favourites for the competition by eliminating Real Madrid, the previous year's winners and thus reaching the semi-finals, and in the European Cup Winners' Cup Rangers had had a good result at Ibrox, beating Zaragoza 2-0. In the estimation of the newspapers and pundits of the time, it was generally reckoned that a two-goal lead was a "cushion", whereas a one-goal lead was "wafer-thin".

However, pessimists in pubs and professional ones in the newspapers now began to worry about Celtic. They felt they had taken on too much, basing this assumption on the fact that they had drawn one game and lost one since the New Year. But this Celtic team had not got to where they were by being pessimistic – indeed confidence permeated the team – and once they touched down at Glasgow Airport on the Thursday the game was put to one side and, quite rightly, attention turned to the visit to Love Street to play St Mirren on the Saturday.

St Mirren were a team who seldom did well in the Scottish League, but they had a good Scottish Cup tradition, including eliminating Celtic at the semi-final stage in 1959 and 1962. But this year, they were already out of that competition having lost disappointingly at home to Hamilton Accies a couple of weeks previously. Their league form was indifferent at best and dreadful at worst. Yet they had played above themselves to earn a draw at Celtic Park in early November – a huge shock at the time, for it was Celtic's first point lost in season 1966/67 – and St Mirren were never a team to be underestimated, although Love Street had not in previous years been considered a bogey ground for Celtic. The Buddies had a comparatively new manager in Alex Wright, brought in the previous December in a desperate attempt to halt the slide towards relegation. They also had a goalkeeper called Denis Connaghan (as distinct from Eddie Connachan, the man who had denied Celtic in the Scottish Cup Final of 1961), who was in magnificent form, but no-one would have thought that there was much for Celtic to be afraid of. Yet Celtic had had a long trip in midweek and there was also the worst enemy of them all – complacency.

If there had ever been the slightest doubt that Celtic were back in Scotland, they only needed to look out of their windows on Saturday morning to see the rain. Celtic had already taken the precaution of postponing their reserve match against St Mirren on the Friday night to keep the pitch in good shape for Wednesday's return tie against Vojvodina, and as they travelled the short distance to Paisley they must have entertained serious doubts about whether the game would be on. Whether this would have suited Celtic is open to question. It would have given them a rest before Wednesday, certainly, but Stein always preferred to play. In any case, referee Bert Crockett of Dundee had passed the pitch, even though it had rained solidly for well over 24 hours, and the game was on.

It would be the second Saturday in a row that Celtic had to play on a wet pitch, and this time Stein took the decision to keep Jimmy Johnstone on the bench and deploy John Hughes on the right wing. John needed a game. He had been poor in Yugoslavia, and Stein felt that wet Scottish conditions were the ideal circumstances for the quixotic "Yogi Bear" to shine. Relationships between Stein and Hughes would dip alarmingly in future years, but in 1967 "Yogi" was reckoned to be an integral part of the squad and, having on occasion in the past suffered some appalling abuse from the terracings, he needed the occasional ego massage.

Jock got that one right for Hughes was brilliant that day, with relegation-threatened St Mirren, who had planned to be facing Jimmy Johnstone on the right wing, totally at sea when faced with the rampaging Bear. The Celtic fans started to sing "Feed The Bear, the Bear, he's every f***in' where, Feed the Bear!" Chalmers, like Johnstone, was rested, and Wallace, of course, who had had his enforced rest (because of ineligibility) in Yugoslavia on Wednesday, started the game. The game finished 5-0, but it could have been a lot more. The refreshed Wallace scored first and last, Lennox scored just after half-time, Gemmell converted a penalty for the fourth goal, but the best goal of them all was that scored by John Hughes. He had made it with a charge through the defence, then flicked the ball to Gallagher, got it back and tapped home, as the crowd erupted into a sea of appreciation of such brilliance. It was a trademark Hughes goal.

The crowd, given as 18,000, loved this as they huddled together under the inadequate Love Street shelter or tried to hide under someone's umbrella on the terracing. It was generally agreed that if Celtic played like this, they could beat anyone. There were two slight dampers on the day. One was that Rangers had also won, equally emphatically beating Motherwell 5-1 at Fir Park, and the other was the injury to Bertie Auld, who had played brilliantly but limped off near the end. It was still, however, reckoned to have been a good day for Celtic. Things might have gone differently in the aftermath of a European trip.

The focus, however, was now clearly on the visit of Vojvodina on Wednesday, March 8 to a packed Parkhead. European nights at Celtic Park were always great occasions and this particular night was arguably the greatest of them all. It was not as if there was not excitement elsewhere as well. Rangers had played Airdrie the night before in the Scottish League and had gone to the top of the table in spite of a desperately awful performance, in which they won 1-0 with a penalty. Celtic anger at that result was almost tangible, but we simply had to get it out of our system and move on. Then, on the day after the Vojvodina game, there was to be a crucial by-election scheduled in Pollok, a seat won by Labour in their General Election triumph a year before, but one which was looking decidedly shaky given the government's temporary unpopularity. In addition, Dundee United were also in action in the Inter Cities Fairs Cup against Juventus at Tannadice, although their chances were rated slim as they were 3-0 down from the first leg.

A student at St Andrews University, impecunious and simply lacking the transport to get to Celtic Park and back, I was compelled to sit in my room attempting to study, listening fitfully to a radio programme called *Scrapbook for 1922*, which I would, in normal circumstances, have been fascinated by – all about Lloyd George and the creation of the Irish Free State – but hoping that they would interrupt it to give updates from Parkhead. But this was 1967, and Scottish Home Service simply didn't do that. Highlights would be on TV at 10.25pm, and I decided to give up any attempt at studying and simply walk round the streets until that time.

I tried to avoid anyone I knew for I feared they would make jokes or tell me the wrong score, although with apparent and consistent sincerity, claiming they had heard it on some radio station or saying that they had phoned some newspaper office. But this was no laughing matter. I slipped into the TV room at precisely 10.25pm to join some other chaps who shared my ignorance of the outcome. To their credit, STV did not reveal the score in advance, but Arthur Montford, wearing a stereotypical checked jacket, used words like "cliffhanger" to describe what they were about to show.

More than two hours earlier, at 8pm, the game had kicked off in Glasgow. Steve Chalmers, who had been reputed to be injured, was included (Jock occasionally circulated such rumours to confuse the opposition), as indeed was Charlie Gallagher, given the nod over Bertie Auld, who was still slightly under the weather from his knock at St Mirren. The first half was frankly a bore. The crowd shouted and encouraged, but the Yugoslav defence simply soaked up all the pressure that Celtic could bring to bear on them. There were a few half-chances for both teams, but little for anyone to get enthused about, even though "We Shall Not Be Moved" and that other hit of 1967, "The Merry Ploughboy", reverberated around the stadium along with the awe-inspiring chant of "Cel-tic", followed by three handclaps.

It was such a total non-event as the Yugoslavs, in white with a diagonal band, passed the ball around so well and so confidently. Celtic, in their all-green outfit, did most of the running but Vojvodina were clearly the better football team, and the half-time whistle came with most fans in an almost catatonic state of anti-climax and disappointment. The silence as the teams left the field told its own story. But there were still 45 minutes to go.

Stein apparently did not often go in for the "hair dryer" treatment with his players – at least not at half-time, when there was still a game to be won. Instead, there was a quietly encouraging homily, a few individual chats to various players and a final reminder that 75,000 – a sell-out crowd – were hoping to go home happy. Gemmell was encouraged to go upfield more and Johnstone was given even more of a roving commission, for Stein knew well that he would take several men with him wherever he went, and Celtic needed to upset and disorientate the Vojvodina defence. Johnstone even started the second half lining up beside John Hughes on the left wing.

Slowly, gradually, as the second half developed, Celtic began to gain more of the ascendancy. Now playing towards the old Rangers end of the ground (the Lisbon Lions stand, as it is now), where Jimmy Johnstone would normally be on the stand side of the ground, he now began to appear all over the place, but the Yugoslavs did not lose their composure, with their goalkeeper, Pantelic, looking particularly capable of dealing with any cross balls or shots from a distance.

A hint of desperation was beginning to be felt in the Jungle as the hour mark approached. Nowadays, in these circumstances, the manager would make a substitution or two, but in 1967 there was no such option for the only substitute allowed would be a goalkeeper, and then only in the case of injury.

About a decade previously, Elvis Presley had released the single "It's Now Or Never". This could hardly have been more appropriate to Celtic's plight, but the reckoning was that it would be better not to "die wondering". Pushing men forward might lead to the loss of a goal, but the team were losing anyway, and the Yugoslav side were beginning to pass the ball around with the accuracy that is bred of confidence and indeed experience of dealing with such situations.

But then Tommy Gemmell picked up a pass from John Clark and started on one of his overlaps down the left. He crossed, and Pantelic, instead of coming out for it but staying vertical, decided to dive for it. He missed it, and the ever-alert Steve Chalmers poked home a simple goal. Vojvodina claimed a foul for a handball or a push, but the Swedish referee had no doubts as mayhem took over the frenzied terracings of Celtic Park.

Celtic were now back in the tie, but Vojvodina recovered from their reverse and steadied their ship. A lesser team might have folded under the onslaught of Celtic and their fans, whose sheer passion was something they had never seen before, but this Vojvodina was no poor team, and although they possibly now reckoned their chances of an outright victory at Parkhead as rather poor, they began to think that the play-off in neutral Rotterdam might by no means be the worst thing in the world. In Rotterdam there would be no, or certainly very few, Celtic fans, who seemed to exercise such a demonic influence on their team.

It had sometimes been the fashion with Celtic writers to portray these last 30 minutes as if Celtic were attacking relentlessly and Vojvodina Novi Sad defending desperately, conceding free kicks galore and clearing their lines with increasing panic. This was not entirely true. Yes, Celtic were on top, but their opponents never lost their composure under the pressure, and were even occasionally able to launch a few counter-attacks, which fortunately came to nothing, with Clark, McNeill and Craig defending well and Bobby Murdoch increasingly taking control of the centre circle.

As often happens, even today, at Celtic Park, the weaker brethren were beginning to depart as full time approached. I have never understood this. Some say it is to avoid the queues and traffic jams, but I suspect it is because there is a limit to the sheer amount of tension a human being can take. So when, almost at full time, Celtic won a corner on the stand side of the ground I could imagine quite a few saying: "Ach! Nothing will come o' this! Ony chance o the gemme being televised fae Rotterdam next week?" and departed. Others said: "Wan last chance."

Charlie Gallagher trotted over to take the kick. It had, of course, been Charlie who had taken the kick in the 1965 Scottish Cup Final from which McNeill had scored the glorious winner. That one had been on the left. This one was on the right. McNeill himself started his run, combining the ability to keep his eye on the ball and evade the baulking of opponents. Meanwhile, Steve Chalmers did his own bit of baulking to prevent, as if by accident, Pantelic getting up for the ball and Charlie's cross was the perfect height and direction for the elegant head of Billy McNeill to do the job.

Pandemonium ensued. You really have to be among a Celtic crowd in a standing area when a vital goal is scored to know what it is like. I, of course, was not there, but the scene could be imagined. Kissing, cuddling, tears promiscuously intermingled with friends, complete strangers and even the guy with whom you had been having an animated and not entirely pleasant discussion about the value to the team of Jim Craig or Charlie Gallagher. Shoes can come off, wallets and keys can drop out of pockets, you can be crushed… and you may well end up some ten yards or so away from where you were originally. The mayhem had not yet subsided when the referee blew for full time immediately after Vojvodina had taken their centre. Oh, how I wish I had been there.

About 100 miles away, and an hour later, I incurred the wrath of some other students by shouting, crying and bawling in the company of a few other like-minded characters who had, like myself, been watching the TV "cliffhanger" without knowing the score. The common room of St Regulus Hall, normally sedate, august, dignified, with people discussing Homer's *Iliad* or Gide's philosophy, or the theory of numbers or even the treatment and cure of venereal diseases, was in uproar as Celtic supporters treated themselves to an impromptu dance. A few patronising English students got told where to stick their World Cup, while Rangers supporters remained silent. Supporters of East Fife, Forfar, Hibs and Morton, however, expressed mild delight that a Scottish team were now in the European Cup semi-finals, emulating the achievement of Dundee in 1963.

Another friend of mine, who was upstairs in his room, entertaining, shall we say, a young lady, heard me shouting and made a mild complaint the following day. I asked him blandly if he had spilt the coffee because of my ecstasy and he uttered the immortal words: "No, it wasn't coffee." Another coarse fellow who had overheard all this said: "It was more like milk." Whatever all that meant, I simply did not know – nor really did I care. I did know, however, that Celtic had won a famous victory of intense significance and that Billy McNeill and Charlie Gallagher, who had changed my life for the better that day two years earlier, in April 1965, had now done it again. The only difference was that the Dunfermline corner in 1965 had been from the left at Hampden, whereas against Vojvodina, it was from the right at Parkhead.

"Aye, Jock cut it fine the nicht" was the general opinion among the gentlemen of the press, and in all the long history of Celtic Park it would be hard to parallel such a night for passion, drama, tension and eventual triumph. It was even put as a cause for Labour's defeat at the Pollok by-election the following day in that Celtic supporters were all too traumatised and shell-shocked (in a nice way) to do anything else than talk about their triumph, and could not even be persuaded to attend the polling stations. Conservative voters, however, had been less overwhelmed by the exploits of Queen's Park and the Scotland rugby team, and duly turned up to vote.

Jock Stein himself paid tribute to the Celtic fans who "encouraged the players and helped them regain confidence for renewed effort in the second half to break down the Yugoslavs' strong, efficient defence. The players went out for the second half believing that they could win the tie, and they were further (sic) confident when they heard the crowd willing them to victory". Credit was also given to Tommy Gemmell for his great run which led to the equaliser and more than made up for his bad mistake the previous week.

Everyone at Celtic Park was on a high after this result, and it was the job of Jock Stein to bring everyone down to earth and remind them that there was a Scottish Cup quarter-final on Saturday against Queen's Park. Those of us who can recall 2003 will remember with horror how Celtic, having defeated Liverpool in Europe, then went up to Inverness bristling with misplaced confidence and complacency and blew a Scottish Cup tie, thereby gifting Rangers with a treble. Thirty-six years previously, Stein had to make sure that something similar did not happen.

The Scottish Cup quarter-finals had always been one of the big days of the Scottish football card, and still was in 1967, even though Celtic had been frying other fish in midweek, and the other big Glasgow team was no longer invited to the party. The tie of the round was quite clearly Hibs v Aberdeen at Easter Road, but there was also Dundee United v Dunfermline, Clyde v Hamilton Accies and Celtic v Queen's Park, the amateurs of Scottish football.

The time was when Queen's Park and Celtic were the deadliest of enemies in a rivalry which even pre-dated Celtic v Rangers. Celtic won the Scottish Cup finals of 1892 and 1900, but lost that of 1893 to the Spiders, and they had had many clashes in the Glasgow Cup. Queen's Park and the SFA were often seen as virtually the same thing, with Queen's Park allegedly having all sorts of unhealthy influences over the referees' committee. The referee of the 1893 Scottish Cup Final was a Mr Harrison of Kilmarnock. At one point in the game, there being no goal nets, Queen's Park claimed a goal while Celtic claimed that it was a goal kick. But the amateurs had won the day by saying: "It's a goal, Mr Harrison!" The said Mr Harrison took their word for it, for amateurs and gentlemen did not lie!

In addition, it had rankled in the early days that Queen's Park had knocked Celtic out of the Scottish Cup in 1896, using their influence, it was claimed, to organise the suspension of the great Barney Battles from that particular game (although, in fact, frost and the postponement of the fixture from its original date played a part as well). Many years after that, in the Glasgow Charity Cup Final of May 1926, the day after the collapse of the General Strike, Celtic fans had wholeheartedly sung "The Red Flag" in a class-war attempt to unsettle the Glasgow bourgeoisie which Queen's Park represented, singling out a few perceived strike-breakers in the Queen's Park team who had volunteered to drive milk lorries and buses.

Celtic in the 1890s represented the professionals, the working class, Queen's Park the amateurs and the middle classes in a clash for hegemony of Scottish football, which led to the two teams trying to outdo each other in building stadia for the purpose of hosting the Scotland v England international. Celtic did this in 1892, but Queen's Park won the battle with the building of the present Hampden Park in 1903. Queen's had ruled the roost in Scottish football until the rise of Celtic in the 1890s, and with their ten Scottish Cup victories remain third in the list of teams who have won the Scottish Cup most often. (Jock Stein knew most things about Scottish football, but he got that one wrong, apparently, in a quiz question.) The Hampden side had also, until early in the 20th century, refused to have anything to do with the Scottish League, seeing it as the creation of John H McLaughlin of Celtic, who was also the champion of professionalism.

Now, in 1967 (the centenary of Queen's Park, as it turned out), Celtic and Queen's Park were hardly rivals, for there was a huge gulf between them, and they co-existed peacefully with respect for each other's traditions, tending to vote with each other at SFA and Scottish League meetings. Indeed it was often rumoured that, on one or two occasions when Queen's Park in the First Division were in danger of relegation and Celtic couldn't win the Scottish League, the teams would perhaps draw, and then Celtic would pull out all the stops to hammer Queen's Park's rivals. It didn't always work out, and the Spiders' natural habitat was now the Second Division. But, in any case, everyone had a nice word to say about Queen's Park, that quaint anachronism of Scottish football. There was something pure about them, as distinct from the brutal and sometimes dirty world of professional football, and Latin scholars looked with approval on their motto *Ludere causa ludendi* – "to play for the sake of playing". With my own eyes, I have seen once or twice Queen's Park supporters actually reading books in the stand at half-time!

Yet they would be no pushovers in the Scottish Cup. Indeed, Celtic were painfully aware that only two years earlier, in February 1965, in the interregnum between Stein's appointment in January and his arrival in March, Celtic had struggled at Hampden against Queen's Park, who had, frankly, in the first half at least, been the better team. Eventually, Celtic wore them down and Bobby Lennox scored in the second half to ease the tension. But it had been a nervy 1-0 victory to prove the adage that there is no such thing as an easy Scottish Cup tie.

But on this March day in 1967, the Jungle roof was nearly lifted off when Celtic appeared. Again, they were wearing their all-green strip, which they had worn against Vojvodina, and they appeared now as European Cup semi-finalists. They had a special guest as well in no less a person than 007 himself, alias James Bond. Sean Connery appeared before the game, kicked a ball around for a while, then went to the stand to watch the game, as if he had been watching Celtic all his life. Certainly with a name like Sean Connery, you really should be a Celtic supporter, although we were sad to see him in later years shamefully flirting with David Murray's Rangers, and he also told everyone that he had once supported Hibs. Clearly a man who was "all things to all men" or, as the less charitable would put it, a "chancer".

Nevertheless, on this particular day, James Bond was a great propaganda coup for Celtic. Students of the body language of Jock Stein and some of the more serious-minded players (the photograph in *The Celtic View* showed several players looking away from 007 in the direction of a banner being raised by the crowd) might have detected a certain feeling that 007 was getting in the way of some rather serious business. Nevertheless, this whole stunt, particularly in the context of what had happened on Wednesday night, gave everyone the impression that Celtic Park was the place to be. Even Her Majesty's Secret Service were here to bow the knee of homage to the great Glasgow Celtic. Celtic's decision to invite him may even have had something to do with Mr Kosygin of the Soviet Union watching Rangers a month earlier. Celtic were now "the good guys". Rangers, incidentally, were elbowed even further out of the way when a waterlogged pitch led to the postponement of their league match with St Johnstone.

Indeed, up to mid-morning, it might have looked as if the Parkhead game was also likely to be off, but a wind sprung up and referee Mr Callaghan sanctioned play at 2pm. It would be the third Saturday in a row that Celtic had to play on a heavy wet pitch – not that it need have bothered them, for they had the players to deal with it. It was a typical Glasgow day in mid-March – showers of rain, sunny periods, wind, more rain – but the conditions were no more turbulent than what transpired on the field of play. It was, in fact, an excellent game of football, won 5-3 by Celtic, but one in which the amateurs emerged with a great deal of honour and thoroughly deserved the sustained round of applause given to them by the appreciative and respectful Celtic crowd.

Queen's actually scored within the first minute with a Tommy Gemmell own goal. But you can't keep the irrepressible Tommy Gemmell down, for he equalised with a penalty kick (by no means the most obvious penalty kick ever awarded at Celtic Park) within ten minutes. Chalmers then scored for Celtic after some magnificent work from Bertie Auld, but Queen's Park would not give up and Niall Hopper scored a great goal for them. Celtic went ahead again with a Wallace counter, then seemed to put the game out of sight, just as half-time was approaching, when they went 4-2 ahead with a great goal by Bobby Murdoch after a touch of Jimmy Johnstone at his best.

That seemed to be that, but Hopper scored again for the visitors soon after the break, and the second half, with the score at 4-3, was marvellous entertainment for the fans as both teams attacked with all their might. It was only when Bobby Lennox scored in the 85th minute that Celtic were able to breathe easily in the knowledge that they had made it to the semi-finals of the Scottish Cup. A replay would have been exactly what Celtic didn't need in their crowded schedule, even though, the cynics noted, it would not have done any harm to the already swelling coffers.

And that should have been the end of it all. That it wasn't was due to something snapping within Jimmy Johnstone. One of the qualities that Jimmy had been slowly developing was his ability to keep calm and not to retaliate when fouled. Infamously, he had snapped on New Year's Day 1965 after many fouls by Rangers player Theorolf Beck, but the red mist was seen less often these days. He had kept his cool admirably against Vojvodina, and for 89 minutes against Queen's Park he did likewise. But one foul too many from Miller Hay and Jimmy retaliated with the traditional "Glasgow kiss" – a head butt. Although referee Mr Callaghan either didn't see it properly or didn't think it was too bad and merely booked both players, Jock Stein disagreed.

Johnstone was immediately taken off and was seen to make a comment to his manager as he passed him. Stein then followed him up the tunnel. Legend then had it that Jimmy ran to hide in the toilet to avoid the rage of Big Jock and would only come out when Stein promised not to hit him. To what extent this is true, we do not know, but we do know that Johnstone was told to get dressed and see the directors in half an hour. Stein had then recommended a week's suspension by the club, and the directors agreed.

Cynics, however, noticed that the week's suspension also included the Scottish League v the English League game on Wednesday. Frankly, it suited Celtic for Jimmy not to play in that game, and Jimmy had not given any indication of being all that bothered whether he played in that game or not. It would have been interesting to see how Stein would have reacted had Jimmy's misconduct occurred the previous week, immediately before the Vojvodina game, or before a game against Rangers. As it was, Jimmy was given seven days' suspension from the club and would not play against Dunfermline in the following Saturday's game. Stein himself said that the decision was "far from easy" and he hoped that "the step that has been taken will make him a better player for Celtic".

All of this did not, however, become apparent until we read the Sunday newspapers the following morning, and most supporters departed Celtic Park unaware of all this. The green and white brigade headed back along London Road and the Gallowgate delighted that Celtic had survived this game, which might indeed have been a "Berwick" following the mighty events of midweek. In the other ties, Dundee United had beaten Dunfermline in a close game, but the other ones were drawn. Clyde and Hamilton Accies had drawn in a game after which newspaper reports were far from charitable about the standard of play, and at Easter Road, Aberdeen, now regarded as Celtic's main rivals for the Scottish Cup, had needed a late equaliser to earn a replay.

Arguments raged into Sunday and Monday about the wisdom of suspending Jimmy Johnstone. Gair Henderson of *The Evening Times* was full of praise for what Stein had done, saying that "it was in the tradition of fair play for which Celtic are renowned". Some supporters thought that Stein was mad to do such a thing, risking Celtic's chances in the various competitions they were involved in and possibly permanently alienating the man whom many considered to be the best player in the world, while others (myself included) saw it as part of the ongoing territorial personality struggle between Stein and Johnstone. Johnstone was good, but Stein was the boss. No-one was bigger, in any sense of the word, than Jock Stein. It would, however, have been interesting to know what would have happened if Jimmy had *not* made that unfortunate remark to Big Jock, for it seemed that what caused the trouble was the challenge to Stein's authority rather than the violent indiscretion in the first place.

Celtic were drawn against the winner of Clyde or Hamilton (it would turn out to be Clyde) in the semi-final, to be played at Hampden on April 1, but the big game that midweek was the league international between the Scottish League and the English League, which insisted on rubbing everyone up the wrong way by calling itself the Football League. As far as Scotland was concerned, it was often used as a practice match for the "big" international between Scotland and England, but Scotland could only choose players who played for a Scottish team. Anglo-Scots, like Billy Bremner and Denis Law, were not allowed. Indeed they could have played for the English League.

Even in 1967, it was generally accepted that such league internationals had had their day, and the 1967 game did little to keep interest alive in this game. The weather was foul yet again, with wind and sleet, and the amazing thing was that 29,000 were persuaded to turn up at Hampden Park, where cover was minimal, to see such a terrible game in which the Englishmen won easily 3-0. Four Celtic players – McNeill, Gemmell, Clark and Chalmers – played for the Scottish League, but none of them did much to enhance their reputations.

League business resumed on Saturday, March 18. Celtic had Dunfermline at home, while Rangers went to Ayr United. With the points being level, Rangers were marginally ahead on goal average, but Celtic had a game in hand, and they were to play this game on Monday night. It was against Falkirk at Celtic Park. It followed then that Celtic's next 48 hours were vital ones in their attempt to regain their league title.

Dunfermline, managed by Willie Cunningham, were still a good side. Like quite a few provincial sides, they often gave the impression of being a "ceiling" club, in the sense that they felt that they could go so far and no further. They sometimes seemed to lack belief in themselves on big occasions.

Celtic had got the better of them in recent times, notably in the game at East End Park the previous November, when Celtic won breathtakingly 5-4. Celtic had also beaten them twice in the Scottish League Cup quarter-finals and a common factor in all games had been goals and loads of them. They were sufficiently attractive visitors to draw a crowd of about 41,000 to Celtic Park to see how Celtic, without Jimmy Johnstone and forced to play John Hughes on the right wing instead of the wee man, would do against the Pars.

In fact, it was one of Celtic's many good performances that season. Celtic always seemed to do well against the Pars and this was no exception. The score was 3-2, but that was slightly misleading, for Dunfermline scored late in the game through Alex Ferguson to reduce the leeway and give Celtic supporters a few palpitations. It would, however, have been a gross injustice if the Pars had equalised. The first half had seen some superb Celtic football, with Chalmers heading home a Wallace cross and Wallace doing likewise from a Chalmers cross. Tommy Gemmell also scored a penalty kick. The second half continued in the same vein, but Celtic were unable to add to their tally.

The game was another interesting example of the unconventional nature of Stein's tactics. Hughes was theoretically the right-winger, but in fact played in his normal role on the left. Chalmers, of course, was a recognised right-winger, but he was not there all the time. Sometimes it was Wallace, sometimes Murdoch, other times Tommy Gemmell (playing at right-back that day) on the overlap. The Dunfermline defence, normally methodical and organised, were totally bewildered by all this. Interchanging of the forward line was, of course, a great Celtic tradition. McMenemy and Quinn's team of the 1900s had done this to devastating effect, as had Jimmy Delaney's side of the late 1930s.

Although Rangers also won, thereby keeping, temporarily, their advantage of goal average, Celtic played off their game in hand on Monday, March 20, and their 5-0 beating of Falkirk at Parkhead gave them a two-point advantage, with both teams having played 27 games out of 34. Twenty-five thousand saw another superb Celtic performance. Johnstone was back after his suspension –

Stein was as always an expert with his carrot-and-stick policy – and was given a great welcome. Chalmers, Auld, Hughes, Gemmell (penalty) and Chalmers again scored the goals against a very weak Falkirk side, whose only method of resistance seemed to be an ineffective offside trap.

This result put pressure on Rangers, who were travelling to Spain to play in the second leg of their European Cup Winners' Cup game against Zaragoza, in which they held a 2-0 lead. Tuesday, March 21 brought news that Celtic would be pitted against Dukla Prague in the European Cup semi-finals while Rangers, if successful against Zaragoza, would play Slavia Sofia. Celtic were delighted to have avoided Inter Milan, the favourites, but were also aware that Dukla, the team of the Czechoslovak Army, would be tough.

Czechoslovakia, of course, no longer exists, and about 18 months after they played Celtic, their players would have a difficult decision to make when the Soviet Union invaded their country, afraid of the "liberalising tendencies" of Alexander Dubcek, who showed signs not of turning capitalist or siding with the NATO countries, but of allowing some freedom of speech. Not even acknowledged left-wingers like myself, with a certain ideological sympathy for communism, could defend the Soviets on that. The soldiers of the Czech Army, some of whom played for Dukla, would have been compelled in August 1968 either to join in the suppression of their own countrymen or themselves risk brutal elimination by the merciless Soviets.

It is difficult to parallel this sort of thing in Scottish history, although there was the time in Glasgow in 1919, in the immediate aftermath of the First World War, when the British government, panicked by the fear of revolution at the time of the George Square Riots and constantly terrified that the Irish problem might spread to Glasgow, felt obliged to confine some soldiers of the British Army to the Maryhill Barracks. Lloyd George feared that their loyalty could not be depended on.

It was clear then that Celtic were in for a tough time in Czechoslovakia, although the first game was at Parkhead. But the immediate concern was the visit to Hearts on league business on Saturday, and even before that, the events of the Wednesday, March 22 were not without significance for Celtic and their supporters. In the first place, there was the Rangers game in Zaragoza, and although everyone around Celtic Park – managers, players and supporters – always say things like "I don't care" and "no concern of ours" whenever Rangers are playing, in fact it is always a very great concern of all Celtic supporters, with "Hoo did the Huns get oan?" a constant question.

But there were also two Scottish Cup replays which would have a bearing on Celtic. Clyde were at Douglas Park, Hamilton for a tea time kick-off (Hamilton Accies did not, as yet, have floodlights) and then, later on, there was the game that had lit up the North East of Scotland into some passionate crucible of enthusiasm which had not been seen in that quarter for many years. This was the replay of Aberdeen v Hibs. Celtic would, of course, play the winners of Clyde and Hamilton in the semi-final and, if successful, would meet in the final the winners of the other semi-final, Dundee United v the winners of the Pittodrie quarter-final.

The Celtic View of that day, incidentally, gave an excellent example of how insidious a weapon propaganda, in this case benevolent propaganda, could be. The previous Friday night, Celtic's reserves had lost 0-3 to Rangers reserves at Ibrox. "Kerrydale" skilfully avoids talking about the game, but concentrates on how the Celtic party in the main stand was "subjected to insults" by a "large section of the Rangers followers in the stand". Well, yes, but why is anyone surprised at that? Did they expect anything else? And then comes the brilliantly subtle sentence, "Celtic are very sorry for the officials of the Rangers club who *say* (my italics) they have done everything to eliminate this type of obscenity of language which appears to be prevalent at their ground and who apologised to their visitors for the latest outbreak".

Under the guise of being forgiving and gracious, there are at least three unpleasant and subtle hits at Rangers. Rangers "say they have done everything" – but apparently they haven't. Bad language "appears to be prevalent at their ground" – you mean, it isn't at Parkhead? And the "latest outbreak" – so it has happened before? It then goes on to express their confidence that Celtic supporters will not retaliate – yet it has just put that very idea in their mind, and also those of us who attended Celtic games regularly were far from sanguine about Celtic supporters' ability not to "descend to such obscenities".

The dominating topic of general conversation in March 1967, however, was not Celtic FC, nor was it the Beatles, nor Prime Minister Harold Wilson, nor was it even the Vietnam war. It was, in fact, the SS *Torrey Canyon*. This was an oil tanker en route to Wales from the Middle East which had hit some rocks off the coast of Cornwall, threatening to cause the biggest environmental disaster of all time. Every night, the BBC showed pictures of an oil slick moving towards the British mainland and distressing pictures of birds, unable to fly because they were covered in oil. The problem was that the stricken ship refused to sink, and needed to be bombed by the RAF to do so. This was, of course, great fun for the RAF, who had begun to question their continued existence since the Battle of Britain of nearly 30 years previously, but there was a serious side to it as well, and now gradually people began to think more deeply about pollution and the environment. It would take some time, however, for environmental issues to become the hysterical obsession that they are with some people today.

On Easter holiday now from university, I was offered a lift by some friends to Pittodrie to see Aberdeen v Hibs. We were genuine neutrals. One of us supported Rangers, one supported Dundee, one played for East Fife but supported Hearts, and then there was me. It was an odd experience to visit the Granite City and discover that football had, temporarily at least, taken over that strange city. It was like visiting Newcastle on a football day when everyone is going around with a black and white scarf. In Aberdeen, that pleasant Wednesday afternoon and evening, everyone was wearing red, talking animatedly about what Eddie Turnbull had done for the city, how they were going to win the cup this year (they had not done so since 1947, having lost three finals in the interim) and how they were particularly enthused by a chap called Jim Storrie, who had recently joined the club from Leeds United.

In this, they were fuelled by Grampian Television, a spectacularly dreadful Aberdeen-based TV station. Mercifully, they took most programmes, like *Coronation Street, The Saint* and *Take Your Pick,* from the ITV network, but now and again they produced their own cringeworthy attempts at local culture. There were local music programmes like *Bothy Nichts,* the presenter who kept saying "Oh, fit a rare nicht we're hae'n of it the nicht," a quiz programme where you got two points if you told them that Paris was the capital of France, and one for a close miss if you said that David Copperfield was written by Robert Louis Stevenson. And, of course, the adverts. "Do you need a perr o shoes? Weel, come tae oor shop in Buckie High Street and we'll get ye a perr o' shoes." Archie Glen, a fine Aberdeen half-back of the 1950s, hosted a football preview programme on a Friday night, when it was not unknown for someone to talk at length about the prospects for the next day's game, which had already been postponed. There were also teams called Queen of the Sooth, Patrick Thistle, Stenhousehouse and Hib.

Aberdonians are, in football terms, a breed apart – infamously hard on their own players when things are not going well, critical, sometimes downright anti-social and torn-faced, unfriendly but with a deep sense of fair play and what is right. They are not all that bad (at least they weren't in 1967), but they could be more than a little boorish at times with their inane chants. They have loads of women supporters, one of whom confided to me in a matronly way at a game in 1964 (pre-segregation days) that she wanted to take Jimmy Johnstone home with her after he had been brutally fouled by a coarse Aberdeen defender called Hogg. Her husband was a lot less sympathetic, shouting "Get aff the parrk, ye wee durrty green bastarrt!" before realising, from the look of disapproval from his wife, that I was of the other persuasion. He then became politely reasonable for the rest of the game, won 3-0 by Celtic.

Forty-four thousand turned up that night, almost a record, and Hibs supporters were few and far between. It was thus odd to be in such a large, biased crowd with no-one talking about anything other than Ernie Winchester, Harry Melrose and Jim Storrie. It was actually quite a refreshing experience, and interesting to see such passion from a part of Scotland which had not hitherto been linked to such commitment and enthusiasm.

Ernie Winchester, the cult hero who had recently fallen from grace, was restored and scored the first goal in Aberdeen's easy 3-0 win. The douce Dons had rarely seen anything like this, and were to a man and woman convinced that the Scottish Cup would be theirs. The taunting of the Hibs fans was at once triumphalist, gloating and none too intelligent, going along the lines of "Yerr out, yerr out" delivered *ad infinitum* and *ad nauseam* in that sing-song accent, with the rich burr in the way that they emphasised the letter "r". A poor lonely Hibs fan, shamefully mocked and jeered at, was heading along King Street to get his last train home to Edinburgh. He had one last shot, however, reminding one of a "my big brither will get you for this" type of riposte when he turned to his tormentors and said: "Celtic will win the cup and they'll beat you, ye bastards!" It was somehow touching and even prophetic. He then shouted "corn beef", an obscure reference to the typhoid epidemic which had hit Aberdeen in summer 1964.

That city had not yet been revolutionised with North Sea oil (although there were rumours), but it had certainly been touched that night by the richness of expectation. But their enthusiasm was dampened ever so slightly as they got into their cars and drove home to be told the news that Rangers had qualified for the semi-finals of the European Cup Winners' Cup. Rangers had done so in a way which defied belief and the circumstances had to be confirmed several times on the sports news. Rangers had, in fact, lost their two-goal lead and the game finished 2-2 after extra time. The tie then went not to a replay at a neutral venue, nor to a penalty shoot-out (no-one had ever thought of them in 1967), but to the toss of a coin. John Greig did many fine things for Rangers in his career – let us not deny him that – but one of his best decisions was to call "tails" that night.

Clyde had decisively beaten Hamilton Accies at Douglas Park to earn a Scottish Cup semi-final tie against Celtic, but Celtic were now preoccupied by the visit to Tynecastle on Saturday. In some ways, this would prove to be Celtic's most decisive victory of the season, and it was a watershed in Celtic's visits to Edinburgh. Not since April 30, 1955, when Neil Mochan and Bobby Collins had done something to attempt to expurgate the awful memories of the loss of the Scottish Cup Final replay to Clyde in the previous midweek, had Celtic beaten Hearts in a league match at Tynecastle. Celtic had famously won a Scottish Cup tie 4-3 in 1962, and a Scottish League Cup game in August 1964, but Hearts had either won or drawn the league games, the wins being normally very convincing.

But this game also had a more sinister element as well, and indicated the rapid deterioration in the relationship between the two sets of supporters. It all seemed to stem from the sale of Willie Wallace to Celtic in December 1966. One could, to a certain extent, sympathise with the Hearts fans, but their grievance was surely against their own pusillanimous management for their lack of ambition and desire to make money, rather than with Celtic. Previously, Celtic and Hearts games had passed with a minimum of trouble, with even a certain grudging respect between the fans of both teams, but now, at Tynecastle, on this windy, rainy day, we began to hear blasphemy about the Pope and songs about sashes and walls. This aping and copying of Rangers fans sadly continues to this day, and sounds absolutely bizarre and absurd when sung by people who live in Edinburgh's Dalry and Gorgie.

This did not mean, of course, that all of west Edinburgh had converted to extremism and bigotry. Indeed many Hearts fans were embarrassed about all this, but it did reflect the frustration of the Edinburgh fans who could, of course, have become Scotland's establishment team in the capital in the same way that Arsenal were the establishment team in England, had their management shown more ambition and determination. In addition, their day had passed. They had won the Scottish League as recently as 1958 and 1960, and had near misses in 1959 and 1965. But 1965 was also the day of Celtic's defeat of Dunfermline in the Scottish Cup and their blowing up against Kilmarnock on that day would have many long-term consequences. Indeed, with the benefit of historical perspective, one could say that Celtic and Hearts changed places that day.

The poor weather conditions kept the crowd to a little under the capacity for Tynecastle, but they saw a good game with a very even first half before Bertie Auld put Celtic ahead just before half-time. Bobby Murdoch had been injured early in the game after what looked like an innocuous fall on the ground, but the fall had aggravated an earlier ankle injury sustained, by coincidence, against Hearts at Tynecastle in December 1963. Bobby was off for a while but came back before finally having to withdraw near the end. By this time, the on-form Celtic side had scored two more, Willie Wallace from a free kick against his old team-mates and then Tommy Gemmell with a twice-taken penalty kick. Hearts had put up a good fight in the first half, but were outplayed in the second. Willie Wallace was outstanding throughout and never was the folly of the Hearts directors more exposed than on that day.

This game kept Celtic's two-point lead at the top of the table. They might even have increased it, but Rangers also won that day, beating Hibs 1-0 at Ibrox. But Celtic had another game to play on the night of Monday, March 27, one brought forward from April 15, which was scheduled for the England v Scotland international. Stein had wanted the postponed Ibrox game to be played that night, but Rangers had to turn it down because of John Greig's wedding. Frustrated by this, Jock then turned to another Glasgow team, Partick Thistle, and found them a great deal more co-operative, agreeing to play their home game that night.

Bobby Murdoch was out injured at Firhill – a potentially serious problem, for Murdoch was as good a player as any this season – but he was replaced by the versatile Willie Wallace at right-half. Celtic gave Charlie Gallagher a game in place of Bertie Auld, and he was superb as Celtic won 4-1. Charlie had another reason to celebrate for his wife had just had a baby boy on the Saturday. Lennox scored Celtic's 100th goal of the season and after Partick Thistle equalised, Chalmers scored twice and Wallace once to give Celtic a comfortable victory, an assessment agreed with by the ever-chivalrous Willie Thornton, one-time centre-forward for Rangers. (Thornton, a winner of the Military Medal in the Second World War, was often given a reluctant ripple of applause at Parkhead.) Annoyingly for Celtic, a couple of days later Rangers won again, this time 4-3 against St Johnstone at Ibrox, an exciting game but celebrated with relief rather than ecstatic rejoicing by the Rangers supporters.

And thus ended the month of March. Now for April, the month when things were usually decided. It was already possible to detect in Celtic fans, and certainly in *The Celtic View,* a barely concealed excitement about what was about to happen. Certainly, Jock Stein in *The Celtic View* and in his ghost-written column in *The Sunday Mirror* was at pains to keep everyone's feet on the ground. This season could be the best of them all. On the other hand we could all fall flat on our faces, as had happened to a certain extent the previous year. What was certain was that, one way or another, April 1967 would not be easily forgotten.

Two semi-finals beckoned in the Scottish and European Cups, the league race had now, as it were, turned Tattenham Corner (the famous turn in the Derby at Epsom in June) and we were heading down the home straight with a two-point lead and five games remaining (home to Dundee United and Aberdeen, away to Motherwell, Kilmarnock and Rangers). There was even the unprecedented possibility of a European Cup Final. And, just in case anyone had forgotten, two weeks later there was the international against the world champions England. Quite a few Celtic players would be involved in that, one felt, so the month of April would be anything but a sedate, relaxing end to the season. These were tumultuous, tempestuous and torrid times – and we were all looking forward to them with relish.

APRIL

· · · · · · ·

Clyde were Celtic's opponents in the Scottish Cup semi-final at Hampden on April 1. Celtic supporters had, and still have, an affinity and even a certain sympathy for Clyde. They are one of the teams that a Celtic supporter would happily confess to having as his "second" team. Hibs, Albion Rovers and Dundee United can occasionally share this honour, perhaps; Rangers, Hearts, Motherwell, Airdrie and Aberdeen certainly not.

Indeed there was a great deal to admire about the Bully Wee Clyde in 1967. Playing at nearby Shawfield, home of the famous greyhound racing track, Clyde were actually, at that moment in time, third in the Scottish League. Moreover, this had been achieved by employing part-time players, all of whom were enthusiastic and gave every impression of enjoying their football under the equally enthusiastic Davie White. Their manager was in his prime and had not yet over-reached himself by making the fatal mistake of taking on the job at Rangers – as he would do at the end of the year. That was, as events would prove, too much for him.

Clyde, founded in 1876 and one of the oldest teams in Scotland, were an excellent example of how to cope with economic reality. They were too close to Celtic to have any huge support, but had had their moments. In the 1950s, they achieved the unprecedented feat of winning the Scottish Cup in 1955, suffering relegation in 1956, winning promotion in 1957 and then the Scottish Cup again in 1958. This sort of thing is hard to parallel in world football, but the first of these achievements remained a painful one for Celtic.

Several of the 1967 Celtic side – notably Billy McNeill and John Fallon – had vivid memories of watching that awful night in April 1955, when Clyde beat Celtic 1-0 in the Hampden rain in the replay of the Scottish Cup Final. The first game had been surrendered through a ghastly late goalkeeping error, but the replay was far worse. Inexplicably, Celtic opted to drop Bobby Collins, by some distance their best forward, and went down 0-1 to a second-half goal scored by Tommy Ring. Allegedly, Collins' non-appearance was because he had tried to shoulder-charge Clyde's goalkeeper. If that was true, it was Celtic who were the sufferers.

The situation was dripping with irony. Tommy Ring, like many of that Clyde side, was Celtic-daft and the fact that he was never given the opportunity at Celtic Park speaks volumes about the coaching set-up there in the early 1950s. He was a superbly talented outside-left and the night after that final he visited his mother's house in Glasgow's East End to show her his Scottish Cup medal. He found himself shunned by his brothers, who refused to eat with him, such was the pain of losing a Scottish Cup Final. But it didn't bother Tommy all that much. He had already won five Scottish caps and went on to win another seven.

Clyde's victory in the 1958 Scottish Cup was against Hibs, a team who could be predicted with a certain degree of accuracy, even in 1958, to blow up at Hampden, but Clyde had beaten Celtic en route to the final in an unusual match. It was Clyde's home game but had to be played at Celtic Park after a wall collapsed, injuring a few fans, at the previous league game between the two clubs at Shawfield.

They were also the team who had famously held the Scottish Cup for eight years in a row. They won it in 1939 and as the tournament was not contested again until 1947, El Alamein, Stalingrad, Anzio, D Day and V E Day all became famous throughout the world while Clyde were the Scottish Cup holders. They had also lost to Celtic in the Scottish Cup Final of 1912 a week before the *Titanic* set sail, and in 1910 to Dundee, who recorded their first and only triumph in the tournament. The final took three games and in the first of these Clyde were leading 2-0 late in the match until Dundee scored what looked like a consolation goal before they equalised with virtually the last kick of the ball.

Clyde were clearly a team of some character and history, but the conventional wisdom was that "you never get a good game between these two" Glasgow East End sides. Perhaps it was because they knew each other too well; perhaps because their supporters did not really hate each other enough; more likely, it was because Clyde were professionally determined to play a good defensive game and give nothing away.

There had also been a tendency for Celtic to play Clyde immediately after a game against Rangers. Whether successful or not, games against Rangers did leave some legacy or fall-out. Either Celtic had lost to Rangers and felt despondent and depressed, or perhaps they had beaten Rangers and were complacent and over-confident. For whatever reason, games against Clyde, whether at Shawfield or Celtic Park, tended to be miserable 0-0 or 1-1 draws on rainy days.

Celtic's main problem in the Scottish Cup semi-final on April 1 was the absence of Bobby Murdoch through an ankle injury. Willie Wallace played at right-half, as he had done on the Monday, but if there had ever been any doubt that Willie was a better forward than a midfield player, the proof was here. It also showed what a great player Bobby Murdoch was. Celtic put on one of their poorest performances of the season in the Hampden drizzle. Things were pretty miserable as half-time came, with nothing happening and the tiny pocket of Clyde fans in the impressive crowd of 57,000 growing in confidence at the weaknesses in Celtic's forward play. Jimmy Johnstone and Bertie Auld in particular both had what is commonly known as a "stinker".

One must always be suspicious of statements like "Celtic supporters are the best in the world" and "faithful through and through". Great European nights with impressive singing and commitment must be balanced against games like this one, when some Celtic supporters turned on their team with boos, catcalls and slow handclapping. There were even a few statements like "I always knew that c*** Lennox would never make it" and "Chalmers simply canna f***in' score goals". It was incredible. Here, we had the European Cup semi-finalists who had already won the Scottish League Cup and the Glasgow Cup, were ahead in the Scottish League and were now contesting the Scottish Cup semi-finals against tough opponents. Admittedly, they were having a poor day but then again they were without their star man, the injured Bobby Murdoch. But they were now, as this game petered out, being told by some of their fans that they were useless.

My depression, such as it was, centred more on the fans than the team, whose poor performance I simply put down to a bad day. But in any case, by the time that we had reached Buchanan Street Station on the way home, Celtic were world-beaters again. And why was that? It was because Rangers had lost 0-1 to Dunfermline Athletic! This meant that Celtic were now two points ahead with a game in hand in the league race. In any case, the Scottish Cup semi-final saw no harm done – it finished 0-0, and really Celtic should have had a penalty in the last few minutes, when a shot was elbowed away by a Clyde defender, something that was visible to everyone in the Hampden drizzle but the referee, Mr JRP Gordon of Newport-on-Tay, who would go on to disgrace himself in later years.

The semi-final replay was scheduled for Wednesday, April 5. By then, we knew that the opponents in the final would be Aberdeen, who had needed their own share of luck to beat Dundee United in the other semi-final at Dens Park. This came in the shape of an own goal by Tommy Miller who, everyone joyfully told me, was the brother of Rangers' Jimmy Miller.

Celtic had hoped that Bobby Murdoch might be back in the team for Wednesday night, but in fact he wasn't, although he was in the party and was seen in the stand. In the meantime, Jock Stein must have said a few words to his players, for the performance was like chalk and cheese compared to Saturday. Charlie Gallagher was also given a game and he revelled in the conditions with silky, inch-perfect passes. The difference was also in sheer speed,

Stein realising that Saturday would have taken a great deal out of the part-time Clyde. Within three minutes, Celtic were ahead, a Chalmers shot blocked by the goalkeeper but poked into the net in the ensuing scramble by Bobby Lennox. Some 15 minutes of total Celtic dominance later, Bertie Auld, who had been distinctly out of sorts on Saturday, scored a wonderful goal from the edge of the penalty box to show the sort of form of which he is capable.

The 55,000 who turned up, a large crowd for a Wednesday night replay, must have wondered what all the fuss had been about on the Saturday, for this was truly a splendid Celtic performance. Clyde were a beaten team long before half-time, and Celtic showboated for the entire second half. They were able to take off Jimmy Johnstone, who was apparently suffering with flu symptoms, and replace him with John Hughes as the game finished 2-0.

One says "apparently" in the case of Jimmy's illnesses, because we could never be sure. Jimmy was prone to quite a lot of neurotic illnesses, and there can be little doubt that he lived in mortal terror of Big Jock. It is also possible that Jock was playing games. Jock had complained about Clyde's manager, Davie White, putting out stories about his team suffering illnesses and injuries, but he was capable of doing the same himself. He was aware that the most vital part of the season was now approaching and that Jimmy Johnstone, that stormy petrel but still undeniably his star man, often needed to be wrapped in cotton wool.

There was an extra dimension to all this. The Wembley international was approaching in ten days' time. Normally, the team would have been announced by now but Bobby Brown, the Scotland manager, had decided to delay naming it until the Monday of the week of the game, so that he could check on injuries.

Such was Celtic's form this year that a case could have been made for every one of the XI being chosen for Scotland. There was even a campaign for the 36-year-old Ronnie Simpson to be chosen as goalkeeper, but most people thought that such a choice would surely be the heart ruling the head. It was widely believed that the reason for Brown's delay in naming the side was because he wanted to see how Bobby Murdoch was, as speculation grew that Brown could indeed choose all eleven Celtic players – the only precedent for that being the very first international of them all in 1872, when Queen's Park supplied all eleven players for Scotland.

While arguments raged about the possibility or desirability of "Celtic" playing England, one wondered about the attitude of Jock Stein. He was normally very keen for his players to play at international level. One recalls how delighted he was for Charlie Gallagher in February, when Charlie became the first Scotsman to play for Ireland, something that was now allowed because of Charlie's Irish parentage. But he was also worried about the possibility of his players getting injured, and in particular suspected that some brutal English defenders (like Jack Charlton or Nobby Stiles, who had been no shrinking violets in the winning of the World Cup) might target Jimmy Johnstone who had, they would remember, scored two goals against them the previous year at Hampden. Perhaps then, we wondered, the illness of Jimmy Johnstone, and indeed the injury of Bobby Murdoch for that matter, might have been exaggerated and prolonged to deter Bobby Brown from picking them.

If this was so, it was a decidedly high-risk strategy for Celtic travelled to Motherwell on Saturday, April 8 for a difficult Scottish League game without either Murdoch or Johnstone. Murdoch had been supposed to be on the bench, but when Charlie Gallagher was injured and had to limp off, it was Jim Brogan who replaced him. Murdoch had still not recovered. The game itself was tough in every sense of the word. Motherwell, once famous for their fine silky football, had fallen on bad times in recent years, but the way they played reminded the old-timers of the Stevenson and Ferrier days of long ago.

They were also capable of putting in a few fierce tackles as well – and the game was played on a fiery pitch on a rather windy day, albeit noticeably drier than some of the days that season. It was one of Celtic's tougher tasks, but they emerged 2-0 victors, one of the goals a brilliant shot from distance by Willie Wallace, the other a Tommy Gemmell penalty. Yet many honest supporters felt that it would not have been the biggest injustice in the world if Motherwell had earned a point, and the predominant emotion in the Celtic camp was relief rather than triumph. Unfortunately, Rangers had also won that day at Stirling Albion, but Celtic now had only four games left – at home to Aberdeen and Dundee United and away to Rangers and Kilmarnock.

Saturday, April 8, 1967, however, was a lot more famous in sporting circles for what had happened at the Grand National at Aintree. An unknown horse called Foinavon, with an equally unheard-of jockey called John Buckingham, won the race at 100/1. This had all come about because of a huge pile-up of horses at the fence after Becher's Brook on the second circuit, but Foinavon was so far behind that John Buckingham saw the problem, evaded it and won the race by hundreds of yards. Jokes abounded about Foinavon being the first blind horse with a wooden leg to win the Grand National. Those who had picked Foinavon – including the inhabitants of a village in Angus called Finavon, which sounded like the winning horse – or drawn it in the works lottery won a fortune. On a more serious note, several of the horses involved in the pile-up had to be destroyed or "euthanised" (as it was euphemistically put), and not for the first or last time questions were asked about the Grand National.

It had been a good week for Celtic, with big steps taken towards the Scottish League and the Scottish Cup. The European test, however, was now the important one. Over 75,000 tickets were sold for the Parkhead tie, a crowd which in itself would terrify most teams and certainly the Czechoslovak Army side who would seldom have played in front of attendances even half that size. But for me, it was the end of my Easter holidays and the return to university.

Once again, I was forced to miss out travelling to see a European match. Even though it was my first week of the new term at St Andrews University in the vital first year, the Latin Department, with their deserved reputation for academic eccentricity and even cruelty, decided to hold exams on the Prescribed Texts that very week. The carrot was what was called an "exemption" from having to do that part of the exam when the proper degree exams were held in May. Thus, necessity to study was added to finance and transport issues, which prevented me from travelling to Celtic Park on April 12. *Cicero Pro Murena, Virgil Georgics IV, Horace Odes III, Livy XXX* and the *Poems of Catullus* all demanded my attention.

I consoled myself with the thought that, unlike the Vojvodina game in March, nothing would be decided that night. It was just the first leg. This did not in any way lessen or relieve the tension, but I resolved that this time I would not hide from mankind while the game was on, but would try to follow it as best I could through the intermittent newsflashes on radio and TV and, of course, watch the highlights on TV at the eccentric time of 10.52pm on BBC. BBC TV did give the half-time score at the end of the news at 9.10pm, but there then followed a programme about the Budget, which the Chancellor of the Exchequer, the admirable James Callaghan, had presented the previous day, and no full-time score. I was, meanwhile, trying unsuccessfully to study.

And yet these great works of literature were all so irrelevant. Bees swarming on an Italian farm, a Roman general having (or trying to have) sexual relations with an African Queen before the Battle of Zama in 202 BC, and even Catullus asking Lesbia for a thousand kisses were nothing at all compared with the passion that was being enacted on the grass under the tall lights of London Road. That was real love, heart-stopping, lung-bursting, bowel- and bladder-filling love. I believe it is now called "stress incontinence". It was put more crudely then – "burstin' for a p**h" – but it still affected the way you looked at life. I was always told that I took Celtic far too seriously. Maybe that was true, but it was a problem shared by many, many thousands.

In the meantime, on the Monday between the Mother-well game and the arrival of Dukla, Scotland's team had been named for the visit to Wembley. Four Celts were in the team, yet they were not necessarily the ones that

Celtic supporters would have chosen. Johnstone was in, as indeed was Gemmell. No surprise there, but there was Bobby Lennox, who was not always an automatic choice for Celtic, and then the choice that made the headlines – veteran Ronnie Simpson was to become the oldest Scotland debutant and the nation's oldest player since Jimmy "Napoleon" McMenemy in 1920.

Many eyebrows were raised and supporters of men like Jim Cruickshanks of Hearts and Bobby Ferguson of Kilmarnock (fine goalkeepers both) were naturally disappointed, but there could be little doubt that Ronnie Simpson was as good a choice as any. Ronnie told a reporter that it was "the greatest day in his life". Jock Stein, who reputedly had not liked Ronnie when they were both at Hibs, was delighted, as indeed was Ronnie's father, the ex-Rangers centre-half Jimmy Simpson, who had played for Scotland 14 times in the 1930s. Jimmy, now a publican in Govan, was frequently seen at Celtic Park for games in which his son was playing, talking to his old adversary, Jimmy McGrory, and frequently using the pronoun "we" when discussing Celtic's progress.

The two Jimmys, Simpson and McGrory, would have been distressed that week to hear of the death of Sam English in a Vale of Leven hospital. Sam was, of course, the unwitting cause of the accidental death of John Thomson in 1931. He was suffering from what is now called Motor Neurone Disease and was only 58. It is not entirely true to say that the John Thomson incident ruined his life, because he did win medals and Irish caps after that, but he would use the word "joyless" to describe his later career, even after Celtic FC and John Thomson's parents publicly exonerated him from any blame. This did not, however, prevent cretins from shouting "killer" and "murderer" at him. It was often said that the death of John Thomson was a double tragedy, for the effect it had on the blameless Sam.

Such events were now pushed into the background on that dry but slightly cold night of April 12 at Celtic Park. Celtic had started playing towards the Rangers End. Stein had said he would attack. That was pure rhetoric, we thought, because he would say that, wouldn't he? But Celtic did attack. Johnstone, fit again, was fed repeatedly by Murdoch, who had also returned to the team, although if you looked closely you could see that his right ankle was heavily strapped up under his stocking. Johnstone was brought down several times, but the courage of the wee man was obvious in his willingness to come back for more. It was he who put Celtic ahead just before the half-hour mark, just managing to get the ball past the goalkeeper before a crude challenge sent him up in the air.

But then Celtic seemed to throw it all away. A curious hesitancy and reluctance to tackle in the middle of the defence allowed Strunc to run through and score just on the stroke of half-time and reduce the heaving cauldron that was Celtic Park to a more introverted and quieter interval than might otherwise have been the case. But as this was before the away-goals rule – the tie would have been decided by a play-off in a neutral country if the scores were level over two legs – the loss of a home goal was not as damaging as it might have been. Celtic still had the second half to play, having been the better side in the first half, and there were still 75,000 to cheer them on.

The second half belonged to Willie Wallace. Purists among the support, and that might have included me, had certain reservations about buying a player from another club, preferring to see the club rear their own, as indeed they had done with most of that team. Such pious scruples were immediately swept to one side that night as Wallace scored the two goals which gave Celtic a 3-1 win. The first was a deft flick from a Gemmell punt, the second was a pass from an Auld free kick. Another attempt of Wallace's hit the bar. It might have been more than 3-1, indeed it should have been, but the general consensus was that a 3-1 scoreline did at least give Celtic more than an even chance in the grim land called Czechoslovakia less than a fortnight later. *The Celtic View* decided to be very optimistic, however, by issuing an appeal to supporters to stay away from Glasgow Airport in the event of a triumphant Celtic return.

Wallace's two goals earned him a call-up for Scotland. Jimmy Johnstone, badly bruised by the Czech defenders (as Stein always knew would happen), did not respond as well as he might have done to treatment on Thursday morning, and had to withdraw from the Scotland team. Bobby Brown immediately replaced one Celt with another as he invited Willie Wallace to join the team. Willie did, of course, have the same name as the famous Scottish patriot of the Battle of Stirling Bridge in 1295, whose monument dominated the landscape around the Stirling area. He also appeared in the first line of "Scots Wha Hae", so he seemed an ideal choice!

These were indeed stirring times. The European Cup semi-final was good enough, but now there was the Scotland v England international at Wembley as well. England had, we all knew, won the World Cup the previous year, and Scotland now had the chance to become the first team to beat the World Cup winners. Scotland v England games, often called "the international" as if there were no others, were always important, but this one even more so. As the Yogi Bear character, to whom John Hughes owed his nickname, might have put it: "More important than the average."

The town of St Andrews is, by definition, Scottish-named after Scotland's patron saint. It is also undeniably on the Fife coast. Yet the university has always been heavily populated with English people, not least the university staff. It took me some considerable time, for example, to work out that the name of the distinguished scholar of Alexander the Great was, in fact, Sir William Tarn, rather than the "Taah" that my well-meaning but unreconstructed Oxford-educated lecturer, with his distinct reluctance to pronounce the letter "r", seemed to be telling me.

By and large, English people were full of respect for Scotland and its heritage, occasionally patronising without necessarily meaning to be so and even expressing support for Scotland in various sporting endeavours. Jim Clark, the racing driver, was much praised. Sometimes English students tried to be more Scottish than the Scottish, enjoying any opportunity to wear a kilt and ostentatiously enjoying haggis and neeps at Burns Suppers. But April 15, 1967 was different. England were the world champions and as yet undefeated.

In St Andrews, Saturday, April 15 was the day of the annual Kate Kennedy parade to celebrate the university's history. Kate Kennedy was the "niece" of Bishop Kennedy, who had had something to do with the formation of the university. Most people believed that the relationship between the bishop and his "niece" was somewhat more basic, more agricultural and a lot less pure than what was traditionally portrayed, but it was usually a good day.

Students were dressed as people like Herbert Asquith, at one time the town's MP, and Tom Morris, the famous golfer, walking the streets.

Latin and Greek proses – pieces of difficult English to be translated into the ancient tongue – often began with "An uncertain rumour, as often happens" and I was already an expert at saying "*incerta fama, ut plerumque fit*". Well, it so happened that, just as the parade was finishing, "an uncertain rumour" reached our ears that Scotland were winning 1-0 at half-time, and forever the classical pedant, I then told everyone that "Lex" had scored the goal. ("Lex" is the Latin word for "Law"), when a radio confirmed that Aberdonian Denis had indeed put Scotland ahead.

We then rushed back to our residence to listen to the old radiogram giving the commentary. The game was not on TV – football seldom was in those days – and radio was the best we could find. The game was tense. It has subsequently been portrayed as a comprehensive Scottish victory, with much unwarranted stress being put on Jim Baxter's "keepy-uppy". In fact, it was nothing like that. Scotland scored again, with Bobby Lennox becoming the first Celtic player to score at Wembley, but then England scored. Scotland scored a third, England a second – and we were all sweating and swearing at the referee to blow the full-time whistle. He eventually did so after an inordinate amount of injury time, it seemed, and bedlam ensued at Wembley and in every Scottish household.

It was a day in which the four Celtic players distinguished themselves, but there was no real failure for Scotland. The two much-vaunted superstars of Scottish football – Denis Law and Jim Baxter – both played well that day (they hadn't always in the past). Naturally, we would have preferred McNeill at centre-half to McKinnon, but we had to admit that big Ron played well. Yet the hero of the day was surely the other Ron – the great Ronnie Simpson. The last time he had been at Wembley had been in 1955, when he won an English Cup winner's medal with Newcastle United (he had done similarly in 1952), and now he had played in a winning team for Scotland against England at the age of 36.

All Scotland glowed for days afterwards, and there was even some grudging admiration from the English media and public, who had perhaps begun to feel that their heroes of the previous year had grown too big for their boots and that a little deflation was no bad thing. It was no secret that the England manager, the humourless Alf Ramsey, who did not like Scotsmen and seemed to include the phrase "most certainly" in nearly every interview, was not well liked by the English press. Others, however, were. No-one could dislike Bobby Charlton, although his brother Jack was less popular. Gordon Banks, England's goalkeeper and arguably their best ever, earned much admiration in Scotland for the dignified way in which he accepted defeat. He was full of praise for Scotland and in particular for his opposite number, Ronnie Simpson.

There was, in contrast, almost a mundane feel to Celtic's next game. This was on Wednesday night at Celtic Park against Aberdeen. It was, in paper talk, "a cup final rehearsal". The game had actually been scheduled for Saturday, April 22, but both teams agreed to bring it forward to the Wednesday so that Celtic would have more time to concentrate on Dukla Prague. Stein went out of his way to be gracious, using words like "sporting" of Aberdeen, but in fact it suited the Dons just as well as it did

Celtic. Aberdeen now had ten days to prepare themselves for the Scottish Cup Final.

There was also an element of trying, unsuccessfully, to take a little away from Rangers, who would otherwise have had centre stage playing Slavia Sofia in the Cup Winners' Cup semi-final in Bulgaria that afternoon. Rangers did very well, winning 1-0 in their 4pm kick-off, while in the evening at Celtic Park, 33,000 saw a very disappointing 0-0 draw in which both Celtic and Aberdeen seemed very much to be holding back. Aberdeen, in particular, seemed to show little ambition or inclination to get the ball over the halfway line. In defence of both teams, it must also be said that conditions were difficult, with a strong gale blowing and the pitch still sodden from the persistent April rain, which had resembled sleet on occasions. The crowd were by no means happy with the performance, but the point gained meant that Celtic were now three points ahead of Rangers in the Scottish League with three games left.

Celtic now departed for Seamill Hydro for intensive training before the Dukla game. They had, as we have seen, no game on the Saturday, but even so they had a good day. Rangers could only draw with Clyde. This meant that Celtic had 55 points and Rangers 53, but Rangers now had only two games left – at Dundee the following week and the much-postponed game against Celtic, which was provisionally scheduled for May 6. The maximum tally they could reach was 57. Given Celtic's better goal average, one more win or even a draw at Ibrox would do it. But Celtic's schedule could not really have been much heavier – Dukla Prague on Tuesday, April 25, the Scottish Cup Final against Aberdeen on Saturday, April 29, Dundee United at Parkhead on Wednesday, May 3 and then Rangers at Ibrox on Saturday, May 6. A game against Kilmarnock had to be fitted in some other time, but the picture was complicated by Kilmarnock's European commitments in the Inter Cities Fairs Cup.

Celtic flew out to Prague on Sunday to begin what was probably the most important week of their 79-year history. The kick-off would be at 4pm BST on Tuesday and arrangements had been made for the team to be back in Glasgow late on the Tuesday night. Instructions had already been issued to supporters to stay away from the airport to avert potential traffic congestion so that, European Cup finalists or not, they could then direct all their attention to the Scottish Cup Final.

The media, even the English media, had cottoned on to the fact that Celtic were on the brink of becoming the first British team ever to appear in a European Cup Final. At long last, the BBC were taking some interest. There would be a live radio broadcast of the last 15 minutes or so from Prague, beginning at 5.25pm, and on TV there would be a highlights programme across Great Britain at the odd time of 6.17pm after the news and the weather. The commentator on the network TV programme was to be Kenneth Wolstenholme, a man well known for his clichés, such as "a pretty kettle of fish" and "the fat is really in the fire now", not to mention his infamous "they think it's all over – it is now" of the previous year's World Cup Final.

He was, however, as far as Scotland were concerned, a Celtic sympathiser and he had been since, as a young man, he attended the Empire Exhibition Trophy Final at Ibrox in 1938, when he had been impressed by Johnny Crum's Highland Fling after he scored the goal and the "revolutionary" songs of the Celtic faithful. He was also a lover of good attacking football and saw in Celtic the way that the game should be played, as distinct from some of the more sterile English teams. Sometimes Jock Stein treated Wolstenholme with a certain amount of suspicion and sneered at his conversion to the cause of Celtic. Jock was being rather too ungracious on these occasions, for Ken was a genuine man.

The weather in Czechoslovakia was unpleasant and very cold in that strange stadium called the Juliska, which had trees growing halfway up the terracing. Ironically, it was a great deal warmer in Scotland, where it was pleasant and spring-like that evening. Dukla Prague had virtually gone into hiding to prepare for the game, in contrast to Celtic, who were far more open with the press. Back home, the tension that Tuesday afternoon was almost unbearable. How could lecturers deliver their lectures on Roman Britain or Homer's *Iliad* in such circumstances? How could people live their normal lives as if nothing of such huge import was going on? Women were doing their shopping, people were taking their dogs for a walk and shopkeepers were selling their wares, as if it were a normal day.

There are times when one wishes that one was not born a "Tim". How great it must be to worry only about gardening or bridge or music or chess. None of this gnawing inside your vitals, none of this constant going to the toilet, none of this inability to concentrate on anything else, not even the blandishments of pretty young girls. These are the superficial attractions of a life without Celtic, but yet the adrenalin is there and one must always recall the words of Willie Maley, who said that, as far as he was concerned, if it hadn't been for Celtic, life would have been a very empty existence indeed.

There are those, myself included, who claim that they kick every ball with the team. That was certainly true during that commentary of the last quarter of an hour. We had joined the game with the score still 0-0. Ronnie Simpson had made one save early on, but apart from that the Celtic midfield and defence had taken control. It is often said that Steve Chalmers was a one-man forward line, as if Jock Stein had decided that that was the way it was going to be. The truth was a little more complex than that. Celtic were virtually forced into that position for they had no other choice, and just occasionally someone like Bobby Lennox might have a foray to help the exhausted Chalmers. But men like Murdoch and Gemmell, who normally liked to come forward, were under strict orders to stay in their own half. Just occasionally, Celtic broke out but had no-one to pass to and simply had to hoof the ball up the park and out of play. Years later, Jock Stein would admit that chairman Bob Kelly was "far from happy" with the way Celtic set out to defend, but after you become the first British team to reach the European Cup Final it is hard to criticise your manager.

It is never easy to listen to a game on the radio when it means something. Even today, for example, I will never, for reasons of public safety, listen to a Celtic game while driving my car. I will happily listen to an English Premier League game, for example, or even a Scotland international, but Celtic is far too important for that. And with radio, when you cannot see and are totally relying on one man's impressions, your mind plays tricks and your imagination takes over as you try to anticipate the tones of his voice.

So there I was that tense tea time in my friend's bedsit, pacing the wooden floor while my friend, just as excited himself, tried to tell me to calm down. Unable to sit down, constantly needing the toilet, worrying even about a heart attack and visualising the headlines of "18-year-old St Andrews student dies while listening to the radio", I was now far more concerned about whether we could last out these 15 minutes. The minutes were indeed steadily decreasing and, with McNeill in total command and Celtic two goals to the good, a rational assessment would have had to be that Celtic looked safe and in control.

But there is nothing rational about following Celtic. That late goalkeeping error in the 1955 Scottish Cup Final was branded on my young heart, and I recalled Tannadice Park in January 1962. Celtic had been 5-1 up and coasting, but had then relaxed and Dundee United had pulled things back to 5-4. The well-dressed, respectable, magnanimous, genial, cheerful gentleman (almost middle class, one might say) beside me grew more and more tense as United piled on more and more pressure. Once, when left-back Jim Kennedy miskicked, he cracked altogether and, to the mortification and embarrassment of his son, bawled "Christ, kick it, ye c***!" I wonder how he got on with the tension that night.

Twice my legs gave way under me. Once was when Bobby Murdoch brought down a Dukla player and the commentator feared a penalty. Everyone looked at the Swiss referee, Gottfried Dienst. Dienst had, of course, been the referee in the World Cup Final and was reckoned to be one of the better referees. He might have made a mistake about the ball being over the line at Wembley the previous July, but here he was correct. No penalty. Years later, Bobby Murdoch told me that he himself thought he had given away a penalty on that occasion.

The other occasion when I almost fell to the floor in a senseless heap was when a Dukla player put the ball over the bar, but by then the minutes really were ticking past and you could tell from the background noise of whistling and booing that the Czech crowd were far from happy. But then came that glorious final whistle, and after a brief rest and prolonged stay in the toilet, purging myself, it seemed, of all that I had had to eat and drink for about a week, I emerged to resume my normal life.

Normal? Not really. Euphoric and chirpy, I went around telling everyone "I knew we would do it" (a blatant lie) as we settled in the TV room at 6.17pm to see the highlights of what was really a pretty dreadful game of football, but in which every touch by a Celtic player was cheered to the echo. It would be wrong to say that all Scotland was proud of Celtic – there were a few bigots still around – but most people, of moderate opinion, were impressed by this feat. Even if they were to lose the European Cup Final, they had already made history by reaching it. A few minutes after the end of the TV programme came the inevitable and predictable phone call from my father, trembling and incoherent and shouting a few things down the phone about Patsy Gallacher and Tommy McInally of old, saying that he thought it was "meant" for them to win and finishing with: "If ye want tae go tae the final, I'll get you the money – somehow." As I say, there is nothing rational or logical about loving the Celtic.

It was probably the best goalless draw of all time and in Prague, after the interviews with Jock Stein visibly trembling with emotion, it was pack up and go, job done. But that night on the plane, Jim Craig reported feeling a little shivery, as if he had flu. He was immediately isolated, as far as that is possible on an aeroplane, and sent home to bed whenever they touched down. In the event, he was OK for the next game on the calendar, the small matter of the Scottish Cup Final against Aberdeen.

Wednesday morning's newspapers were universally ecstatic. There is a fallacy that some newspapers do not like Celtic. There may be an element of truth in that in the minds of some editors and journalists, but a successful Celtic team does sell newspapers. They certainly sold well that Wednesday morning, and if there was ever any doubt that Scottish football was on a high in 1967, it was swept away when Kilmarnock beat Leipzig that Wednesday night and qualified for the semi-finals of the Inter Cities Fairs Cup, where they would meet Leeds United.

It certainly meant that, in England, the patronising comments about Scotland became distinctly muted. The "know-it-all" stuff about "Raith Thistle" and "Partick Rovers", whom Arsenal could beat playing with a team of one-legged men, came to a shuddering halt. Not only had Scotland beaten England a fortnight ago, but one Scottish team was in the final of the European Cup and two others, Rangers and Kilmarnock, seemed to be on the point of doing likewise in other European tournaments.

But now there loomed the Scottish Cup Final. Celtic had won the trophy 18 times. Rangers had edged ahead during Celtic's lean years and their victory in the previous year's cup final replay remained an open sore. The Scottish Cup had been looked upon as Celtic's own trophy. What Celtic youngster had not been told about Jimmy Quinn's hat-trick in 1904, Patsy Gallacher's somersault with the ball wedged between his feet in 1925, the late own goal that earned Celtic a replay in 1931 or John McPhail's great goal in 1951? The Scottish Cup was axiomatic to one's childhood and, of course, it had been the epic final of 1965, two years earlier, which had propelled Celtic to where we were now.

As famous as any cup finals were the two that we had played against Aberdeen in 1937 and 1954, both won 2-1 by Celtic. On both occasions, the Granite City had virtually emptied itself to come to Hampden to support the black and golds in 1937 and the reds in 1954. On both occasions, defeat had been accepted honourably by the people from the North and both sets of supporters, as a result, had a tremendous respect for each other. Celtic fans, for example, in the bad old hooligan days of the 1950s and early 1960s, often wrecked Perth, Dundee and in particular Falkirk, which received a real pasting on many occasions, but Aberdeen usually survived intact, with even, I recall, a half-hearted attempt to sing "The Northern Lights Of Old Aberdeen" by Celtic supporters, who didn't really know the words, on the train home one night in 1964.

The Dons had only won the Scottish Cup once, in 1947. They won the league in 1955 and the League Cup in 1955/56, but apart from that their record had been a sorry one for a club with the potential dormant support of the city itself and those who lived in places like Newtonhill, Muchalls, Milltimber, Cookney, Tarves, Maud and Fyvie, where there once lived a bonny lass much pursued by the captain of the Irish Dragoons.

But in 1967, things were more optimistic for football in the North East. Eddie Turnbull was in charge. He was tough, swore loudly and vociferously and was very aware that, although when with Hibs in the Famous Five forward line he had won the Scottish League three times, he had never won the Scottish Cup. Now that he was with the

Dons, a grim, steely determination was shining through. No more Mister Nice Guy in Aberdeen. No more of the long trip to see the quaint stadium with its funny wee stand in the corner of the main stand, supporters with funny accents and then those lovely fish suppers before you went home after a comfortable victory. Eddie was making changes.

It was often claimed that he and Stein did not like each other. Whether this was true, we do not know, but they were certainly two of a kind. Capable of jovial geniality with reporters and supporters on occasion, but grimly determined to the point of boorishness with their players. These were characteristics that Stein and Turnbull both shared. But above all, they both liked to win.

Turnbull had a fine old warhorse in Harry Melrose as their captain. He had, of course, played for Dunfermline in the Scottish Cup finals of both 1961 and 1965, and was a good player and a good captain. There was an excellent goalkeeper called Bobby Clark and solid defenders like Ally Shewan and Tommy McMillan. But the star man of Aberdeen, in some ways the joker of the pack, was a chap called Jimmy Smith. He shared Jimmy Johnstone's name of "Jinky" and was a similar sort of player, although not nearly as good, with a reputation for being moody but occasionally turning it on and winning games.

It was rumoured that Rangers were "after him". This was demonstrably false for reasons that will become apparent and may have stemmed from the fact that Rangers had in the 1930s had a Jimmy Smith in their team. As things stood, they already had two Smiths in their current team, Dave and Alex, both bought in summer 1966, and it would be nice, would it not, to make that three? The story went that Rangers did indeed make a few discreet inquiries about this guy, but suddenly withdrew their interest. They knew that he had a disciplinary record, but that was not the problem. They knew that he had his games when he didn't seem to care, but that was not the problem either. The problem was more basic than that. You see, Jimmy Smith, I was reliably informed by a drunk man on the train to the Scottish Cup Final, was "a Tum". It was hardly a piece of ground-breaking news, for everyone knew it anyway.

The man didn't pronounce it correctly, for he meant that he was a "Tim" – i.e. a "Tim Malloy", a Glaswegian of Irish descent and a Roman Catholic. So, such was Rangers' bizarre and scarcely believable policy in 1967, Jimmy Smith couldn't play for them. Not only that, but my inebriated companion informed me that it was only a matter of time before Jock Stein came for him. "Efter the-day, you'll see. Mark my words." Rangers had been deceived by his name – Smith – by no means overtly Irish or Catholic, and simply meaning a "worker", as in "blacksmith", "goldsmith" or "silversmith". It is not unlike another trade name, such as Mason, for example. Now that might have made things different.

I had decided that I was going to go home for the weekend to Forfar and to travel to the game by train from Forfar Station. It would be one of the last times that I would have the opportunity to do so, for Forfar Station was under sentence of execution under the Beeching cuts, the rather short-sighted and ill-judged way of closing what were seen as uneconomic lines. (In later years it would be much deplored, and even reversed, in the Borders.) The train had come from Aberdeen and was packed with people from both persuasions. Curiously, the cup final was not all-ticket. It might have been an idea to have made it so, thought the morning papers. In the event, the limit of 134,000 was not reached, but it was only a few thousand short.

The Celtic support were naturally upbeat and cheery, singing "We're off to Lisbon in the green, in the green" – a slight change from "Dublin" in the current favourite Irish rebel song of the time. The Aberdeen supporters were a shade less optimistic – but then they seldom were, as my friend kept saying, pointing out that the stereotypical greetin-faced Aberdonian was well in evidence, moaning about the price of things, and telling everyone what was wrong with Harold Wilson's Labour government, which seemed to make them pay income tax.

Unknown to everyone, even the press, all was not well in the Aberdeen camp at Gleneagles. Eddie Turnbull had first felt ill when coming back from Wembley a couple of weeks previously and had then been diagnosed with a form of hepatitis. He had struggled on over the previous two weeks with the aid of antibiotics and other medical drugs, but on the morning of the game he was simply too ill to travel. Possibly nerves and tension played a part in all this as well, but poor Eddie had to be left behind to listen to the game on the radio when the bus departed for Hampden. They had delayed the bus for as long as possible to give him every chance of feeling better, but eventually decided to leave him. They then got caught up in traffic, and arrived a lot later than they would have liked.

This was unfortunate for the Aberdeen team, but to what extent it can be used as an excuse, I'm not sure. Even if Turnbull had been there, it is doubtful whether Aberdeen could have lived with the rampant Celtic of that day, and in any case, Jock Stein produced his magnificent tactical ploy of giving Jimmy Johnstone his normal "roving commission", as I was told by a man with a huge razor scar down one side of his face and no visible teeth. He had clearly been a victim of the "razor gang culture" which had caused so many deaths and injuries in Glasgow in the 1940s and early 1950s until the famous police chief, Percy Sillitoe, aided by a few draconian judges, had stamped it out. This wee guy, now in his 50s at a guess, was a clear living monument to this awful but widespread crime. He was happy, though.

The day was bright but windy, with it blowing into our faces in the packed King's Park End commonly known as the Celtic End. In fact, there was no Aberdeen End. Their fans, about 30,000, or a quarter of the total crowd, had opted to stand in pockets all around the ground, including a few at the Celtic End, although most of them were in the North Stand enclosure. Confirming the belief that Celtic and Aberdeen fans generally got on quite well in the 1960s, there was no outright hostility. Plenty of banter, but no offensive songs about each other. The songs about Glasgow scum finding a dead cat in a dustbin and thinking it a treat had not been invented – in fact, it originally came from Edinburgh – nor did the Celtic support say anything about anyone having carnal knowledge of sheep. No, we were all too busy telling everyone that we would not be moved, or singing about the echo of the Thomson gun and definitely, definitely telling everyone about how we were going to Lisbon.

When the teams did come out, we did indeed see that Jimmy Johnstone was all over the place or, as my learned friend said, "had a roving commission". He might even have used the word "ubiquitous". It was clear from an early stage that although Aberdeen could be dangerous on the break, Celtic had settled more quickly, with Murdoch spraying intelligent passes on the ground and Gemmell making his usual forays up the left wing. Jim Storrie of Aberdeen had clearly been told to shoot on sight when the wind was behind him, but most of his efforts were erratic. Once or twice, he brought out a save from Ronnie Simpson but, as the first half wore on, there had been no real cause for alarm.

That Celtic were getting the upper hand became apparent with the fouls that Aberdeen were forced to commit. One on Steve Chalmers by Aberdeen's stormy petrel Jimmy Smith was dreadful, for which he was rightly booked by referee Willie Syme. This referee was, apparently, quite happy to say that he was a Rangers supporter in his spare time, even though his father had played two games in the goal for Celtic at the end of World War One. (His son, Davie, would also be a referee in the 1980s.) Syme was, on this occasion, very fair – indeed he was generally a good referee – and when the name of Jimmy Smith went down in the book (this was before the use of yellow cards), it was made clear to Jimmy by voice and gesture that a long, lonely walk to the dressing room was likely to follow any more conduct like that.

Poor Jimmy Smith! Aberdeen's talisman knew that he could not foul again, he had no mentor to guide him, for Turnbull was ill in bed in Gleneagles, and like quite a lot of Celtic supporters he did not really enjoy playing against them in any case. He dropped out of this game when his team needed him most, and it is probably true to say that what he did that day guaranteed that any chance of an immediate transfer to Celtic was not remotely likely. He would, a few years later, go to Newcastle United, where his talent would occasionally impress, but his lifestyle wouldn't. He once earned notoriety for getting sent off within a minute of the start with a truly vicious tackle on a Birmingham City player. He eventually got his wish of coming to Celtic (on loan) in that dreadful 1975/76 season, but this was far too late in his career and he never really made it into the first team.

Another foul, this time on Jimmy Johnstone by Ally Shewan, had the Celtic fans in uproar as half-time approached, but then in the aftermath of a corner kick Celtic went ahead. To someone low down in the King's Park end of the ground, there was no clear view, but I recall seeing Steve Chalmers raise his arms in triumph after Bobby Lennox had passed to Willie Wallace to put Celtic ahead.

Half-time on that heaving terracing was no comfortable experience. Everyone seemed convinced that the game was over, but I, neurotic as always, had to try to calm everyone down with the sobering realisation that we were only one goal up. My concerns were dismissed with contempt as everyone told me that this team simply wouldn't lose, either at Hampden or next month in Lisbon. "By the way, ma brither and me are gaun. Are you, Jum?" (Everyone was, of course, called "Jum" in Glasgow. For a while, it had been "Mac", but now it was definitely "Jum" or "Jimmie".)

If I did not get a good view of the first Willie Wallace goal, that could hardly have been said of the second. I can see it yet. Wee Jimmy Johnstone on his right wing, reaching the byline, cutting it back straight through the Aberdeen defence, Willie Wallace, unmarked and "like a man waiting for a bus", the ball speeding from his right foot and coming straight towards me certain to hit me on the face, I thought, if the net hadn't stopped it, then the heaven-splitting roar as about 30 crazy punters jumped on my back. Hugging and delirium, the man with the razor scar kissing everyone in sight and me ending up with my arms round an old granny with tears in her eyes!

The game had started again by the time everyone had settled down, and I restored the lovely old granny to her husband, who thought he had lost her. "Dae ye think Wallace'll score a hat-trick? Like Jimmy Quinn? I was here when he did that, you know, in 1905!" he assured me. In point of fact, it was 1904 but this was no place to argue with the veteran and his wife, who had now gained some equilibrium on the terracing and was holding her own with anyone in the foul language stakes. "Watch that wee c***, referee!"

Once more, I was assailed by doubts but neither Jock Stein nor the Celtic players were, and the second half began to tick away as I spent half my time watching the game and the other half pleading with the minute hand on my watch to go round quicker. Around me, it got noisier and noisier and then came a really poignant moment of which I remain really proud.

A family of Aberdeen supporters decided with five minutes to go that the game was up and that it was time to leave. Most Celtic supporters shook their hands and I did as well. It was a respectable, decent family, the father downcast but sporting, the mother smiling tolerantly but clearly concerned about the sheer size of the crowd, the daughter of about my age, whom in other circumstances I might have tried to be even more sociable with, and then the wee boy of about 12 or 13, in tears and with his dreams shattered. Aye, football is a cruel game, but I put my arm around him, told him that his day would come and then suddenly, instinctively, irrationally took off a rosette I had bought that day with "Celtic Lisbon 1967" on it, and pinned it on the boy's red and white scarf, saying something about friendship and souvenirs.

Whatever possessed me to do that, I will never know, but the wee boy with the glasses and the tears in his eyes looked at me, then his pleasant-faced mother took him to resume their battle up the terracing with full-time approaching and everyone in green and white going crazy with delirium. That wee boy will now be approaching retirement age. He would have been a grown man, maybe with children of his own, at the time of Gothenburg, when they had their own moment of ecstasy. I hope he enjoyed that. I wonder if he still has my rosette.

I was further made proud of being a Celtic supporter when I saw everyone making way for Aberdeen fans, shaking hands with them and allowing them free passage up to the top of the huge terracing – no easy task when everyone was dancing about. We had lost cup finals before, and most of us recalled what a dreadful experience it could be. Indeed I had a flashback of that same terracing emptying in eerie silence that awful night in 1963. But we now had to be magnanimous in victory.

Full time came. The Scottish Cup had been won for the 19th time, we saw the cup being presented, but much as we shouted for them, the team would not come out for their lap of honour. They were forbidden to do that, as we all knew since the previous year's Scottish League Cup Final, when a few mentally challenged Huns had tried to attack our men.

But we tried to see the heroes at the front of the South Stand when they came out to their bus, and that was where we went, with everyone still pummelling each other on the back, putting arms around each other and singing sporadic snatches of supporters' songs. There was even someone singing "Penny Lane" of the Beatles – all about "blue suburban skies" and things like that – which was incongruous in the context of other people singing about a lorry load of volunteers, bayonets slashing Orange sashes and Erin's green valleys looking down, once again, on Parkhead. And, of course, the ever-present "And we're all off to Lisbon in the Green" with, I regret to say, the three added words, the last one being "Queen".

How this happens, no-one can explain, but there does seem to be some cosmic force that determines that whenever one member of the Old Firm does particularly well, the other member seems to gild the lily by doing badly. It happens both ways. In 1962, on the same day Rangers won the Scottish Cup, Celtic collapsed miserably to Raith Rovers in the league at Parkhead, and here we saw it happening, only the other way round. It was like a game of Chinese whispers, with a message being passed along the line and people getting it wrong. We were told first of all that "we had won them all", including the Scottish League, because Rangers had blown up at Dens Park against Dundee. "3-0 for Dundee," I was earnestly informed by a man who was making it all up. That result would indeed have given us the Scottish League, but in fact my friend's transistor radio said that the score was, in reality, Dundee 1 Rangers 1 – still a good score, but not yet enough to win the league. Almost, though.

Then the players came out to board their bus. We were pushed back by the police – none too gently, but they had a job to do and it was nothing like the police brutality that the anti-Vietnam war rallies in the USA experienced – and only in the distance did we see the bulky figure of Big Jock, the red hair of Wee Jimmy and the auburn hair of captain McNeill. The bus passed very quickly, but we glimpsed them all, as they waved back at us with the Scottish Cup sitting resplendent in its green and white ribbons. Oh, what a glorious sight.

Was it only four years earlier, at that other cup final, when we experienced the depression, the curses, the sullen faces, the mass departure? Yes it was, but it seemed more like a lifetime, that awful night when we folded miserably 0-3 to Rangers. If anyone had said then, in 1963, that this team would be the first to bring the European Cup back to Britain, what a cruel mockery that would have seemed. But perhaps it was, as my father said, all "meant". He had also said quietly and with sincerity in 1963: "They'll come again." Now they had, and how.

And then back to the centre of Glasgow and the train home. It was green and white all the way, with even the hooter on the trains sounding like "Cel-tic". Someone in Buchanan Street said that I was a "Fenian b******". Many people heard, and on another occasion there might have been real trouble. This time, however, the sound was mocking laughter, as the isolated bigot scurried out of the way of the triumphalist Celts.

Aberdeen supporters on the train home were quiet and dignified. Naturally disappointed, they realised that they had been up against a truly great team, and that they had nothing to be ashamed of. I ended up talking to a man who turned out to be an old friend of my father's. He was not wearing any colours, but he was Celtic to the core.

We were even home quickly enough to see the highlights on BBC TV at 10.05pm. My dad, with his increasing fear of crowds the older he got, had not gone to the game with me but had followed it in agony on the radio. He was smiling and happy, my mother was glad that I got home safely, but I thought of nothing but the game being replayed on the TV, looking for myself in the crowd. "There I am," I shouted improbably, pointing to the heaving masses after the second goal. Billy McNeill dropped the lid off the cup as he was presented with it – that had not been obvious from the naked eye on the terracing, but the TV camera showed it.

I slept the sleep of the just that night, I went to church on the Sunday to thank God for all he had done, and returned to St Andrews on the early bus on the Monday morning, still whistling, humming and singing to myself "We will cha-a-ant 'The Soldiers' Song'". Come to think of it, I don't know why I bothered with the bus. I could have flown like Peter Pan. I was certainly walking on air.

MAY

• • • • • • •

Those who celebrated May Day on Monday, May 1 saw the sun rising with Celtic the winners of three trophies, the Glasgow Cup, the Scottish Cup and the Scottish League Cup, and apparently on the cusp of winning the Scottish League. Rangers dropping a point at Dundee on cup final day meant that Celtic only needed to take one point from their three remaining fixtures. They had Dundee United at home on Wednesday, May 3, the much-postponed New Year game against Rangers at Ibrox was now on Saturday, May 6, and the game against Kilmarnock had not yet been arranged because Killie were still in the Inter Cities Fairs Cup, playing Leeds United in the semi-final. There was also a Scotland game against the USSR on May 10. Eventually, the Kilmarnock game would be fixed for Monday, May 15, four days before Kilmarnock's first leg in the semi-final.

This all seemed irrelevant, for surely Celtic would finish the job when Dundee United came to town on Wednesday night. It was not the only game on in Glasgow that night, for Rangers, 1-0 up from the first leg, were playing Slavia Sofia at Ibrox in the Cup Winners' Cup semi-final. It would be one of the very few nights in 1967 when people could honestly say that Glasgow actually belonged to Rangers, rather than Celtic.

Rangers duly won their way through to the final in Nuremberg but Celtic, in a strange, strange performance which in some ways defied analysis, decided to blow up against Dundee United and break the hearts of the 44,000 fans who had come to Celtic Park to see the team win the Scottish League. Cynics, of course, were not slow to seize on the fact that the unexpected defeat set up a great game at Ibrox on Saturday, when Celtic would have another chance to win the league, this time at the home of the enemy. There was even a safety net beyond that, for there was another chance to do it when Kilmarnock came to Celtic Park.

The disgruntled fans who turned on Celtic that night could be sympathised with, but it would have to be said that they had very short memories and they were probably wrong to detect any sniff of corruption. Yet the game which disillusioned so many otherwise bouncy and exuberant fans deserves some sort of examination. The facts were that Celtic were without Chalmers and Auld from the cup-winning team, and Hughes and Gallagher were therefore given a game. Celtic opened the scoring with a Gemmell penalty, Dundee United equalised, Wallace put Celtic ahead with about half an hour remaining, United veteran Dennis Gillespie scored with a header from a corner kick as the Celtic defence stood and watched him – and it was this goal which looked particularly bad – before Dundee United scored again a few minutes later, then held out against strong Celtic pressure near the end. A draw and a point would have been enough for Celtic to win the league, but it was not to be.

It was a strange night in any case, not least because a chunk of the new Jungle was closed for maintenance. The supporters who had at half-time cheered the appearance of the Scottish Cup bedecked in green and white ribbons now departed in silent anger into the dusk. Some indeed welcomed the possibility of winning the league championship on Saturday at the home of our rivals, who would, of course, purr their pleasure at this turn of events for the next couple of days. There were mutterings about the game being thrown, but more were angry at this superbly talented team simply underestimating the opposition.

The Glasgow Herald talks about a "nervous and ill-knit" Celtic side "lacking the confidence and determination" which had characterised their play at home and abroad. It criticises both the defence and the attack, as indeed did the mass of Celtic supporters as they trudged along the Gallowgate and London Road. It was in some ways, a savage reminder of the fickleness of Celtic fans. On Saturday night, their team was the greatest team on earth; tonight, according to some, the players were not worthy of the money they earned, and the hope was expressed that Big Jock would kick a few backsides. Some of them were not fit to wear a green and white jersey, and yes, the question was asked, was this game thrown?

Yet all this was grossly unfair to Dundee United. They had beaten Celtic by the same score on Hogmanay at Tannadice, and had even, that very season, beaten Barcelona. They were a good side, although most of their good results were at Tannadice, and none of us could remember when they had ever won at Celtic Park before. (It was, in fact, their first-ever victory at Celtic Park.) On the night, they had fought back well, taken their chances, and although even their most loyal fans (lucky if there had been enough of them to fill a bus) had a look of surprise about them, they were well worthy of their victory.

It was also true that Celtic, even this Celtic, had a few bad games in 1967. My own personal opinion was that Celtic were actually a better team in 1968 and 1969, but the difference was that the bad games in seasons 1967/68 and 1968/69 were games that mattered. (One thinks of the European heartbreaks against Dinamo Kiev in September 1967 and AC Milan in March 1969, and the feeble performance against Dunfermline Athletic in the Scottish Cup in January 1968.) The bad games in 1967 – Clyde in the first game of the Scottish Cup semi-final, the half-hearted 0-0 draw with Aberdeen in the Scottish League, and now this glitch against Dundee United – all ultimately did not matter, for the team, in all three cases, were able to steady the ship immediately afterwards.

The truth was that Celtic had set their standards high, and everyone would therefore try that little bit harder to beat them. The demeanour of the Dundee United players at the end of the game made that clear. It was their cup final, and to this day they are proud to remind everyone that they were the only team to beat the team that won the European Cup – and they did it twice. By the same token, a defeat, a rare event in 1966/67, was all the harder to take for the Celtic fans who found it difficult to believe that anyone could defeat their team.

In fact, it was probably a timely reminder that the team was mortal and fallible. Two trophies remained to be won. Jock Stein would make sure that there would be no complacency. It was, however, a rather chastening experience to wake up on the Thursday morning to endure a few quizzical looks and the odd sneers from those who had found it difficult, the previous weekend, to cope with 19 Scottish Cups.

All this was forgotten on the Saturday in one of the best Old Firm games of all time. Indeed those who had "wondered" about Wednesday's result would have had some vindication when they saw the enormous queues on the Underground, and the undeniable fact that this game was the sole topic of conversation in Glasgow. Indeed it was a typical Glasgow spring day in the drenching rain, so different from the cold and frost of January 3, and the very antithesis of the previous week's Scottish Cup Final. At one point, trains on the Underground had to be suspended following a few lightning storms, but fortunately service was quickly resumed.

The thing that never fails to amaze a visitor to Celtic and Rangers games is the amount of fans who arrive inadequately clad, without bonnets and coats, even on a day like this, when it was obvious from very early in the morning that there was going to be a great deal of rain. Enterprising street vendors, however, had clearly been to "the Barras" in the morning, bought up every Celtic and Rangers bonnet in sight and sold them in great numbers to the punters arriving at Copland Road Underground Station. Those without the wherewithal to buy a bonnet or a tammy employed the age-old Glasgow method of tying four knots in a handkerchief and putting it, precariously and inadequately, on one's head, thus giving one a passable resemblance to a cleric or religious leader.

All Old Firm games have their own momentum, of course, but this one had added impetus in that Celtic could win the Scottish League with a draw, whereas a Rangers victory would put it in serious doubt. Aye, and the cynics said, it would guarantee a sell-out crowd to see Kilmarnock in Celtic's last game. But an Old Firm game is surely too important to be fixed (isn't it?) and the cynics were generally shooshed into silence.

There was even more to the game than that. Within the month, both teams would be playing in European cup finals – Celtic v Inter Milan (who had now won their way through to the final by beating CSKA Sofia of Bulgaria) and Rangers v Bayern Munich. There were at least two special guests there. One was James Bond, Sean Connery, back again to see the Celtic, and sitting near him in the Ibrox stand was no less a person than Helenio Herrera, the manager of Inter Milan, who sat taking notes.

Herrera was not above a little gamesmanship. He had flown in on Inter Milan's private jet and given Jock Stein to understand that he could give him a lift back to Italy, so that he could see Inter Milan v Turin on the Sunday. Jock had agreed but also taken the precaution of booking on a scheduled flight just in case. His suspicions were justified, for suddenly there was no room for Big Jock (he would indeed have taken up a lot of room on a small jet) and "Sorry, Mr Stein". Stein smiled politely, but I have it on good authority that the phrase "little bastard" was used in private afterwards. It did not matter, for Jock, prepared as always for the duplicitous nature of the much-detested Herrera, went anyway on the scheduled flight.

There was no cover at the Celtic End, and not very much at the Rangers End either, but that did nothing to curb the enthusiasm of anyone. It was the day that the infamous "Gemmell's a Bas-tard" chant was born at the Rangers End, and heard loudly and clearly on the TV highlights programmes that night. Tommy Gemmell himself was a little shocked, but then made a joke about it in his ghosted newspaper column that it was merely the Rangers fans warning their defenders to keep an eye on Tommy because he could score a goal and "Gemmell's a Ban-dit", was what they were chanting. Celtic fans later started chanting "Gemmell's an An-gel", as well as retaliating with less complimentary chants about Rangers players.

It was easy to see why the Rangers fans had a problem with Tommy Gemmell. He was the man who, in some ways, typified the Jock Stein Celtic with his bravado, enthusiasm and general swagger. Such qualities did not always endear him to Jock himself necessarily – they would have several serious dust-ups in years to come – but Jock, at this stage, did little to discourage Tommy's style of play. Tommy was the archetypal attacking full-back. He had never been a great defender, more than once losing out to Willie Henderson in the days before Stein arrived, but he was never afraid to go upfield and attack. He also had a tremendous shot – various studies in *The Sunday Mirror*, for example, coming up with impressive but meaningless statistics comparing him to racing cars and fast bowlers in cricket – and seemed to have no nerves at all, banging in penalty kicks with what he himself called the "terrible dunt", and never seeming to get upset if he missed the occasional one.

But there was, of course, another reason why Rangers supporters detested him. He was actually one of them, a Protestant. They were never likely to understand this, but it was now beginning to be a topic of conversation among the brighter Rangers fans (and yes, there were quite a lot of them), and certainly in broader Scottish society, that it might be not a bad idea for Rangers to consider signing a

Roman Catholic. There was a joke going around Glasgow that one day in a closed-doors friendly, Rangers did indeed play a Catholic – but he beat them 2-1! Fingers were pointed approvingly at Celtic, whose broad-based selection was clearly not doing them any harm, but still at Ibrox, the no-Catholic policy since the 1920s, never written down but never really denied either, prevailed.

Religion, of course, was for Sunday. This was Saturday, May 6, the day that Celtic won their first-ever Scottish domestic treble. The pitch was barely playable – words like "paddy field" were used by the press, and even the toss for ends saw the coin stuck in the mud. Thirty-five people were arrested and the huge crowd saw a tremendous game between two evenly balanced sides with, curiously, one great goal and one scrappy goal for each side. The Celtic End was distinctly short-changed, for the good goals were scored at the Rangers End, and the scrappy ones in front of us.

The game was even, but it was Rangers who took the lead through Sandy Jardine with a great shot from the edge of the box. This was near half-time, and just as depression was sweeping over us, we equalised, Jimmy Johnstone on hand to prod home a rebound from a Lennox shot. Thus half-time was spent with us in the ascendancy, and as the second half progressed, confidence – often a dangerous emotion – began to spread and Celtic looked to be in charge.

When Jimmy Johnstone scored his wonder goal with 15 minutes to go, it looked all over. It was a brilliant goal, but from the far end the ball didn't seem to have entered the net, for it came to rest in the mud some distance from the Rangers goal. But everyone accepted that it had crossed the line, and Celtic now had to lose two goals inside 15 minutes to lose the league.

"Glas-gow Cel-tic" (to the same rhythm as the vile Gemmell chant from the other end) was the cry, but those of us of a melancholic disposition had cause to shout about complacency yet again when Ronnie Simpson made one of his rare errors, and Roger Hynd earned a late equaliser for Rangers. Goodness knows how long it was between that goal and Willie Syme blowing the final whistle, but I was aware that my "stress incontinence" was playing up again, and was only relieved in the primitive Ibrox Celtic End toilets after a great deal of pain. It was a "pleasurable pain" or a "painful pleasure", for by the time I was able to relieve myself, Celtic had won the league for the second year in a row and the 22nd time overall. The domestic treble was ours, and all that remained that day was to get back through the Huns to central Glasgow via the Copland Road Underground Station. Actually, they were surprisingly civil and the place was very well policed with horses and dogs. There were even a few – but only a few – handshakes exchanged. One even sensed a certain feeling of relief among Rangers fans that Celtic had not given them a complete pasting.

And so the treble had been achieved. Rangers had done this in 1949 and 1964, but this was Celtic's first. There were a few celebrations, not least among the Celtic players, one imagines, for Jock Stein flew to Italy that night to see Inter Milan v Torino and was not therefore around to stop the Bacchanalia. The supporters certainly enjoyed themselves. There were now two schools of thought about the European Cup. One was that we had had a good season anyway, which would long be remembered even if we blew up in Lisbon.

The other was that all this would count for nothing if we did not beat Inter Milan, and a defeat would lead to renewed sneers about all our domestic success being achieved in what was "just" Scottish football.

In the meantime, there was still a great deal of football going on. Rangers, for reasons best known to themselves, disappeared to America – a move that would be much criticised by their supporters and the followers of Scotland, for it meant that none of them were available for the Scotland game against the USSR on May 10 at Hampden – while Celtic went to Seamill Hydro and trained. But Tommy Gemmell proved yet again to be a difficult man to keep out of the news.

He scored a goal in the international at Hampden. The trouble was that it was against Ronnie Simpson and was for the USSR against Scotland! What would James Bond have made of that one, we wondered? It was the downside of Tommy Gemmell. He was very aggressive, full of himself, confident – but he could be a careless defender, and in this case, he was just too sure that Ronnie Simpson read his mind as he lobbed the ball gently over him. It was one of the worst own goals of all time, and Tommy was indeed fortunate that his other deeds that very month meant that it has not achieved the historical notoriety it perhaps deserved.

Remarks were made about Celtic's attacking full-backs, but although it was a friendly international it was embarrassing nevertheless, for the side contained seven Celtic players. Simpson, Gemmell, McNeill, Clark, Johnstone and Lennox were in the starting XI and then Willie Wallace came on as a substitute for Denis Law. Scotland, having beaten England a month earlier and on top of the world, went down 0-2 to the USSR at Hampden in front of 53,497 disillusioned and angry Scottish fans. It had been a poor game and a chastening experience.

Back in St Andrews, the heat was rising as exams approached. The first year was the vital one, for if you passed these exams, you would usually get some degree or other. But the end of the first year usually saw a pretty severe and brutal "chucking out" for those who had not performed well. The polite euphemism was the "discontinuing of studies", but basically you needed to pass at least two of your three subjects, and what would have been the point of winning the European Cup if you had to return home in disgrace to a job in the factory and the severe disappointment of your parents?

It was just as well that there was not a choice in this, because there is little doubt that I would have plumped for the European Cup and to hell with the university. I debated this with myself often enough and came back time and time again to the lyrics of the rebel song,

"I want no gold to nerve my arm,
To win a woman's heart,
To free my native land,
I'd gladly give the red drops from my heart."

Yes indeed, "the red drops from my heart" – and that was how highly I valued the Celtic. I was fortunate in that I had none of the usual student distractions of women and drink (they would both, sadly, plague me in later years), so I could concentrate on my twin passions of classical languages and Glasgow Celtic. I had passed the Latin exam in April that took place in the week of the Dukla Prague game, so Latin was not a problem, but I still had Ancient History and Greek. The Ancient History exams were on

Monday, May 22, but the Greek ones (three papers) were scheduled for the morning of Friday, May 26, the afternoon of May 26 and Saturday morning of May 27.

This clearly knocked out any small chance of me getting to Lisbon on Thursday, May 25. I probably could not have afforded it anyway, even with my father's offer to impoverish himself to facilitate things, and I realised that studying on the day of the game would be next to impossible, so I would have to get down to it at an early stage. Ancient History was a "swot" subject, so it was just a matter of learning, and the Greek Prescribed Texts were OK as well, but there were a few rogue and unusual things in Greek, like Vase Painting, not to mention the normal unseen translation from Greek into English, and from English into Greek.

The English into Greek was what was called a prose. It was generally considered to be the most difficult part of the course, but I rather enjoyed it and was prepared to spend a lot of time practising putting bits of English into Greek. I was generally looked upon as rather studious and it was frequently predicted that I would do well, even though I had my fatal flaw of the Glasgow green and white. In my honest moments, I knew within myself that I was bright enough.

I also found myself rather enjoying Homer's *Iliad* with all the stock epithets – Agamemnon, for example, was "lord of men", and Achilles was "swift of foot". With a little dexterity and thought, one could easily transfer some of these adjectives to the Celtic players, so that Stein became "lord of men", Lennox was "swift of foot", Johnstone was "nimble-footed", McNeill was "god-like", Auld was "rich in counsel", Gemmell was "of the large nose" and could one have ever found a better description of Ronnie Simpson than the Homeric one of old Nestor "who knew all things, past and present"? And I imagined myself going to the Delphic Oracle to ask who would win the European Cup. Back came the answer, ambiguous as always: "A mighty club will fall in Lisbon." Yes, yes I know that, but which mighty club?

The football continued. Celtic finished off their domestic programme on Monday, May 15 with their game against Kilmarnock at Celtic Park. A crowd of 21,000 appeared to see a pretty uninspiring game of football, won 2-0 by Celtic, the goals coming from Bobby Lennox and Willie Wallace. Lennox's goal at first sight looked to be offside, but the match officials called it right. It was a typical Lennox goal, Bobby moving so fast that it looked as if he had started from an offside position, whereas in fact he was simply too fast for anyone. Fortunately, on this occasion, the linesman kept his flag down. John Cushley was given a game and actually played alongside Billy McNeill as double centre-half in one of Jock Stein's experiments to attract a few more to the game. In the goal, the ever-faithful John Fallon was also given a game.

At half-time, a car appeared with all the trophies on its roof – an extremely rare chance to see all of Scottish domestic football's trophies at the same time – and as everyone remarked, there was symbolically room for another one, which could now be won in ten days' time. Then, at full time, the team carried Jock Stein shoulder-high on to the field and off again. It was as well that there were 11 players, for it was no easy task to lift on high Big Jock.

Kilmarnock, never the best-loved of opponents for their perceived Rangers sympathies when Willie Waddell was their manager, but now better regarded with ex-Celt Malky MacDonald as boss, were given best wishes as well. They were due to play at Leeds United in the Inter Cities Fairs Cup semi-final first leg on Friday, May 19 and then on the Wednesday before Lisbon at Rugby Park. They went down 4-2 in heavy rain and experienced for themselves a little of the wild side of life in the unforgiving and notorious atmosphere of Don Revie's Elland Road, but the two goals they scored gave them a little hope for the second leg.

Then, on Saturday, May 20, was the English cup final. In those days, the game was televised throughout the world – but not to Scotland. The SFA had traditionally blocked the FA Cup Final before and predictably turned awkward again on the dubious grounds that the game, if televised on TV, would deter people from going to junior football games. On this particular day, the Scottish Junior Cup Final between Kilsyth Rangers and Rutherglen Glencairn was taking place at Hampden, but the blackout looked like nothing other than the malign grip of Calvinism trying to spread its icy fingers over Scotland once more to prevent people from being happy and enjoying themselves. So we had to listen to the English cup final on the radio and it was a good game, with Tottenham Hotspur beating Chelsea 2-1. It was the first-ever all-London FA Cup Final, and Spurs had now won the trophy three times in the decade of the 1960s.

On Sunday, Charlie Gallagher played his second and last international game for the Republic of Ireland. This was at Dalymount Park, where a poor Irish side went down 0-2 to a disciplined but uninspiring Czechoslovakia side in front of a paltry crowd of just over 6,000. Charlie would have been forgiven for not giving the game his undivided attention, for he had to fly back the Glasgow the following day, and then depart for Lisbon on the Tuesday morning.

It was announced early in the week that the European Cup Final would be televised live at 5.30pm on the Thursday. In 1967, one must remember, television coverage, even of a game like this, could not be guaranteed, and it really made a huge difference to one's approach to the game. Television in 1967 could still be primitive, as events would prove, coloured TV had not yet made its appearance in Great Britain, and the coverage would lack the sophistication that the next 50 years would bring. But then again, people will not complain about anything if they've never experienced anything better. Indeed it was a rare treat. Arrangements were made by supporters all over Scotland to watch the TV, in my case in the Common Room of my residence, St Regulus Hall.

My Ancient History exams came and went on the Monday. I had the comfortable feeling that I had passed, for it was, as I said, a "swot" subject and if you bent down and worked, you would get through. Basically, I knew enough abou Alexander the Great, the Gracchi and the Roman Emperors to pass. As yet, there was no great stress laid on "skills" and "analysing events" or if there was, they were generally ignored for exam purposes. I learned that, in so far as one had to express an opinion, it was never a good idea to disagree with the orthodox, if you wished to pass an exam. The point was to get through. An examination hall, like an interview room for a job, is no place to show off, express one's own opinions and be "clever" – lessons that I absorbed in 1967, but sadly seemed to forget in later years.

Getting "uptight" for exams was a common phenom-enon. It was even a trendy and therefore dangerous thing to phone home threatening to give up university, to suffer from a mini (and bogus) nervous breakdown, to take a mild sedative in order to get through the day and to smoke cigarettes and drink alcohol to "ease the tension". I was spared all these things, for, frankly, exams were only half of my life in mid-May 1967. Such tension as I had was resolved to a certain extent by singing. Naturally, I had a wide repertoire of Celtic and rebel songs but depending on what company I was in, I might or might not sing the three add-on words after "I'm off to Dublin in the green". I also became a fan of Manfred Mann – I actually thought that it was the name of the singer, but in fact it was a group – and went around singing an inane ditty which began with the words "Ha! Ha! Said the Clown".

This very group, the following year, 1968, released a great song called "The Mighty Quinn". What a shame it had not been released 60 years earlier with lyrics that applied to the one and only Mighty Quinn, the great Jimmy from Croy! I remember trying to make up words that were appropriate to the miner boy from Croy, but as far as "Ha! Ha! Said The Clown", I only really learned the next few words "as the King lost his crown" and hoped to apply that to the appalling Herrera. I never really got round to learning the rest of the words, though. Lisbon and the game that would determine the rest of our lives was approaching.

It was not all that was approaching. Some sort of war was brewing up in the Middle East with everyone in the Arab world ganging up against Israel. Unaware of the complexities of that situation, I was rather taken aback by the passions it aroused in the student community with most people, surprisingly perhaps in view of later events, siding with Israel. Mercifully, the benign Harold Wilson, the Labour Prime Minister, decided to stay neutral. Frankly I couldn't be bothered with it, and asked the simple question, so often asked by so many Western people and still not entirely irrelevant today: "Why can't they just get on with each other?" There still is no answer to that one, is there?

The Celtic team flew out to Portugal on the Tuesday morning. The players knew what the composition of the team was going to be and most of us could guess correctly, although some of us felt that John Hughes might just have got the nod over Bobby Lennox. The team was officially announced soon after they reached Lisbon, where they were given a good reception by the locals. Jock Stein showed that he was manager material by courting the world's press, in sharp contrast to the boorish Herrera, who ignored them and gave the impression that they were just getting in the way. It is never a good idea to treat the Fourth Estate in that way, and world public opinion was pretty soon on the side of Celtic.

It must be recalled that, in 1967, Portugal and Scotland did not really know very much about each other. To the Portuguese Scotland was a cold, misty, rainy land where everyone played the bagpipes and wore kilts. They used to fight the English quite a lot but had kissed and made up many centuries ago. To a Scotsman, Portugal was a hot, languid, lazy country where everyone went on fishing trips. That would have been the average Portuguese impression of Scotland and vice-versa. But they had loads in common. They both lived next to imperialist neighbours in England and Spain, so there was a natural inclination for the Portuguese to support the Scots, and when the Portuguese locals discovered that there was an Irish connection as well,

Lisbon turned green and white, for Portugal was definitely a "Catholic country".

By this time, the advance guard of what was called the Celticade had arrived in Lisbon. That was the name given to those who had travelled by car all through England, France and Spain. Others flew in and it was believed that 25,000 were there. Now, as I have said previously, one must always be suspicious of bland statements like "Celtic fans are the best in the world". There is, after all, a downside as well. But Jock Stein had worked hard since becoming manager to rid the support of the hooligan element which had disgraced Celtic in places like Dundee, Perth, Falkirk and, on one notorious occasion, in Sunderland, and here he reaped the benefit. The supporters charmed the locals, visited the tourist sites, talked to the local girls, bought local goods, showed total respect and even veneration for the local churches and bought Portuguese flags to wear on their Celtic scarves and jerseys. Those who wore kilts were particularly cossetted, looked at and photographed by the Lisbon population.

The eve of the game was not without its interest elsewhere in the footballing world. Kilmarnock's brave quest for the Inter Cities Fairs Cup came to a halt at Rugby Park when they could not penetrate the tough Leeds United defence, which contained a man called Norman Hunter, who rejoiced in the nickname of "Bites Yer Legs". Scotsman Billy Bremner was resoundingly booed for repeated fouling. *The Evening Times* was happy to use the word "skulduggery" to describe the tactics of Leeds United.

Kilsyth Rangers won the Scottish Junior Cup in a replay of the final against Rutherglen Glencairn, one-time nursery of the great Jimmy McMenemy. The Kilsyth side contained a young man called Pat McMahon from the nearby Celtic-orientated village of Croy. He would join Celtic a day or two later and play a few games for the club, coming off the substitute's bench one day in the rain at Tannadice Park in January 1969 to score the final goal in Celtic's 3-1 victory. England beat Spain 2-0 at Wembley, a result that caused a certain rejoicing among the Portuguese population, if not the Celtic support. Some Celtic players apparently watched that game at their hideaway outside Lisbon.

But now, the great day dawned. It was now impossible to ignore, even if you wanted to. As to who Scotland wanted to win, there was now less and less doubt in that most people were giving their sometimes reluctant, sometimes hypocritical but more often their full and sincere backing for Celtic. The hardcore Rangers fans, a shrinking band since their dominant days of the early 1960s, obviously were not in favour of a Celtic win, but the moderate element was. Ibrox itself declared that it wanted Celtic to win, albeit couched in terms of hoping that they could do likewise next week in the European Cup Winners' Cup Final "for the good of Scottish football", and most supporters of other clubs expressed support for Celtic. Mind you, many of them were doing a little fence-sitting. If Celtic won, they could share the glory. If they lost, they could shed crocodile tears.

Most Scottish people who cheerfully admitted to knowing little or nothing about football wanted Celtic to win. The rugby-playing fraternity of Edinburgh and the Borders, for example, had no axe to grind and, other things being equal, wanted a Scottish team to do well. Old ladies who normally did gardening and went to coffee mornings were usually sufficiently interested to want Celtic to do well. Students and academics were generally broad-minded enough to want a Celtic victory. The Celtic paranoia about everyone hating them finally took a massive blow when the Church of Scotland's General Assembly, then in session in Edinburgh, sent a telegram of good wishes. In the 1920s, this august body had passed resolution after resolution deploring the "Irish menace", which was in danger of "diluting the Scottish race" if any Protestant ever had sexual relations with a Roman Catholic. The Kirk had now clearly moved on to being a benign group of harmless old duffers.

English people do not, as a rule, hate Scotland. The other way round, it can be different, certainly as far as football is concerned. The World Cup of 1966 was by no means a highlight of a Scottish person's life. But English people do not see Scotland as a threat. The country is quaint, has beautiful scenery, and produced in the 1960s loads of good football players like Dave MacKay, Ian St John, Denis Law, Alan Gilzean, Pat Crerand and Jim Baxter to play in the English league. There was respect for Scotland. But now a Scottish team had had the temerity to be the first British team to reach the European Cup Final.

But if Celtic were to be the first British team to lift the trophy, then at least it wasn't another English team. Like other countries, supporters of one English team are often insanely jealous of other teams in their own country. The idea of "Manchester United representing England" was much peddled by the BBC, but in fact had very little basis in reality. Manchester City and Liverpool supporters would have considered it better for a Scottish team to be the first to win the European Cup rather than their rival. In any case, what they had seen of Celtic on TV was impressive, and most people in England, if they tried hard enough, could usually come up with a Scottish or Irish ancestor, so

Celtic had a great deal of moderate and grudging support from England. In any case, it gave them all something to be interested in.

Conversely, Inter Milan had their detractors. Not only were they looked upon with suspicion for their ultra-negative and defensive-orientated approach to the game, but there were other factors as well. The Willie Maley song, written many years later, has a line about "to Portugal we had to go, to meet the team that Italy adored". This was, frankly, not true. Italy did *not* adore Inter Milan. Reasons of local rivalry and petty hatred meant that AC Milan supporters cheered for Celtic, but there was also a general dislike of Helenio Herrera, the little Argentinian who was the manager of "Grande Inter" widely suspected of nobbling referees and officials, and well known for being a bully with his players. He had a pathological suspicion that players were drinking wine and plotting against him – a bit like Stein in that regard perhaps, but a hundred times worse and without Stein's redeeming features. Herrera being humiliated would have gone down well in many areas of Italy.

Stein won the first round. It was a matter of no importance whatsoever, but it was symbolic. There were two benches for the officials of both sides, but neither had been assigned to either team. Stein decided that he wanted one, and told his reserves, John Fallon and John Cushley, to grab it and sit on it, so that Herrera would have to take the other. It was pure psychological warfare, but Stein was able to declare later that he was not going to be Herrera's fall guy. Jim Craig would later describe Celtic players as "gallus", meaning confidently naïve, but Jock Stein was no fool.

I have no clear memories of what I did in the morning of Thursday, May 25. I presume I studied my Homer's *Iliad* for tomorrow's exam. In the afternoon, I bagged my seat in the Common Room of St Regulus Hall where I lived, and sat there with loads of others, discussing matters like whether the absence of Luis Suarez would be significant for Inter Milan. Most of us were of the opinion that Suarez might suddenly reappear in any case for Herrera was considered an untrustworthy character. Inter Milan were the winners in 1964 and 1965, and we feared that that experience might just tip the balance. They also had the advantage of being more accustomed to the fierce heat. Funnily enough, almost all the pundits of all the newspapers thought that whoever scored first would win the game. In this respect, they were all gloriously wrong.

Finally, 5.30pm arrived. By this time, the Common Room was full and the atmosphere was electric. It was a warm day, the sun was still out and the curtains had to be drawn as we all strained to watch the pathetically small TV screen. Neil Mochan and Bob Rooney came out chewing gum, but we found it difficult to identify the players. Jimmy Johnstone was obvious, of course, but the others were all going past so quickly, and this was 1967, remember, when TV camera work was far from brilliant.

The game started. Jimmy Johnstone was given the ball to run with for a while so that the Portuguese would identify with the small redhead. Red hair was not common in Portugal, and large-bosomed, matronly, maternal ladies would naturally fall in love with him. The TV audience did not see the red hair, but they knew it anyway. We cheered, but then ominously our TV began to splutter and flicker. However, it righted itself until the Inter forward, Renato

Steve Chalmers in 1962

Prague, April 25, 1967. Jimmy Johnstone and Tommy Gemmell in Dukla strips celebrate reaching the European Cup final

Scottish Cup Final, April 29, 1967. Captains Harry Melrose (Aberdeen) and Billy McNeill (Celtic) shake hands while referee Davie Syme looks on

Prague, April 26, 1967. John Fallon, the reserve goalkeeper shows his delight at the full time whistle. Bob Rooney (half hidden), Sean Fallon, Neil Mochan and Jock Stein are also in the picture

On the road to Lisbon, Celtic celebrate the winning of the Scottish Cup against Aberdeen on April 29, 1967

Jock Stein congratulates Bobby Murdoch and Willie Wallace after winning the Scottish Cup against Aberdeen at Hampden on April 29, 1967

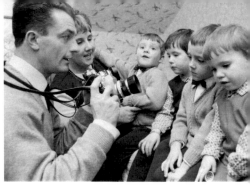

Bobby Murdoch with his wife Kathleen and young Bobby

Stevie Chalmers and his wife have problems in getting the young Chalmers family to smile for the camera

Jimmy Johnstone is about to score the goal that helped to win Celtic the Scottish League at Ibrox on May 6, 1967

Jimmy Johnstone prods home at Ibrox in the rain on May 6, 1967

Action in the rain at Ibrox on May 6, 1967 as Bobby Murdoch stretches to clear

Poor fellows! They don't know what is going to hit them

Stevie Chalmers turns away after scoring the winning goal

Inter Milan couldn't stop the players, and neither a moat nor a wall nor the Portuguese police will stop the fans!

Scenes of jubilation in Lisbon

Celebrations at the final whistle

Billy McNeill is mobbed by fans at the final whistle in Lisbon

Willie Wallace is lifted in the air by exultant fans

Billy McNeill is hugged by triumphant supporters. Observe the fan in the kilt

The iconic image of the first British team to win the European Cup

Billy McNeill was brought round in a car with the big trophy to the dressing room in Lisbon

All there apart from Big Jock! Maybe he is taking the photograph!

The night after the night before as the team drive round Celtic Park on a lorry to show their fans the European Cup

The Daily Record *of Friday, May 26, 1967*

Jock Stein receives his special trophy for winning the European Cup from Bill Nicholson of Tottenham Hotspur

Bobby Lennox, Willie Wallace and Jimmy Johnstone are the Celtic players in this shot from the game against Spurs in August 1967. Jimmy Greaves is the Spurs player beside the referee

Action from the game against Spurs in August 1967

Mrs Kelly unfurls the league flag at the start of the new season while her husband and Jock Stein look on

Off to South America!

Celtic players don't seem to be all that happy with an Argentinian after a bad foul on Jimmy Johnstone in the Hampden game

Trouble in Montevideo with the steel-helmeted police

A show of affection from Bertie Auld to one of his Racing Club opponents in Montevideo

Trainer Neil Mochan attends to Ronnie Simpson after he has been hit by a missile before the game started in Buenos Aires

Jock Stein kisses the new Mrs Tommy Gemmell

Never exactly his favourite people! Jock Stein has just been talking to a Summer School of referees. The famous referee Jack Mowatt (now a Supervisor) is in the front on the extreme right

Billy McNeill discusses the finer points of theology while Jock Stein and Bob Kelly talk to Glasgow's Lord Provost

Racing Club's vice chairman Senor Cuneo signs autographs for youngsters before Celtic play Partick Thistle at Firhill on October 14, 1967

Jock Stein at the wedding of Mr and Mrs Bobby Lennox

John Hughes in action in the first game against Racing Club at Hampden on October 18, 1967

When not leading Celtic to unbelievable success, Billy McNeill is a somewhat harassed looking family man

Jim McLean (in later years the legendary manager of Dundee United) scores against Celtic for Dundee in the Scottish League Cup Final of October 28, 1967. Celtic would eventually win 5-3

Scottish League Cup final of October 29 1966. Willie O'Neill makes his famous goal line clearance

Scottish League Cup Final of October 29, 1966. Bobby Lennox scores the only goal of the game

Celebrating the winning of the Scottish League Cup in October 1967

Matt Busby presents Celtic with the Award for the Best Team of the Year at the Sports Review of The Year on BBC TV in December 1967

Bobby Lennox and Willie Wallace reminisce over old times

The Bhoys of the Old Brigade

Twenty years on, and some of the strips are struggling to hold the expanding waistlines

Showing the big cup off at Celtic Park once again. Jimmy Johnstone's red hair has now gone

Cappellini, ran across Jim Craig on the edge of the box and fell down. As our hearts sank, the referee, Kurt Tschenscher, of Germany, pointed to the spot. Frankly, it looked for all the world like a typical Italian con trick. Our TV seemed to protest about it as well, for the picture disappeared. The sound, however, remained and we were able to hear that Sandro Mazzola had scored. Sadly, I lowered my moral standards by shouting loudly my wishes that the "w*p c**t" would miss it. I subsequently apologised and regretted the word "w*p", but not the other one.

But what could we do with the television, which had now earned the word "f***ing" as an honorary title? A guy who claimed to know something about TVs tried but failed, and in an atmosphere in which "desperation" seemed to sum everything up, we realised we would have to abandon ship and move to the Residence up the road called Southgate.

We charged up the road, in my case with the tears rolling down my cheeks, ignoring the quizzical looks of those I met, swearing like a trooper, charging across the road with no thought for my safety and generally looking and acting like a demented nutcase. Was this to be the end of all my dreams? I knew my dad would be similarly distressed – but, of course, looking at it in perspective, the game had not yet gone 15 minutes, even when we burst into Southgate Hall to join the agonised faces of those already there.

Finding a seat, I settled down, my heart beating to an extent that, had I been an older man, the medics would have been extremely worried. But it was vital that we did not lose another goal. That would certainly kill us off, and maybe me too. Celtic had taken a grip of the game. Bobby Murdoch, his ankle well strapped up, was spraying passes, Bertie Auld was in the thick of things, Ronnie Simpson showed tremendous composure with a back heel when well out of his goal – but it was only days later when the game had been shown *ad infinitum* (but not *ad nauseam*) that we realised just how much Celtic were on top. Half-time came, however, and we were still one down. Were we going to show the world how football should be played, but lose the European Cup?

By half-time, I had recovered sufficient equilibrium and was able to speak. With me was my friend Colin, one of those moderate Rangers supporters I had talked about, but now more vocal in his encouragement of Celtic than even I was. In truth, I was glad of the temporary relief of tension that half-time brought.

Across in Lisbon in the Celtic dressing room, according to veterans of the event, everything was quite restrained. Stein was never a manager to go in for hysterics at half-time (he could be different at full time), and in that strange dressing room, which was more or less divided into two parts by the toilets and showers, Bobby Lennox recalls that Stein simply went around encouraging everyone, telling them to continue doing what they were doing and things would be all right.

But the second half started, and once more, thousands of Celtic supporters and I prepared to kick every ball. Often it is said that the last ten minutes of a game are "kitchen sink" time as you throw everything at the opposition, including the kitchen sink. The "kitchen sink" time in this game lasted all the second half, with Inter penned back as Murdoch and Auld orchestrated the attack. Gemmell and Chalmers were particularly unlucky, the ball hit the bar, went over the bar, appeals for penalties were turned down and goalkeeper Sarti was having the game of his life.

Twenty minutes of the second half had gone. It was thrilling but unsuccessful, and I at least was beginning to drop my head, reconciled to hearing and reading tomorrow about how they "had done Scotland proud" but hadn't won. But then it happened. Thankfully, Jim Craig disobeyed the instructions of Jock Stein. Tommy Gemmell was upfield on the attack as always. Therefore Jim should have been back, for Jock did not like both full-backs to be upfield at the same time, but there Jim was, passing the ball to Tommy Gemmell, who belted home from the edge of the box.

Fatuously, Gerry McNee, not a particularly well-loved or respected journalist, would claim that several Celtic players were offside – a point I once mischievously raised with Tommy Gemmell years later. The reply was "Affside (sic)! Affside! The baw would have been in Paris if it hadnae been for that net." That was years later, however. All that mattered now was that Celtic were level. "Catenaccio", the Inter method of defending, had been broken by Big Tam, and history was about to change.

Those who decided to be wise after the event, and I would have to admit I have been guilty of being one of them, said that they now knew that Celtic would win, whether in the 90 minutes, extra time or the replay provisionally arranged for Saturday night. This frankly was not the case as the game was in progress. We did *not* know that. Certainly Celtic continued to attack, but although the Inter midfield was overrun, their defence held firm, they had their share of luck with refereeing decisions and they looked able to hold out. Indeed, I was beginning to get a premonition (I always got these things, so that I could say "I told you so") that Inter might sneak up and score a winner against our exposed defence, which seemed to consist sometimes of

Ronnie Simpson and John Clark, for even Billy McNeill on occasion joined the attack.

But we were well within the last ten minutes when we struck again. Once more, Tommy Gemmell was involved, dancing about on the edge of the box, then a cutback to Bobby Murdoch, who was now on the left of the field rather than the right, where he would normally be (because his right ankle was giving him pain, presumably). Bobby shot and the ball was touched in by Stevie Chalmers. To be frank, I have a memory blackout of the next few seconds, other than everyone jumping on top of one another, but I remember thinking "Stevie Chalmers! Stevie Chalmers! My boyhood hero!"

Irrationally – for no-one thinks straight in these circumstances – my mind went back some four years to May 1963, when Celtic went down 0-3 to Dundee United at Tannadice Park. Stevie was playing on the left wing – he was no left-winger – and he was having a bad game. But he was trying hard, and getting the most dreadful of foul-mouthed abuse from a few loutish, drunken cretins standing next to me, while I was almost in tears at what they were shouting at that man, who was always one of nature's gentlemen. Oh, how I wish I could have seen them now.

But I do recall everyone asking how long to go, and someone coming into the Common Room and asking when *Top of The Pops* was on. (It was a Thursday night and *Top of The Pops* was usually on at 7.30pm). The unanimous reply was "F*** *Top Of The Pops*". The crowd coming over the moat, Kenneth Wolstenholme saying "Not long now", curses from my fellow students "Keep the f***in baw up there! Watch that c***", praying, gripping the arms of the chair, two pretty young girls coming in to the foul language and profanities, me trying to do a deal with God about going to church on Sunday, thinking about my dad, Jock Stein leaving the bench unable to watch, and then the glorious, glorious sound of the final whistle, as I collapsed back in the chair, a physical and emotional wreck. "Ha! Ha! Said the Clown. The King's Lost His Crown".

Everyone charging about the field with kilts and flags and T-shirts with "Jock Stein" written on them. Then Billy McNeill, seriously pummelled by well-meaning but ill-advised fans, and looking very ill indeed, fighting his way across the field to get that big ugly cup. He eventually got there, and the iconic moment on which history looked down on us when he lifted that trophy. "Glory hovers over Parkhead" said Kenneth Wolstenholme as the tears flooded down my cheeks.

"Still o'er these scenes my memory wakes
And fondly broods with miser care
Time but the impression stronger makes
As streams their channels deeper wear."

This quote from Robert Burns on the death of his Highland Mary is ludicrously out of context here, but the following few hours I recall vividly and with relish. The trouble is they are all in cameos and I can't remember which order, but I recall being hugged in the street, buying chips from an Italian shop owner who did not like Inter Milan and who was as pleased as anyone, meeting, of all people, the Professor of Greek, who smiled tolerantly as we all sang "Cel-tic! Celt-tic", an old tramp who claimed that he remembered Tommy McInally, going back to St Regulus Hall where the TV had now been repaired and watching Celtic fans celebrating in Glasgow with one image in particular touching me even yet. It was the sight of three young boys, street urchins whom the welfare state had not yet quite reached, holding up a Celtic dish cloth. They were the risen people.

As for me, I had to stay sensible. I didn't even take a drink that night. I was not entirely unfamiliar with alcohol and its effects. My previous encounters had produced Herculean hangovers, and I knew that I still had an exam the next day. Although I could not exactly concentrate on studying, I was beginning to develop confidence. It was not just simply the confidence that I knew enough Greek to get through, it was more the general confidence in oneself that if you put your mind to it, you can do most things. What I had seen in Lisbon that night would stay with me all my days. The inferiority complex and homesickness were things of the past. In fact, nothing else now seemed to matter at all, other than that the Celtic were the champions of Europe.

My dad had apparently phoned that night but I was out. I knew he would. It didn't bother me that he had missed me because I knew he would be happy, and I would see him on the Saturday anyway. I later discovered that he had disappeared in the last desperate, entrails-devouring five minutes after Chalmers had scored. My mother had been in another room and had come through to see the TV on but no-one there. She thought he was in the toilet – something that would have made sense in the physical state that he was in – but he wasn't there. Genuinely concerned for his health and well-being, she eventually discovered him hiding in the garden shed, and was able to tell him that they had won! Yes, a self-confessed coward in those last few minutes – yet no-one had said that about him at El Alamein and Mersa Matruh!

So that Thursday gave way to Friday. Friday dawned beautiful with all the seagulls in St Andrews apparently crying "Cel-tic! Celt-tic!" I got up early, bought the papers from a triumphant wee man saying things like "They've won everything" and "They're the best team I've seen". He'd always been a miserable, grumpy little bastard before then too! I devoured all the papers with my cornflakes, and have never seen so many smiling faces. People came up, shook my hand, said things like "I knew *we* would do it!" I smiled my way to the exam hall, grinned at the invigilator and proceeded to devour the exam with contemptuous ease.

Lunchtime was still happy, the afternoon exam paper was even easier, and I even earned a smile from a girl who didn't like me, as I thought. There was still an exam on the Saturday, but this time we did go for a drink. Singing songs about volunteers approaching the border town, and vowing never to shelter the despot or the slave, we got back to see on TV the return of the team to Glasgow. It would be described as VE night, Hogmanay and the Glasgow Fair all rolled into one, and things would never be the same again. I must strongly deny, however, any profane behaviour concerning Patrick Hamilton, the Protestant martyr of the 16th century.

There is, in St Andrews, a spot outside St Salvator's College in North Street with the letters PH written there on the pavement. This was where he was burnt to death for disagreeing with Roman Catholic orthodoxy. Tradition had it that one did not stand on that spot. This was until May 25, 1967, when someone, apparently, did a little dance on that every spot, shouting "Ha! Ha! You Protestant bastard!" It wasn't me, honest... but it was funny!

My dad did phone that night, and he asked: "Did you see it?" He could ask some really stupid questions, that man! Saturday morning saw another exam and my last. It was easy. Then funnily enough, I met my mother. She had come to St Andrews with the Women's Guild trip and oh, how proud she was of her son with his red gown. But her son was still thinking green and white, as indeed were most people. It would not die down for many days yet.

And then I went home to see my father. He had intended to come and meet me at the bus station and give me a hand with my suitcases, but I got an earlier bus and lugged them home myself. And you can guess what we talked about. He still averred that Patsy Gallacher was the greatest player of them all, but agreed that 1967 was the best team of them all, better than the six leagues in a row team of 1905–10, the Empire Exhibition Trophy team of 1938 or the Coronation Cup team of 1953. The game was on TV again that night. We watched it, father and son, unashamedly in tears, and then I went to my own little bed, having achieved the dual triumph of completing my first year and having won the European Cup.

I had read Catullus in Latin. The racy, sexy poems about Lesbia were all very fine, but I could not help thinking of his poem of his island Sirmio.

"O quid solutis est beatius curis
Cum mens onus reponit ac peregrino
Labore fessi venimus larem ad nostrum
Desideratoque acquiescimus lecto"

"Oh, what is more blessed than being free from worries, when the mind lays aside its burden, and tired with foreign travel we reach our own home and lie down in the much longed-for bed"

Or what about John McCormack when his beloved Mavourneen will one day respond to his pleas to "Come Back To Erin" and come home "and sure Killarney will ring out with mirth!"

Life could not have been happier than it was on that blessed night of Saturday May 27, 1967.

There was a postscript, however, and one that did not really reflect very highly on my good self. It concerned Rangers, who were playing in the final of the European Cup Winners' Cup against Bayern Munich in Nuremberg on the last day of May. Ibrox historians may not agree with me on this one, but I think that 1966/67 was actually a good season for Rangers. Other than their unmitigated disaster at Berwick, they had pushed Celtic hard in the Scottish League, and surely to come within a few points of the European champions, as Celtic now were, was no disgrace. Moreover, it had been the opinion of several journalists and indeed some Celtic supporters, myself included, that they had been the better team in the Scottish League Cup Final in October, but they had gone down 0-1. (A total reversal of roles from so many occasions in the past, notably the League Cup Final of 1964/65, when Celtic had been the better team but had gone down 1-2.) And now Rangers were in a European final of their own. You do not reach these dizzy heights with a bad team.

Indeed had this been any other team, such as Aberdeen, for example, or perhaps an English team, this would have been considered a good season with words like "glory" and "triumph" worked into the conversation of their supporters, and books produced on it in time for the Christmas market. But this was Glasgow, and Rangers could only really be judged against Celtic, to whom they were clearly second best. Indeed this would became a sad obsession with Rangers supporters, one of whom some 50 years later would say that the thought of 1967 remains a "daily kick in the testicles", as if you got up every morning, then someone impaired and damaged you in that painful way every day of your life, like a classical torture meted out in the underworld to someone who had tried it on with a goddess, or mimicked Olympian Zeus.

However, here now was their chance to get something at least out of this season. But Rangers, who had often claimed to be the "Scottish" team, now showed that most deleterious of Scottish characteristics – the penchant for self-destruction. Chairman John Lawrence issued a public statement to the effect that his team was simply not good enough to challenge Celtic and singled out the forward line as "makeshift" in that it contained three men who were originally half-backs. The effect that this had on the morale of the supporters and the players themselves could readily be guessed at. It was bizarre and barely comprehensible.

Their opponents were Bayern Munich, who could hardly believe their luck when they heard this statement, and the final was to be played in Nuremberg – something that seemed more than a little unfair. The Scottish press were surely correct in stating that it should surely have been moved to a neutral country. This was one of the reasons which persuaded me, after a long period of soul-searching, that I might support Rangers in this game. But with deliberate ambiguity, I told everyone that I was going to support "the Huns" without specifying whether I meant the German ones or the Glasgow ones!

There were other reasons for wanting Rangers to win as well. Many Rangers supporters had loyally backed

Celtic the previous week. Indeed their chairman, John Lawrence, had appeared at Glasgow Airport alongside the Lord Provost to welcome Celtic back. It may have hurt – it may have been his own private kick in the knackers – but he had been there, and you had to give the man credit for that. Also, even if Rangers did win this trophy, they couldn't possibly claim that they were anything like as good as Celtic, who had won the more important European Cup and a domestic treble. And how good it would be for Scotland if both trophies ended up in Glasgow in the same year. No-one would ever again be able to sneer at Scotland or Scottish football. Tourists would flock to a Glasgow museum, or even Edinburgh Castle, to see both trophies sitting alongside the Crown jewels!

There was a personal aspect to it as well. I appreciated that for someone from a Roman Catholic background in the west of Scotland, it was pretty nigh impossible to support Rangers, given the fact that they would be debarred from working for that organisation.

The cries of "F*** the Pope" were those of the ignorant, but they had been fostered by an organisation which had deliberately set out in the 1920s to exclude them on some mythical grounds of the superiority and purity of the Scottish race, or some bogus clap-trap like that. But for me it was different. I was from the East of Scotland, and from a non-denominational background, not even having a clear idea of what a Catholic was until someone with a blue scarf had called me one when I was about ten years old. I was a Fenian too, apparently, although how I could have belonged to a Victorian terrorist organisation a century earlier was difficult to understand. But no, above all I was Scottish, I decided.

Some of my best friends were Rangers supporters. There are several layers of Rangers supporters. There are the genuine Orange bigots, with whom one can do very little. There are also the ignorant who have been attracted by the extremity of the views put forward by other supporters. There was also, in the 1960s, a new breed of working-class young man, now reaching manhood, who had reacted badly to the Welfare State in that its benefits had, apparently, to be shared with immigrants and in particular the Irish. They reacted to this by supporting Rangers and voting for the Conservatives.

But many young Rangers-minded men and women were decent people who had been attracted to Rangers simply because in their early years, Rangers had won things in the way that Celtic hadn't. (Hearts had similarly reaped a rich harvest of friends when they won the league in 1958 and 1960.) They were not necessarily bigots, simply people who appreciated Jim Baxter, Davie Wilson and Willie Henderson. Admittedly, they went along with the poison on the terracing about the Pope and sycophantically and uncompromisingly supported the royal family, but that did not make them bad people. Most of my friends were in this category, and in spite of obvious differences, they remained my friends. It was them with whom I now identified.

So it was Rangers, reluctantly, for me. My father, however, felt differently. He had often said that if ever Rangers were playing at the back door, he would draw the curtains so as not to see them. Now he practised what he had always preached. Rangers were playing in the house, as it were, on TV, so he went out to do his garden, ostentatiously taking no apparent interest in what was going on. At half-time, it was 0-0 and I went out to tell him. He said "Oh?"

and continued to foster the potatoes and the carrots. At full time, it was still 0-0 and therefore went to extra time. I went out to tell him this, and again he said "Oh? A goalless draw. That'll be extra time, then."

But then Bayern scored through Roth in extra time and kept it that way to win the trophy. By this time it was getting dark, and he was still there applying the last touches to the onion bed when I went out to tell him the news. "1-0 to the Germans," I said. He looked up, a flicker of a smile beginning to appear, and I was about to say something like "pity" or "shame for them", when I remembered all the arrogance of 1963 and 1964, when Jim Baxter arrogantly stuck the ball up his jersey after that awful Scottish Cup Final of 1963, the taunts of "Easy!" from their crowing supporters, the religious discrimination, the ferocious tackles of their coarse defenders, the air of superiority which permeated their organisation, the way that Willie Henderson had held up his arms in triumph to the Celtic End after scoring one day in 1964, the way that simple-minded souls weakly followed them because they were successful, the adulation they used to get in the *Scottish Daily Express* and from Peter Thomson on BBC TV. Then we, father and son, looked at each other, there was a brief pause, then we both doubled up with laughter.

These were the events of May 1967.

JUNE

· · · · · · ·

The dream world continued well into June. Now and again, we wondered whether it was indeed a dream from which we would wake up, but no, the dream continued. It is not an uncommon phenomenon when something really nice happens to then begin to fear that we are going to wake up to discover that it has all been a dream. I recalled vividly two years previously, after the Scottish Cup Final in 1965, sitting in Lewis Polytechnic's café eating mince and chips after returning from Hampden and fearing that I was going to wake up and that it had all been some cruel dream. I was even scared to pinch myself. But, it was reality – or else it had been a really long and very pleasant dream.

Rangers returned home to total indifference, which was in some ways worse for them than protests and demonstrations. The Lord Provost of Glasgow was there to meet them, as indeed was Celtic chairman Bob Kelly, but not a fan was seen. So much for "we are the people". Rangers fans generally hid from sight that summer, occasionally snarling about their team, sometimes even conceding that Celtic were better, but generally pretending to be interested in things like golf, cricket and tennis. A few even converted to Celtic, claiming that they had been Celtic supporters all their life. One of them confided that to me, saying that the moment of conversion occurred when he discovered that Jock Stein was a Protestant. You couldn't make that up, could you?

It may have been a dream in Scotland, but things turned nightmarish in the Middle East when war, which had been threatening for a few months, broke out between Israel and everyone else. In so far as we understood it at all, sympathies tended to be for the surrounded Israel (a glance at the map showed how surrounded she was), but Israel needed no sympathy as she burst out and was at the Suez Canal in a matter of days, with virtually every Arab aeroplane destroyed or immobilised. The Arab world tried unconvincingly to say that it was all because of the Americans and the British. In fact, it was due to their own ineptitude in not trying hard enough to come to some sort of accommodation with Israel on the diplomatic front in the first place followed by military incompetence on a huge scale. Basically the war started on the Monday and finished on the Saturday night. It would have been nice to say that this war solved the Middle East problem. No, in fact it made it a lot worse, and it continues sporadically and pointlessly to this day.

In the middle of this Six-Day War, Celtic went to Spain. It was ironic, for Alfredo di Stefano, who had been offered the chance to sign for Celtic in 1964, had now retired and asked Celtic to come for his benefit. Celtic were more than delighted to say yes, for here was a chance to appear as winners of the European Cup against the team who had won it the previous season. Not only that, but Real Madrid had won it five times in a row in the inaugural five seasons of the competition. The last of these was the game at Hampden in May 1960 against Eintracht Frankfurt, won 7-3 by Real Madrid, in what was often regarded as Glasgow's best-ever game of football and remembered fondly to this day.

Since then, Celtic fans had an affinity with Real. Real came to Glasgow to play in a friendly for charity in September 1962, and then in 1963 had put Rangers out of the European Cup, 1-0 at Ibrox and 6-0 in Madrid. We really needed that in 1963, for Celtic were floundering. It had really shut Rangers up in those dark days of autumn 1963, and although we still heard in the sycophantic Scottish press that Jim Baxter and Willie Henderson were "world class", we heard it with a lot less conviction and a lot less frequently.

But here we were, now ourselves the champions of Europe, being invited to go and play the mighty Real Madrid. If circumstances had been different, if the whole atmosphere had not been one of euphoria, a few questions might have been asked about the wisdom or desirability of playing this game. For one thing, there was a war on. Granted, the war was nowhere near Spain, and no-one had, as yet, started hi-jacking aeroplanes as a terrorist ploy – that would become common in the 1970s – but there might have been an element of danger in this trip. But there was another more serious objection.

This was the presence of General Franco, el Caudillo or leader of Spain. The word "caudillo" was, of course, a euphemism for "dictator" and Franco's dictatorship was one of the worst. He had pacified Spain after the Civil War of 1936–39 but in circumstances which reminded me of the phrase of Tacitus, the ancient Roman author, about the Roman conquest of Britain – *ubi solitudinem faciunt, pacem appellant*, meaning where they make a desert, they call it peace. Franco, like the Romans in Britain, and using methods by no means dissimilar to those of the Black and Tans and B Specials in Ireland, or indeed the Duke of Cumberland in Scotland, had simply wiped out all opposition. Not everyone had been put to death, but enough had suffered that fate to make the rest aware of the need to shut up and toe the line. *Pour encourager les autres*, the French said. In any case, prisoners were needed for slave labour and in particular Franco's monstrous mausoleum to the Civil War, El Valle de los Caidos, outside Madrid, erected in honour of all those who had died *Por Dios Y Espana* with not a word about the many Spaniards who had died on the other side.

Franco's allies in the Civil War had, of course, been Hitler, Mussolini and, to its eternal shame, the Roman Catholic Church. The last named body had actually created a problem for Celtic supporters in the 1930s. Naturally inclined to support the ailing and stricken Republic, even though it was badly led, ill equipped and fighting with itself in a deleterious internecine struggle, Celtic supporters now found that support for the Republic could earn disapproval, opprobrium and even excommunication from the Church. But then again, Churches of all denominations do have a dismal and predictable propensity to side with the rich and powerful against the poor and oppressed. Yet, I thought in my naivety in 1967 that Jesus Christ gave a different message.

So should we do anything to show any support for General Francisco Franco? To the man's credit, he was a football fan and genuine lover of Real Madrid, and his apologists kept saying that he was mellowing and becoming more liberal now that all opposition had been liquidated, but still he was a man with a great deal of blood on his hands. In circumstances other than the euphoria of 1967, there might have been a few demonstrations and placards against the idea of Celtic taking part in this game but anyway, it was more about Alfredo di Stefano, the prickly little Argentinian, rather than Francisco Franco, the dictator of Spain.

Or was it? Ten years later, there were protests when the Scotland team went to play in Chile, in the very stadium where thousands had been detained and in many cases massacred in the aftermath of the 1973 *golpe*, but it was curious that all left-wing idealists in the 1960s who had a great deal to say about Vietnam, South Africa and the Greek colonels seemed to think that Spain was not quite so bad. In retrospect, there should have been much more shouting about this game. Imagine the reaction there might have been if the European champions had refused to go to Spain in protest at the ongoing dictatorship. Brother Walfrid might have not approved, but James Connolly certainly would have.

Be that as it may, Stein decided that he would change the team ever so slightly to give John Fallon a game in the goal and the worthy Willie O'Neill a chance to shine at full-back. There is a myth going around that Stein never again fielded the European Cup-winning team in their entirety after May 25. This is not quite true, but he was certainly reluctant to allow anyone, even Real Madrid, to claim that they had beaten that team, and he also said on this occasion that he wanted our own supporters at Parkhead to be the first to be given the opportunity to welcome the 11 European Cup winners.

As far as Real were concerned, this was no friendly, for some of the treatment meted out to Jimmy Johnstone in particular was shocking. So shocking, in fact, that not all of the 120,000 crowd approved of such tactics. They whistled at their own men and cheered on Jimmy, for they had never seen anything like him at all, either in ability or looks. Pelirojos (red-heads) are not common in Spain – neither are men of this ability. Celtic won 1-0 thanks to a Bobby Lennox goal and Celtic were thus proved to be worthy champions of Europe. But Real Madrid or not, friendly testimonial or not, no-one ever messes with Bertie Auld. When Amancio of Real threw a punch at Bertie, Bertie threw one back, and both were invited to take an early departure by the referee.

The game had zero coverage that night in Scotland – not that anyone was too bothered, for it was just a friendly – and so it was the following morning at my holiday job at the bakery that I heard the news. A lorry driver came in. The man had a speech impediment but was able to tell us that Celtic had won 1-0 and Bertie Auld had got "sent aff". "What for?" we asked. "Bitin'," he said. We had everyone told that Bertie had been using his teeth too much before we realised that the lorry driver had been trying to say "fightin'"!

And thus ended the football season in 1967. It was indeed difficult to take it all in. I recalled 1962 when I danced a wee jig when I discovered that we had won the Glasgow Cup at a rain-sodden Parkhead against Third Lanark, and 1965 when the world changed because we had won the Scottish Cup and were now back among the best teams in Scotland. But this was several steps beyond that. The champions of Europe. Ronnie Simpson's wife once told me that even the players themselves had found it all too much for them at the after-match banquet. It took a long time for them to realise just actually what they had achieved.

Next season would bring its own problems, but for the next few weeks, it was in order to sit back and enjoy it. Everyone still talked about Celtic, everyone basked in the glory. When children read Shakespeare in classrooms, there was a sudden and inexplicable desire to get the part of Lennox, one of the Scottish noblemen who discovered the death of the King. Fathers in cars driving past the William Wallace monument near Stirling would say "Hey, they've been quick at getting that statue put up!" Even at Wimbledon, where the umpires called for "juice" when they got thirsty, they now seemed to be saying "Bertie Auld" when it was two points each in any game. It was a glorious time to be alive. And then for me, Pelion was piled on top of Ossa – a classical allusion meaning that when something is going very well, it suddenly gets even better.

One day in June – annoyingly, I can't quite remember exactly when – I had the experience which maybe did not change the course of my life but did set me on the track of Celtic historiography to a greater degree than had been the case up to then. It was when the boss at the bakery suddenly discovered that we were short of rhubarb for the tarts. A phone call later, and he came back, told me to get on my bicycle and get some rhubarb from the house of Davie McLean, "ye ken, the auld fitba player".

Davie McLean! I knew a little about this man, namely that he had played for Celtic at the time of the great Edwardian side, but that, brilliant goalscorer that he was, he had been unable to displace the great Jimmy Quinn and that he had therefore moved on to try his luck with various clubs in England, notably Preston North End and Sheffield Wednesday, before returning to play for Dundee and Forfar. I had always wanted to talk to him, but had never had the courage. Now the opportunity was presenting itself.

Trembling, and with a knife in my hand (to cut the rhubarb), I knocked on his door. He proved agreeable and charming, as indeed was Clemmie, his wife. He asked my name, and when I told him, he immediately knew who I was (this is Forfar, remember, where everybody knows everybody). He told me "you'll be a Celtic supporter" because he had known my grandfather, the pair of them having played for a junior team by the mighty name of Forfar Celtic.

He immediately started talking about Lisbon, which he had watched on TV. He even came out into the garden to help me cut the rhubarb and said: "I used tae play for them, ye ken." A happy half-hour was spent while the sprightly veteran – he was 77 – talked about Sunny Jim, Jimmy Quinn and his great friend Jimmy Napoleon McMenemy. He didn't like Maley, he said, but, "Patsy Gallacher! Believe a' ye ever read aboot Patsy. He was the greatest there's ever been."

I would have talked longer but the boss was needing the rhubarb so I took my reluctant departure with a feeling of awe and reverence that I had never felt before. I wanted to go back and talk to him, but never had the courage to do so. I would bitterly regret my dalliance on this matter, for he died in December.

Davie McLean, as I would later discover, was at Celtic between 1907 and 1909. His greatest moments of triumph were the goals he scored to win the Glasgow Cup of 1907 and his contribution in April 1909, when Celtic played eight games in 12 days to win the Scottish League. He left because he would not give in to the bullying of Maley, and the fact that, with the mighty Quinn around, he could not hope to get a place in the team. He then went on to play for various teams – Preston North End, Sheffield Wednesday, Third Lanark – winning one cap for Scotland against England in 1912, and he even played a season for Rangers in the chaotic circumstances of the end of the Great War. His encounter with Patsy Gallacher came when he played against him in the 1925 Scottish Cup Final. Davie was by then playing for Dundee and scored their goal in the first half. Davie actually scored more goals than Jimmy McGrory (and that is some feat), but as a great deal of McLean's were for Forfar Athletic in the Second Division at the very end of his career, they were not considered so important.

You cannot imagine what a thrill this was to talk to a man who had actually played with Jimmy Quinn and others from that great side, and who had actually lived long enough to savour the Lisbon triumph. His friend, Jimmy Napoleon McMenemy, had not quite made it, for he had died in the summer of 1965. There was almost a touch of the Apostolic Succession about all this, I felt, as I shook his hand. He must have shaken hands with all of Adams, McNair and Orr; Young, Loney and Hay; Bennett, McMenemy, Quinn, Somers and Hamilton. He may have fallen out with Willie Maley (in later years he made it up with him), but "once a Celt, always a Celt!" He was a lovely old man, and how impressed was my father when I told him about this. I saw Davie on the street a few weeks after that talking to some of his friends, and he broke off his conversation to nod to me. That in itself was a mighty honour.

In the meantime, I continued with my holiday job at the bakery. It was not all that bad a job for I never had any problem getting up in the morning, and the company was good, for we all talked about football and other subjects of male interest. I was never a great holiday person, so didn't really go anywhere, and I was happy enough watching TV, playing, scoring and umpiring cricket matches, reading books and waiting for the announcements of next year's fixtures. News came also that I had passed all my university exams – not that I ever had much fear on that score – and that I would therefore be returning to St Andrews in October. And then there was my dad and old Frank down the road, who talked about Celtic just as much as I did. Life was good.

JULY

· · · · · · ·

July 1967 was like most Julys, I suppose, for the football fan with nothing of any real import going on. John Newcombe and Billie Jean King won the tennis at Wimbledon, Roberto de Vicenzo won the Open golf, the Test match series against India and Pakistan were particularly dull and uninteresting, England winning both with a great deal of comfort and Geoff Boycott finding himself dropped for scoring 246 not out at a painfully slow rate.

July 12 came and went. It was a lot more muted in Glasgow this year and increasingly the subject of indifference, scorn and ridicule in the rest of Scotland. (Unlike Northern Ireland, where it was showing disturbing signs of veering towards the psychotic.) Humour is, of course, the best way to deal with bigotry, and a TV advert was used by Celtic supporters. The advert was of a housewife who was seen taking a can of Heinz baked beans out of her cupboards, and she sang:

"A thousand housewives every day
Pick up a can of beans and say
Beans Means Heinz!"

This was changed by the Glasgow wits to be:
"A thousand Catholics every day
Pick up their rosary beads and say
Stein! Stein! Stein!"

It was the time of flower power centred in San Francisco, hippies and sustained protests against the Vietnam war, as the USA gradually began to realise that they had bitten off a little more than they could chew. The Middle East settled down at least temporarily, but only a fool would have imagined that the problem was solved, and in Great Britain, the Labour government carried on being moaned at by the right-wing press, and even by its own supporters. Everyone complained about poverty and paying income tax, but in fact it was an era of steady prosperity. Working-class families had never been better off, even though the price of prosperity was a slight rise in inflation. Often they complained about Harold Wilson when they were standing in the queue at the airport for their first-ever foreign holiday.

The pop scene seemed to be dominated by *Sergeant Pepper* and the Beatles. No great pop fan me, nevertheless you had to like the Beatles or you would be considered a wee bit funny, and yes, it was good stuff. The Beatles had now moved on from the simpler "She Loves You, Yeah! Yeah! Yeah!" – something that was considered subversive enough in 1962 and 1963 to "All You Need Is Love" – a message that on, first sight, would seem to be the same as the Christian message of the Churches, but the emphasis from the Beatles was on a slightly different kind of love, one felt – and now they had moved on to a different plane altogether.

The cover of *Sergeant Pepper* saw them all standing around a grave alongside Rudolf Valentino and others, and a man had his hand over Paul's head – which some people thought signified impending death – but what was more than a little worrying was the emphasis on drugs. "Lucy in the Sky with Diamonds" was suspected of being an advertisement for LSD, and there were various mad lyrics like "rocking horse people eat marshmallow pies" and some people wore "looking glass ties". It was all part of a drugs trip, with a new word called "psychedelic" entering the language.

Drugs, peace and love were, of course, the symbols of the anti-war people who, if you watched the television and read the newspapers, seemed to all wear headbands, have long hair and hold flowers. That was, of course, the stereotype, but it was seized upon by the right-wing press as if that was what all anti-war people were like in contrast to the clean-cut, short-haired, neat, uniformed young men who were doing so well against the barbarians in Vietnam. In London, the anti-war protesters were always stupid enough to allow themselves to get caught by a *Daily Express* photographer kicking a police horse. It was all so frustrating trying to tell anyone that it was possible to oppose the Vietnam war without being an idiot or a thug. But Harold Wilson still would not join in America's evil crusade.

Ah yes, Harold Wilson, that much-pilloried and hated man. Working-class people, of course, did not always appreciate that other working-class people could prosper as well. In particular, there was the widespread but erroneous view that you got more money for doing nothing and living off the welfare state than you did for working. This piece of nonsense, widely and fiercely peddled in the right-wing press, notably the *Sunday Post,* was a deeply depressing one because once someone got hold of this idea, it was difficult to reason with them for there were always anecdotes about "That fat lazy pig next door..." It was along with "blacks come here to scrounge off us",! "blacks take the best jobs off us" and "prisoners are treated like guests in five star hotels". People who should have known a lot better began to listen to that dangerous demagogue Enoch Powell who, I was ashamed to say, was a Professor of Greek. It was working-class jealousy at its worst – but, I suppose, it was the price of prosperity.

All this, of course, was annoying but paled into insignificance compared with the football. The air of unreality still hung over Scottish football after the glorious days of late May, but one fact did seem to make an impression. That was that Celtic were the *first* British team to win the European Cup, before any English team ever did. And being first, by definition they would *always* be the first to have won the trophy. Others may win it more often, but they could never be the first.

The football season would not start until August, with Celtic drawn in a League Cup section of Rangers, Aberdeen and Dundee United – an easy one, that – but July was normally in the 1960s a dead month for football. It was here, though, that Jock Stein made one of his few mistakes in that he failed to strengthen his squad with a big name or two – although no-one realised it at the time. It was one of the few times in history when even English-based players (England being a land flowing with milk and honey, according to the newspapers) like Alan Gilzean or Denis Law, or even our very own Pat Crerand, would have jumped at the chance to join Celtic.

Ah yes, Pat Crerand. What did he make of it all? He had left us when we really needed him in 1963, and thus, like

Charlie Nicholas and Kenny Dalglish, our love of him must be permanently tarnished because of that. We all know that there were extenuating circumstances, and that had Jock Stein been the manager in 1963, things would have been totally different. With Matt Busby and Manchester United ("Celtic in exile" somebody called them), Pat had won the English FA Cup in 1963 and now the English league championship of 1967. He was clearly a success, but would he have been able to resist the call back home, if Jock had offered him the bait?

The reason why Jock did not offer that particular bait was, of course, Bobby Murdoch. No team needs two right-halves, and Murdoch could hardly have been displaced by anybody. Yet there were other positions that might have been strengthened or supplemented. The disasters that came our way in the autumn were, to a very large extent, caused by self-satisfaction. This might have been alleviated by just one new signing to gee things up a little. Celtic and Stein maybe made the mistake of standing still. Twenty-one years later, Billy McNeill would make the same mistake. Celtic won a Scottish League and Cup double in 1988, playing superbly in their centenary season. They then stood still in summer 1988, and there followed a 5-1 tanking at Ibrox and the start of ten years of untold misery.

To be fair, it did not seem necessary in 1967 to strengthen the European champions. Nor was there any great pressure from any of the supporters to do that, but then again there is nothing worse than a stagnant pool, and some of the players would soon begin to show every sign that success had gone to their heads, as complacency took over. More of a challenge for places might have made a difference. But that, of course, is being written with the considerable benefit of hindsight. More attention was being focused on the imminent arrival of Tottenham Hotspur, English FA Cup winners and with Jimmy Greaves and Alan Gilzean on board, to play a pre-season friendly at Hampden in early August.

And the weather was good as we drank our beer wearing "Champions of Europe" T-shirts and marvelling at all the new converts who previously used to sneer about "Irish" and "Catholics", but were now talking in glowing terms about "Jock". My maternal grandfather, for example, used to claim that he was a Rangers supporter (although he had never been near them all his life) every New Year just to get an argument, an argument that he was always prone to win for Rangers tended to beat Celtic rather too often at the New Year, but now, well into his 90s, he announced that he had supported Celtic all his days, and that the best moment of his life had been Lisbon. It was as if a bandwagon had come along the road, he had been trying to climb on and I was there, able to lift him on board.

It was, indeed, a glorious summer.

AUGUST

· · · · · · ·

August 1967 was a good month. The season started well with qualification for the Scottish League Cup quarter-finals from the difficult section of Rangers, Aberdeen and Dundee United following a very creditable draw with Tottenham Hotspur in a prestigious friendly. The team played well, although there was a time when it looked as if they were about to exit from the League Cup, and indeed would have done so, had Rangers, now beginning to suffer from a death wish as far as Celtic were concerned, not imploded spectacularly.

But to begin at the beginning, the Spurs match, played at Hampden to commemorate the centenary of Queen's Park in 1867, attracted a crowd of over 90,000 on a hot sunny day to see a thrilling 3-3 draw on August 5. Substitutes were allowed by agreement, and the whole thing was fairly light-hearted, but there was, of course, a serious desire from Bill Nicholson, of Spurs, to beat the European champions. Spurs, on the very same night that Celtic had lost 0-3 to Rangers in that dreadful Scottish Cup Final of 1963, had become the first British team to win *any*

European competition when they won the Cup Winners' Cup by beating Atletico Madrid 5-1 in Rotterdam. Both teams therefore had a strong European pedigree.

The two teams had met in America in the summer of 1966. They had played each other three times, with two wins for Celtic and one draw. The teams had fallen out in one of the games when Jock Stein brought on Jimmy Johnstone for John Hughes. The agreement beforehand had been that substitutes could only be used in the event of an injury, and Spurs basically did not believe that Hughes was sufficiently injured. Possibly, it was simply the thought that Celtic could bring on Jimmy Johnstone, who had scored two goals for Scotland against England at Hampden in April of that year, as a substitute. However, the two teams had kissed and made up and Spurs had had a good season in 1967, winning the English Cup by beating London rivals Chelsea a few days before Lisbon.

An agreeable amount of London fans had made the trip to Glasgow. They were welcomed by Celtic fans, quite a few of whom had admired their winning of the league and cup double in 1961 and their recapture of the cup in 1962, but mainly because of their defeat of Rangers in the 1962/63 European Cup Winners' Cup. There was much to admire about Spurs, who had Dave Mackay (never a favourite when he played for Hearts but a genuinely tough Scottish defender), Alan Gilzean (late of Dundee and a redoubtable goalscorer), Alan Mullery and, of course, the quixotic Jimmy Greaves. In addition, there was a certain affinity in that Tottenham Hotspur were by no means the "establishment" team of London – that honour belonging to their rivals Arsenal – in the same way that Celtic were not the "establishment" team of Glasgow. If one pushed it even further, Tottenham Hotspur were often said to represent the Jewish community of London – and one could see religious parallels there, if one wanted to, that is.

The large crowd saw an excellent 3-3 draw with honours even, although Ronnie Simpson made one of his rare errors, which may have deprived Celtic of their victory. Both teams were applauded off the park by the appreciative supporters, with some of the English players visibly affected by the reception they received from the Scottish crowd. But then again, as had been proved in the European Cup Final between Real Madrid and Eintracht Frankfurt in 1960, Glasgow always has a tremendous love of good football. Such was the attraction of Celtic now that both BBC TV and STV had a highlights programme of this game – a pre-season friendly – with BBC even sending up that now blatant Celtic supporter Kenneth Wolstenholme to commentate for the network. We even heard the clichéd phrases "game of the season" and "Battle of Britain" applied to this game, and that was even before the season started.

It was actually quite ironic that Celtic's run to the European Cup Final had not been well covered by either the BBC or the commercial channels. There were those who detected conspiracies here, of course, but the truth was simply that it was considered too expensive, football not yet having become the major money-spinner that it became in the 1990s. Those who moan about the surfeit of the game on TV might do well to recall the days when there was simply not enough. Yet, for all that, here we had this game well covered, at least in highlight form. Things had changed.

The season itself, I recall, was looked forward to with relish and anticipation, but there was always the nagging thought that it wouldn't be, nay it couldn't be, as good as the previous season. It was bound to be some kind of anti-climax. Even if everything were to be won again, it would still be not quite so good, for it would now be the second time that we had done it. In the event, it turned out to be a rollercoaster of a season with more than a few bumps, although things eventually turned out well.

The real football started on August 12 with the visit of Dundee United to Parkhead in the Scottish League Cup, while in the other game of the four-team section, Rangers were playing Aberdeen at Pittodrie. Rangers had spent lavishly over the summer (in contrast to Celtic and now an annual occurrence at Ibrox), but for the first game of the season, Celtic had said that the European Cup was going to be paraded at half-time, and were rewarded with a crowd of over 50,000. Contrary to the myth that Jock Stein never again fielded the XI who won the European Cup (they were not called the Lisbon Lions until years later), lest someone would claim to have beaten them, the 11 men of Lisbon trotted out to their deserved welcome from the Parkhead crowd. Admittedly, Stein did not do it very often, but for the first game of the season, Simpson, Craig and Gemmell; Murdoch, McNeill and Clark; Johnstone, Wallace, Chalmers, Auld and Lennox did indeed take the field to face Jerry Kerr's men from Tannadice Park.

We arrived to see a far more modern Celtic Park, symbolic of the sea change over the past few years. The "Jungle" terracing steps had been concreted – no more cinders and puddles – and had new modern crush barriers, with even the refreshment stall and the toilets looking as if they had had a facelift to greet the European champions. Neither of them could now be called a health hazard any longer. This was, of course, phase two of the development. The previous summer, the old cow barn, that unsightly construction which had been there since 1907, had been demolished and a new one put in its place, but little had been done to improve the state of the terracings and the facilities for eating and the toilets would not have lasted five minutes if there had been any kind of sanitary inspection. So there was a certain amount of comfort there, although the Celtic End shelter still, annoyingly, only came halfway down and there was nothing at all at the other end. It was hardly luxury, but things were improving.

Dundee United, it will be recalled, were the only Scottish team to have beaten Celtic the previous season – and they did it twice, both home and away – and were determined to take something from this game. They played their traditional and predictable game in Glasgow, namely all-out defence. The team bus and even the 10.05pm train from Dundee Tay Bridge Station to Glasgow Buchanan Street seemed to have been parked along the edge of the Dundee United penalty box. Half-time came with no score, and the worse news that Rangers were ahead 1-0 at Pittodrie.

Celtic redoubled their efforts, and although Aberdeen equalised at Pittodrie, the winner for Celtic simply would not come. Normally a 0-0 draw at Parkhead is greeted with cries of "not good enough", "this won't do", "I don't rate this manager" or "this team will never make it" by our weaker brethren and the air is punctuated with boos, catcalls and slow handclapping. They could hardly do that today, when the team were the champions of Europe, but they still moaned and blasphemed about perceived inadequacies. The said weaker brethren of little faith were trooping along the Gallowgate and London Road when, with literally the last kick of the match, Jimmy Johnstone scored. The same folk who had been hurling all that filth and venom were now jumping on each other's backs and shouting about European champions. I've never been a great subscriber to the "faithful through and through" theory of Celtic supporters being "the best in the world". It is not necessarily always true. It must be tempered by thoughts of those who sometimes seem to hate their own players – until, of course, a vital goal goes in.

The Celtic View in midweek sent out mixed messages. In one article, they fired a broadside at Celtic fans who had hurled abuse at Dundee United fans. It didn't say so, but the abuse was aimed at the Dundee United players who had had Rangers connections, in particular Davie Wilson, who had now cut his losses (and his cords of affection) and moved from Ibrox. On the other hand, the same journal had a go at Dundee United with a picture of seven of their players in their own penalty box defending a Celtic attack and asked, "Is it any wonder that Celtic found it so hard to score against Dundee United?" Jock Stein himself, while refraining from attacking Dundee United, nevertheless hinted at his disapproval when he said that an early goal for Celtic would have made all the difference.

Jimmy's goal was a very significant one in the context of the section, though, for with Rangers and Aberdeen having drawn, a draw at Ibrox on Wednesday night kept Celtic ahead of Rangers. This time, it was Celtic who suffered the loss of a late goal, a free kick from Andy Penman after the same player had had a penalty saved by Ronnie Simpson. This gave Rangers a deserved draw after Tommy Gemmell had scored with a penalty in the first half and Celtic had withstood a certain amount of Rangers pressure in the second half. In the meantime, at Tannadice Park, Dundee United had learned from the folly of defending all the time by venturing over the halfway line occasionally. As a result, they beat Aberdeen 5-0.

Both Old Firm teams then won on the Saturday in Glasgow – Celtic 3-1 against Aberdeen, who had not had the best of starts to this season considering that they had reached the Scottish Cup Final last year, while Rangers narrowly got the better of Dundee United 1-0. Aberdeen's visit attracted over 50,000 to Parkhead, and they saw a determined approach from the men of the North. They were broken down eventually by a Tommy Gemmell penalty kick, then Bobby Lennox finished off a fine Bertie Auld move before Auld himself scored virtually at the death after Jim Storrie had kept Aberdeen in the game. The 3-1 win was well deserved, however.

Normally, there would have been a set of league fixtures to be played in the midweek between the first and second halves of the League Cup sectional campaign, but for some odd reason this wasn't the case in 1967, so Celtic arranged their first-round Glasgow Cup tie against Partick Thistle. The Glasgow Cup was, of course, much prized the previous year when it was freely described as one of the five that Celtic won, and although it no longer held the prestige it once did, it was nevertheless a beautiful trophy, very ornate and a fine example of lovely Victorian craftsmanship.

It also gave Stein the opportunity to try out a few fringe players. Charlie Gallagher was given a game, as was full-back Chris Shevlane, signed from Hearts, but the man that really caught the eye was a youngster called Pat McMahon, who scored two fine goals, much appreciated by the 25,000 crowd, in the easy 5-0 victory. McMahon, you will recall, had been signed a day or two after Lisbon and had already won a Scottish Junior Cup medal that year with Kilsyth Rangers. He came from Croy – and that was no disadvantage in Celtic circles for the mighty Jimmy Quinn had come from there 60 years ago, not to mention Andy McAtee, Tommy McAteer, Jock Morrison and Frank Meechan – and he certainly looked the part that night. Stein was insistent, however, that he would not be rushed.

The Celtic View did a feature on him, telling us that he had been working in London and nearly became a Chelsea player. It even said that he had modelled himself on, of all people, Jim Baxter. Pat strenuously denied that, even though he conceded that he looked like him.

In the meantime, a genuinely good pop song gripped my imagination. It was the "Ode to Billy Joe", released by Bobbie Gentry. Bobbie Gentry had a boy's name but was a woman, but what sex Billy or Billie Joe McAllister was, we could not fathom. All we knew was that he/she jumped off the Tallahatchie Bridge, with the best theory being that "she" was pregnant to a man of another race, something of which her father would never have approved. It was moody, atmospheric, mysterious and a rare example of a 1960s pop song that actually made you think. In some ways, the mood reflected the USA at that time – a country which, with its race riots, police brutality and Asian war, simply hadn't a clue where it was going. Naturally, it was parodied so that "all the Orange b****** jumped off the Kingston Bridge", and it fitted well with the other one about them all jumping out of the new Govan high rise flats "and I hope there's joaby (i.e. prickly) fences when they jump!"

The following Saturday, Celtic won 1-0 at Tannadice – this time another competent performance which would have been more if Tommy Gemmell had scored with a penalty, and if the referee had not disallowed a goal when the ball looked clearly over the line (recalling a previous occasion in 1962 when a similar thing happened at that very ground). Those who hoped that Dundee United might have had a more positive attitude, however, were disappointed – the only difference was they played at home in all black while they were dressed in all white at Parkhead. Meanwhile, Rangers beat an Aberdeen team which had now clearly lost the place, 3-0. Celtic now had seven points, while Rangers had six (two points for a win in 1967) and Aberdeen and Dundee United, of whom more might have been expected, were basically making up the numbers.

All this meant that everything depended on the Old Firm game at Parkhead on Wednesday, August 30. It would turn out to be one of the best Old Firm games of them all, and if it had not happened in 1967, when so many other mighty things happened on the field, it would have been rated in Parkhead folklore as highly as the 7-1 victory in 1957, the "Ten Men Won the League" in 1979 or the 6-2 hammering in 2000, instead of being merely looked upon as another of the many nice things that happened in 1967.

This game also happened to coincide with the last episode of the TV series The *Fugitive* on ITV. The American series had been running since 1963 and concerned Dr Kimble (played by David Janssen), wrongly convicted of murdering his wife. He had escaped from a train en route to the electric chair, and had been pursued relentlessly by the same policeman while he himself pursued a one-armed man, whom he had seen running from the scene of the crime. The final episode was scheduled for 8pm that evening, and we had been well informed that the mystery would be solved that night. In the absence of any recording facilities in the 1960s, it was a harsh choice, but Celtic Park was full that night of people who were happy enough to wait to be told whether Janssen had caught the one-armed man or not. Or indeed whether Janssen was in fact guilty? Or was it someone else altogether?

This game itself had several sideshows, like a yob from the Rangers end trying to attack a Celtic player with the corner flag and having to be disarmed by Rangers' Davie Provan; a goal that looked offside given for Rangers; a goal that looked onside *not* given for Celtic; and many vicious tackles, referee Tom "Tiny" Wharton generally not having one of his better games and the eventual nemesis of Denmark's Kaj Johansen.

Johansen had been the man who scored the winning goal in the 1966 Scottish Cup Final, lauded "not without cause but without end" by Rangers fans, who kept telling stories about how a Celtic supporter shot his dog because it was a great Dane and various less-than-total bellyachers like that. Stein, of course, had ruthlessly exploited this. He knew that it was a fluke, but that Johansen would never be able to resist the terracing pressure to try again. This would leave gaps at the back which the speedy Lennox would exploit as he got the better of John Greig.

Still Kaj remained the Ibrox favourite. Now in this game with 15 minutes left, Rangers were still holding on to their 1-0 lead, earned by the dodgy goal which looked offside. Celtic, attacking the Rangers end, pressed and pressed but luck was not on their side, and the Rangers defence looked steady under the pressure. Then Willie Henderson, who had scored the debatable goal in the first half, won a ball and charged upfield. Tommy Gemmell was too far forward, having been caught out of position. Henderson was not the fastest forward on earth, but neither was left-half John Clark the fastest defender on earth. But Clark sprinted, caught up with him, tried to tackle cleanly but only succeeded in bringing him down. Mr Wharton correctly awarded a penalty kick.

This was now the moment, thought the boys in blue behind the distant goal, that Rangers would go 2-0 up, and Celtic's famous ability to fight back would not be enough. It would be Celtic's first defeat since Lisbon, Celtic would probably be out of the Scottish League Cup and Rangers would have their first win over Celtic since Kaj Johansen's Scottish Cup Final of April 1966. Who better, then, than Kaj to take the penalty kick?

To us behind that goal, prayers were offered that Ronnie Simpson might pull off a major miracle and save the penalty. A few began to wave and shout to put him off, but the main mood was one of quiet resignation to our fate and an imminent departure to our buses and trains. Something about the aged Roman Senators in 390 BC sitting quietly and with dignity awaiting the arrival of the barbaric Gauls to slaughter them was going through my mind as Johansen ran up to take the kick. But he hit the bar and suddenly Tiny Wharton was pointing up the field, having awarded a free kick to Celtic.

It took us all a few minutes to work out exactly what had happened. The ball had hit the bar – crucially, Simpson had not got a finger to it – and then the ball bounced down on the correct (for us) side of the line and up in the air again. Johansen then, having in the heat of the moment forgotten the rules, headed the ball before anyone else could touch it and before some eager Rangers forwards had a chance to shoot. He had touched the ball twice from a penalty kick – a clear, if rare, infringement of the laws – and Mr Wharton had correctly awarded an indirect free kick to Celtic.

Whether it was indirect or not was of no consequence for the goal was about 140 yards away, but the effect on the stadium was electrifying, with the supporters' demeanour reflected in the attitude of the players. Celtic, roared on by their massive support, gained a new lease of life, while for Rangers the old cliché "the heads went down" applied. They realised that they had blown up, and now began to believe in the invincibility of Celtic, as their death wish took over. The next minutes saw Celtic at their best – and in 1967, that was saying something.

One goal would have been enough to give Celtic a draw and to maintain the points' advantage in the League Cup section. We would have settled for that but, in fact, we got three to win the section outright and render irrelevant the last game against Aberdeen at Pittodrie. First Wallace stabbed one over the line in the aftermath of a corner kick that the Rangers defence were unable to clear, then Murdoch hammered one home from the edge of the box before Lennox, in the final minute, ran through the Rangers defence like a knife through butter to make the final score 3-1.

Celtic had duly qualified for the Scottish League Cup quarter-finals, and Jock Stein claimed that this was the best win under his command. Considering that this included Inter Milan, Dukla and Vojvodina, it was some claim but in the context of the ability of his team to show character and to come back in the way that they did, Stein may well have had a point. Once again, Rangers had been compelled to bow the knee and their psychological trauma would continue. Had there not been so many other games happening in 1967, this one would have been talked about for a long, long time. As it was, it was still one to savour.

Kaj Johansen bore a disproportionate share of the blame and scorn that we mercilessly heaped upon him. Kaj, sadly no longer with us after his untimely death in 2007, was anything but a traditional Ranger. He had joined Morton when Morton had started the trend of signing Scandinavian players, and was transferred to Rangers in 1965. A genuinely modest man, he was overwhelmed by the cult hero status heaped upon him because of one goal and he was also embarrassed by being singled out in the ludicrous and offensive Rangers supporters' chant of "Kaj, yay, yippee, the Pope's a hippy". But on this occasion, he was the man that everyone pointed fingers at. It was a classic case of how someone gets built up by the media, and then knocked down again. "The higher you climb, the harder you fall" was the proverb which summed Kaj up.

Meanwhile, back home on TV, David Janssen did now live happily ever after, and it was indeed the one-armed man who had killed his wife, as we were all told when we arrived back in triumph. There were edited highlights of the football on TV, but we were only half joking when we said that highlights of *The Fugitive* would also have gone down well.

For Celtic, there was, of course, a downside to it. We have mentioned that Rangers now believed in the invincibility of Celtic. Sadly, some Celtic players began to believe this as well, it appeared, and the club would endure a rude shock or two in the month of September, caused, it would appear to many of the fans, by a certain amount of complacency and the feeling that everything was going to be all right anyway. In retrospect, it might have been better had they had a shock or two in the month of August. A certain amount of having to pick oneself up, of having to analyse a few deficiencies and of having to realise that a major fight was on our hands, might have been no bad thing.

One stresses "in retrospect". No-one ever thought like this as August came to an end, and the nights began to draw in. Everything was rosy, as rosy as it had been all summer, and Celtic seemed yet again to be heading, inexorably, to more glory. The last day in August was spent in cosy reflection of last night's events and of optimistic expectation of the future. We exchanged thoughts with those who had not been lucky enough to get one of the 75,000 tickets and who had spent the night watching *The Fugitive* on STV. It was exciting, apparently, but the ending was all too predictable – namely that it had been the one-armed man who had done it (but we all knew that because Janssen had seen him running away from the scene of the crime) and Janssen ended up a free man, shaking hands, albeit reluctantly, with the copper who had pursued him relentlessly every Wednesday night at 8pm for the last four years.

The Celtic View had a good cartoon in it the following week. A man with a Celtic scarf was seen coming home to his wife with his arms in the air in triumph saying "Celtic did it!" His wife is similarly delirious shouting "And the Fugitive didn't!"

Yet her feelings of relief that Dr Kimble was innocent were nothing in comparison to what we had felt as we streamed out of Celtic Park, dancing, chanting and singing, "We've got the best team in the land! We've got Ronnie Simpson number one, we've got Jim Craig number two…

etc." And frankly, so we had. Still working in my bakery during the long summer holidays, I got on my supporters' bus, where there was much singing and dancing, got home at about 1am, slept for an hour or two in a chair and was ready for my 5am start at work. Lack of sleep doesn't really matter in such circumstances. It was a pleasant shift, telling all the lorry drivers and the boys who delivered the rolls about how we had won against all the odds, while the lady that I worked with assured me that she had known all along that it was the one-armed man.

Meanwhile, in Glasgow, a Rangers fan found guilty of "breach of the peace" was described by the Baillie as being like "one of the Red Guards", a reference to the elite squad of Chairman Mao in China. Not a particularly nice bunch of chaps, they went round beating up anyone who disagreed with the thoughts of Mao Tse-tung. It was, we felt, an apt comparison for this chap, who boarded a bus in the Gallowgate and challenged innocent old ladies to a fight while cursing and blaspheming all and sundry. And all because Kaj Johansen missed a penalty!

SEPTEMBER

· · · · · · ·

"Uneasy lies the head that wears the crown," says Henry IV of himself in Shakespeare's play of that name. September was the month when the crown began to topple. There were reasons for it. The most obvious one was complacency and resting on our laurels, but the other was, quite simply, that there were other good football teams around, and it brought home in a funny sort of way the enormity of what had been achieved the previous season – just simply how good we had been, and how difficult it was to remain at the top at that level. Maybe we should have strengthened the squad in the summer – but this, one must stress, was hindsight speaking. No-one said it in July.

The disappointment was all the more keen because we hadn't really seen it coming. The successful League Cup qualifying campaign in August had confirmed the calibre of this great side, and the key thing was that the appetite was still, apparently, there. There was little reason to become depressed or lack confidence for the future, but September was a chastening and sobering month. Change in football can happen with devastating suddenness.

But to begin at the beginning of September. To someone who was brought up in Forfar and whose family had worked on the railway off and on for over 100 years, the closing of the local station was a significant and terrible decision. Apart from anything else, the railway line led to Glasgow and that was where Celtic lived and played. So when Dr Beeching was employed by the government to close down railway lines, and when he chose the line between Stanley and Kinnaber Junction for the axe, this meant a cultural disaster. The stations of Coupar Angus, Alyth Junction, Forfar, Bridge of Dun and Laurencekirk were for the chop.

Protest meetings were in vain. No-one listened. Still less did they care when young hooligans like me scrawled obscenities on the notice of closure. Ironically, what probably sealed the fate of Forfar Station was the General Elections of 1964 and 1966, which confirmed Labour in power in Westminster, but not locally. North Angus and South Angus were in the 1960s Conservative strongholds, which meant that local protests counted for little with the government. It was a bitter example of politics in action.

Naturally, we all knew that "they" would regret what they had done. Within six years and another dreadful war in the Middle East, the price of petrol and motoring rocketed. The railways should have been kept. How encouraging it is to see the Borders Railway being re-opened in recent years. How nice it would be if it could happen more often and in other parts of the country. Road travel has, of course, improved tremendously over the past 50 years and continues to do so, but "dull would he be of soul" who could not regret the passing of the local railways and the wealth of local history that they encompassed.

The last day of Forfar Station was to be Monday, September 4. I was therefore determined to go and see Aberdeen v Celtic on Saturday, September 2, even though it was a dead game as far as Celtic were concerned. We had already qualified for the quarter-finals. The players, as usual, travelled with the supporters on the train that left Buchanan Street Station at 10.30am, passed through Forfar at 12.26pm and reached Aberdeen about an hour later.

What they then did surprised and delighted us fans, for instead of getting a bus to Pittodrie, they all walked up with the supporters, talking happily to them, signing autographs as they walked, and with Jock Stein, obeying his own mantra of "football without fans is nothing", leading the way and holding court about who the big problems in Europe would be this year. I recalled the dictum that the great Jimmy Quinn of 50 years ago did things "just like an ordinary man". Here, we had the champions of Europe doing the same, as they walked along Union Street then King Street to get to the game. The douce Aberdeen matrons out doing their Saturday afternoon shopping stopped and stared at these handsome, fit young men, whom everyone knew and recognised whether you were a football fan or not.

The game itself was not without incident, although it ended up a comfortable 5-1 win for Celtic. Pat McMahon, who had been clearly taken aback by the enthusiasm of the fans who escorted him up from the station, was given his second game for the club and scored a fine goal to give Celtic a 2-1 interval lead, but it had been Celtic's first goal that had caused the trouble. Celtic were a goal down, but pressing hard, when Lennox ran in on goal. Out came Bobby Clark and Lennox went down. It would have to be said that it was not a clear-cut stonewall penalty kick, but it was rather of the "I've seen them given" variety, so beloved of modern day pundits. It might have been, and it might not have been, but referee JPR Gordon of Newport-on-Tay said it was.

Mr Gordon was, years later, widely believed to be a Rangers supporter, even to the extent that one of his linesmen before a Junior Cup final claimed to hear him sing "the cry was no surrender". He would certainly let himself down very badly in one Old Firm game in 1978 and was even accused of accepting "hospitality" (as it was tactfully put) rather too eagerly on foreign trips in Italy and Spain. Whether any of this was true, we know not, but here back in 1967, when he was still on the way up, he awarded a penalty to Celtic which rather destroyed the credibility of some wild claims by some supporters of the paranoia persuasion that Celtic get nothing from referees.

We did not even need one. The game was a non-event (so much a non-event that Jock Stein was seen sitting comfortably in the stand with his arms folded instead of shouting and bawling on the touchline) and in any case Celtic would have been good enough, as the second half proved, to win comfortably anyway. The whole Aberdeen team surrounded Mr Gordon complaining, but he said it was a penalty and a penalty it was. He booked two Aberdeen players who would not shut up about it. Goalkeeper Bobby Clark and quite a few Aberdeen supporters had a complex about the mild-mannered and gentlemanly Bobby Lennox in future years. It all started here, one feels.

And then it got worse. Tommy Gemmell took the penalty kick and Bobby Clark saved it, to the loud cheers of the Pittodrie faithful who had not really had too much to get excited about so far this season. Ah well, that's the end of it, we thought, and began to agree with the Aberdeen supporters that it maybe wasn't a penalty anyway. But then Mr Gordon, who might have decided that Clark's save had solved the problem, suddenly ordered a retake, presumably because Clark had moved. Again, the Aberdeen followers erupted in righteous indignation, but this time the protests from the players were a little more muted because they had seen that Mr Gordon meant business. Gemmell then scored to put Celtic level.

Boos rang round Pittodrie and Mr Gordon was described as a "Glesca bastart" by a man standing next to me in these unsegregated days. I realised that trying to reason with him and telling him that Newport-on-Tay might have made him more of a "Dundee bastart" or a "Fife bastart" rather than a Glasgow one was a waste of time, but then in any case our attention was drawn to the fact that someone had come out of the Beach End, knocked Mr Gordon to the ground and was on top of him, pummelling him with his fists. Sadly, some Aberdeen fans cheered this nana, but most were quite glad to see a mixture of Celtic and Aberdeen players handing him over to the Aberdeen Constabulary. Mr Gordon recovered and the Aberdeen police were very particular about protecting JPR Gordon at half-time and full time.

Celtic played well in the second half to entertain their fans, who were at least half the crowd that day. The players got a private bus to take them back for the 5.15pm train while we had to run. Sprinting along King Street, I passed an acquaintance of mine who supported Aberdeen. Too secure of myself to feel that I had to gloat, I just nodded to him as I passed. He glowered at me, and clearly not yet coming to terms with the defeat, shouted "that f***in' fourth goal wis affside". I did not feel that I wanted to argue with him about the penalty!

At about 6.15 that evening, I alighted with a great deal of sadness from the train. It would be the last time that I would do so at Forfar. I walked up the platform a little to take my last look at the Celtic party who were having their meal on the train. Stein sniffed around – there were no bottles of beer, of course – but Bobby Murdoch stuck his head out of a window and asked me if the evening papers were in at the kiosk yet.

Sadly, they weren't. How I would have loved to give a copy of *The Sporting Post* to one of the greatest Celtic players of them all, but it was not to be. Still, it was a fine way to remember the end of my last-ever train trip involving Forfar Station. The train pulled away, slowly, apologetically and melancholically, while the Celtic fans on the platform sang "We Shall Not Be Moved".

There then followed a friendly against Penarol, the current world champions. Stein had arranged this game because he wanted to give his players a chance to play against South American opposition in view of the imminent World Club Championship game against Racing Club of Argentina. Cynics felt that it might be more to do with making money, but 56,000 duly paid for admission that Tuesday night. It will be recalled that Stein did something similar in February with a friendly against Dinamo Zagreb, but this time there were no gimmicks. It was simply a game against the world champions. Celtic played well, Wallace scored twice in the first half and although the Uruguayans pulled one back in the second half, Celtic won 2-1.

This very sadly seemed to expand a few heads more than was warranted. It was only a friendly, after all, against a team on their close-season tour. Celtic were now about to come a very large cropper. But the next two games were good wins – 3-0 against Clyde in the opening game of the league campaign with last year's league flag being unfurled by Mrs Kelly, the wife of chairman Bob – and that was without Jimmy Johnstone, who was ill with flu.

Then, on Wednesday 13th, we beat Ayr United 6-2 at Parkhead in the first leg of the quarter-final of the Scottish League Cup. This was all very well, and we continued to be impressed by the play of young Pat McMahon, but we all knew that sterner tests lay ahead. Indeed the next two or three games would show just how vulnerable we really were, and never has the phrase "the higher you climb, the harder you fall" been more appropriate than it was to Celtic in that autumn of 1967.

The Old Firm defeat at Ibrox on September 16 was unfortunate, but need not have had such an effect. It could have been, if not exactly shrugged off, then certainly lived with. I am often of the persuasion that too much is made of Old Firm games. They mean a great deal, of course, to the two sets of fans on the day, but they needn't shape the rest of the season. Jock Stein got it right when he said that the two points that you get for beating St Johnstone or Partick Thistle are just as valuable as those that you get for beating Rangers. One would hate to get to the stage of where things are in the football-impoverished North East of England. Supporters of Newcastle, for example, will be happy enough to accept third-bottom and relegation, as long as Sunderland are second-bottom. Such a blinkered, sad obsession with local rivalry has effectively prevented either of these fine clubs from having any real impact on English football for many years.

This game was a narrow 1-0 win for Rangers, a goal scored by that man whose previous encounters with Celtic had not been happy ones for him – Orjan Persson. The game was marred by an unfortunate accident early on to Rangers' Davie Provan after a clash with Bertie Auld, Billy McNeill earning a ripple of applause even from the Rangers End by helping Rangers' trainer to carry off the luckless Provan. It was a close-fought game, nevertheless, and but for a poor refereeing decision, Lennox might have scored near the end. Murdoch also came close now and again, Johnstone made a dreadful hash of a clear chance and, generally speaking, a draw would not have been an unfair result. The goal itself was a good one – a great individual goal from Persson early in the second half – but it would have to be said that there was a certain lack of resistance from some of the Celtic defenders.

In some ways, the defending was a throwback to a few years ago. Indeed standing on the Broomloan terracing, one had to recall a similar goal at the same end, and eerily enough at more or less the same time of the game (early in the second half). Willie Henderson scored the goal in the Scottish Cup quarter-final of 1964, which was great, if you were a Rangers supporter, or dreadful if you were a Celt. Both goals could have easily been prevented by a good, timeous tackle. In 1964, it was sheer fear and shortage of belief by a team who lacked confidence when facing Rangers; in 1967 it was a team which had perhaps got too big for its boots.

Still, the defeat was a great deal less than a "hammering" and the damage could have been easily contained or controlled. The trouble is that in Glasgow successes and failures are grossly over-emphasised, particularly in the context of 1967, when Celtic had done so well in Europe. In the same way that Scotland's victory over England in April was made disproportionately much of, so too did Rangers' victory over the European champions become a greater achievement than was warranted. Concomitantly, Celtic's victory over them in the League Cup on August 30 became marginalised.

It may be that there is an inbuilt bias towards Rangers in some areas of the press – it is not universally true, no matter what some Celtic supporters think – and if this is the case, it is all the more obvious in the gloating and triumphalism after a Rangers victory, as here with words like "glory" and "triumph" and "joy" freely splashed all over the newspapers on Sunday and Monday. Journalists tend to become sycophantic supporters of the winning team. One would not have imagined that it was only a 1-0 victory – and really a rather lucky one at that. The phrase "praised not without cause but without end" comes to mind.

The referee was Willie Syme, an old adversary of Jock Stein. Syme had, admittedly, had a poor game, but apart from the offside decision against Bobby Lennox – as often happened with Bobby, who was the victim of his own speed, for linesmen could not believe that he was not in an offside position when the ball was played – the main criticism came for his leniency towards some rough tackles by players of both sides. The only booking of the game was of Steve Chalmers, for kicking the ball away in disgust – "ungentlemanly conduct" as it was called – something that was ludicrous in the context of what had gone before. Ironically, Chalmers was the most gentlemanly of players.

Stein, it would have to be said, did not react well to this setback. *The Celtic View* had a moan about refereeing, with the implication that Celtic were always the victims and generally ill-done by, something that was not the case, and seemed to contradict Stein's oft-repeated statement that if you are 5-0 up, poor refereeing decisions will be irrelevant. In particular, there was a picture of the front of the paper which actually proves nothing at all, but purports to show how Rangers players Ron McKinnon and Alex Ferguson used their elbows to baulk Billy McNeill. The photograph was more than a little unconvincing and earned a fair amount of deserved ridicule even among Celtic supporters. It was not one of Stein's better displays.

Yet the blame for what happened had to be shared. The manager, after all, cannot cross the touchline and play the game. The players themselves have to accept some of the blame, yet the defeat had happened and we had to move on. We needed what was called "bounce back", resilience and the ability to put one bad result to one side. After all, in spite of what people said, little real harm had been done. It was the second league game of the season. Thirty-two more league games and a long hard winter remained to right the damage.

Of far more importance in the long run to Celtic was the European Cup game against Dinamo Kiev on Wednesday, September 20. Sadly, Celtic were to lapse into the deleterious old habit following a defeat by Rangers. In the past, Celtic would sink into a depressive self-pitying stupor and drop a few more points, as if in sympathy. Clyde or Third Lanark were often the beneficiaries in the past, picking up a point as a result of a sub-standard, lacklustre Celtic performance. Momentum is a great thing in football. Celtic now lost theirs and Wednesday, September 20 was a dark, dark night.

The Queen was in Glasgow that particular Wednesday to launch and name the new ship which had been built on the Clyde. The name was a great secret. It was suggested that it might be no bad thing if the ship was to be known as the *Glasgow Celtic* to honour the Lisbon triumph of May, but ship-building tended to be an occupation of Rangers supporters, and it might not have gone down too well. It would have silenced a few bigots, though. On the other hand, it might have created a few more. With an almost total lack of imagination, the ship was named the *Queen Elizabeth II*.

A few hours later, 54,000 (slightly fewer than one would have perhaps expected) turned up at Celtic Park to see Celtic take on Dinamo Kiev, the champions of the Soviet Union. One wonders, again with the great advantage of retrospect, whether Celtic had taken them seriously enough. We had beaten them 18 months previously in January 1966 in the European Cup Winners' Cup, and perhaps jumped rather too easily to the assumption that we could do so again. No great effort seemed to have been made to do any research on them – something, granted, that would have been difficult in the Soviet Union in 1967, when travel was not always encouraged.

It was, of course, the habit and trend for young people of left-wing leanings to assume that the Soviet Union was not as bad as it was painted in some newspapers. In this, we were totally misguided. What the Americans were doing in Vietnam was indeed terrible, and the South African regime was dreadful – there was no doubt about that – but we really should have protested a lot more about the appalling leaders of the Soviet Union. Eleven years previously, they had devastated Hungary, the following year it would be

Czechoslovakia… and goodness knows what they were doing to their own people inside that huge, secretive, paranoid collection of countries whom we loosely and wrongly termed "the Russians".

It was a rare treat for the people of that grim dictatorship when Celtic v Dinamo Kiev was beamed live on TV from Celtic Park to the huge area that is the Soviet Union. They would have enjoyed what they saw.

The Kiev players had arrived on the Sunday, and had been the subject of more than a little curiosity. They always dressed well in blazers, and ate the Scottish food well, with the newspapers making patronising comments about them not asking for haggis. They were seen around Glasgow, but surprised everyone on the Monday by coming to Celtic Park, disappearing immediately to the consternation of Jock Stein, and then having a training session on, of all places, Glasgow Green in full view of people walking their dogs and pushing prams. So much for Soviet secrecy.

Maybe, the Ukrainians were boosted by the thought of being watched on TV at home, but there was a buoyancy and confidence about them that took us by surprise. We had expected a grim, defensive approach. Celtic, on the other hand, were hesitant, lacking in confidence and seemingly out of touch with what the support wanted. It may have been the same personnel as Lisbon, but the achievement was the total opposite. A misplaced pass from Jimmy Johnstone gave a Ukrainian the ball, and Celtic were a goal down within five minutes. OK, we had started badly before (not least in Lisbon) and then fought back, so no need to get too depressed yet. But then, later on in the first half, Billy McNeill made a pig's ear of what should have been an easy clearance, and Celtic went in at half-time two goals down and enduring the whistles and jeers of a mystified and bewildered support.

There seemed no reason for it. All it did was emphasise the fragility of being the champions of Europe. Dinamo Kiev were good, but they were by no means the best in Europe, and surely Celtic did not suddenly become a poor team overnight. The team rallied a little in the second half and Lennox pulled one back. There was a little more confidence about the play but no great flair. There was passion, sometimes misplaced passion from Gemmell ("the ebullient Thomas" as *The Evening Telegraph* termed him), who was very lucky not to be sent off, but the belief seemed to be lacking. We felt that even if we made it 2-2 on the night, we would have some sort of a chance in Kiev, but this did not happen, and we had to face the prospect of the long trek to the Ukraine with a great deal of foreboding, and with a 2-1 deficit.

Naturally, the disappointed support turned on their players. Now those who had said that Stein should not have stood still, and that he should have bought a new player or two in the summer to freshen things up, seemed to have a point. Complacency had set in, the attitude was all wrong, the players weren't training hard enough, they were earning too much money, some were squabbling with each other – all these things were stated by those who claimed to know what they were talking about. The long journey home that night was not a pleasant one.

The hangover was still there when St Johnstone came to Celtic Park on Saturday. The late Bobby Murdoch used to insist that all through the Celtic glory years, the Scottish team which gave them the most bother, apart from Rangers, were St Johnstone. Coming from provincial Perth, by no means a hotbed of Scottish football, the Saints, now managed by the excellent and unpretentious little Willie Ormond, once of the Hibs Famous Five, were showing people that money was not necessarily a prerequisite of success in Scottish football. They were a team on the rise, a young team with many good players – yet they still should have been used to wipe the floor by the European champions.

But Celtic now seemed to be on the slide, with a death-wish in clear evidence. More than that, there was an element of self-destruction, that very Scottish characteristic, in their make-up. There was no-one more Scottish in looks, character and conversation than wee Jimmy Johnstone. Jimmy decided to add to Celtic's woes with a moment of madness. Still 0-0, but with Celtic marginally on top, Jimmy was tackled by ex-Celt Kenny Aird. It did not seem all that bad a tackle, but Celtic would have been awarded a free kick, one feels, had it not been for the sight of Aird lying on the ground. "A fist appears to have been used" said *The Evening Times*. The referee Mr Padden of Ardrossan clearly thought so as well, for Jimmy trudged off looking down at the turf with Parkhead resounding to a mixture of boos from those who had not seen the incident, and resigned silence from those who had. Celtic were down to ten men, having lost their star man (who admittedly had not been playing well for some time) and it was not yet half-time.

Jimmy, in his candid and honest book *Fire In My Boots,* seems to blame it all on the fact that he was buying a new bungalow and needing it renovated and redecorated. "Don't let anyone tell you that the problems of your private life have no effect on your football. Of course they do," he says (rather unconvincingly) before admitting that "my nerves must have been at breaking point because I turned and hit Kenny full in the face and then turned and followed the referee's pointing finger towards the dressing room…it is the longest and loneliest walk in the world". It must have been, Jimmy, and we were all as devastated as you, but then again, you really have to leave your personal problems at home.

St Johnstone then scored early in the second half amidst a cemetery silence at Parkhead. We all wondered what was going on. How could a team fall from its pinnacle as quickly as all that? Naturally rumours spread about dressing room fallings-out, about Stein being tapped up by Manchester United (a recurring and annoying one, that), transfer requests, and everyone seeming to want more money. What no-one denied was that they had all frankly grown too big for their boots, and that this was a nasty lesson in what is likely to happen when the idea that you have to work for everything begins to be lost. Success in May had been achieved with loads of appetite, confidence and a very identifiable team spirit. All these things were less in evidence now.

To the team's credit, the ten men fought back and Bobby Murdoch equalised. With a bit of luck, they might even have won, as the game finished on a high note, but it was depression that was the order of the day as we trudged back to our buses and trains. This was not what we expected September to bring. Newspapers, of course, were not slow to use words like "crisis" and "panic", but all that had really happened was a loss of form at the wrong time. Some people call it "loss of momentum", others more dramatically call it "freefall". I tend to say "infection" in that one defeat leads to another. In particular, as we have noticed, a defeat to Rangers usually does not come on its own, such is the hysteria and over-importance placed on these games in Glasgow.

My use of the word "infection" possibly came not so much from Victorian medicine as Greek tragedy. There was the belief in Greek society that something going wrong was caused by an "infection", not necessarily in the medical sense, but in the moral sense, in that something evil needed to be expunged. For example, in ancient Thebes, a plague was caused by some unpunished crime, and it was incumbent on King Oedipus to do something about this. He set about his task and in the course of his investigations it became clear that it was he himself who was the cause of the "infection" in that he had (unwittingly and unknowingly) killed his father and married his mother. Such an unfortunate set of occurrences meant that he had to be banished, and then the gods allowed the plague to subside, and, after a civil war, normal life was allowed to continue.

In footballing terms, of course, the gut reaction to such things as a bad run of form is to sack the manager. It is simple, and those who campaign for such a thing often do not consider what the long-term implication of this would be. In the case of September 1967, it was hardly likely that Stein was to be given the boot, nor did it seem likely that any of the players needed to be transferred, even though persistent rumours reached the ears of supporters. Disharmony was, we were told, being fomented in the dressing room by one or two individuals. But another way of purging the influence that was causing the harm might be to embark on a good run of form, and lose the pollution this way.

In some ways, however, the "seven days from Hell" was almost a natural phenomenon. No-one stays at the top of the tree for ever, and the very fact that they are at the top of the tree means that everyone tries harder to beat them. It also means that they are under more pressure from the media and their own supporters, who expect nothing other than the best. Nothing, however, had as yet been lost, but that week remains a painful one on the memory.

September's last two games thus now assumed more importance than they might have done. There was Ayr United first up at Somerset Park. This was the return leg of the League Cup quarter-final (Celtic had won the first leg 6-2) on Wednesday night, followed by a trip to the greatest Celtic bogey ground of them all – Annfield, the home of Stirling Albion. On paper, both games should be won easily, but as I kept pointing out, football games were not played on paper, but on grass.

It was a much-changed Celtic team that took the field at Ayr against the "Honest Men" of that transparently likeable but lively character called Ally MacLeod, whom some supporters recalled from his Third Lanark days. Injuries and also a desire to give some fringe players a game, allied with a desire to show some players that they were not indispensable, meant that men like Charlie Gallagher, Chris Shevlane, David Cattenach and Jim Brogan were given an outing, while Joe McBride made a welcome comeback and a youngster called Lou Macari came on in the second half.

Celtic won 2-0, making it 8-2 on aggregate, but it was a victory described as "uninspiring". Brogan scored in the second half from a good Gallagher through ball, and Wallace added a second almost on time, but the atmosphere was one of a training ground practice match, the tie having been won at Celtic Park a fortnight previously. The small crowd headed back home unsatisfied and unfulfilled, yet it was a victory and Celtic were now in the semi-final of the Scottish League Cup, where they would meet Greenock Morton, while Dundee and St Johnstone would contest the other game. A few years ago, an appearance in the Scottish League Cup semi-finals would have been much cherished and prized. In the atmosphere of autumn 1967, when so much had happened and so much was now expected on other fronts, it was hardly noticed.

Of far greater importance in Celtic's redemption was the trip to Stirling Albion on the Saturday. In addition to the bitter memories of 1962, when a guy called Johnnie Lawlor did so much to destroy the confidence of the emerging Celtic youngsters, of 1966, when the team unaccountably went down to a late sucker punch, and of earlier this year in the pelting rain, when they had to settle for a draw, there were two other factors. One was the imminence of our trip to the Ukraine, for which Celtic stated that they were taking all their own food, such was the suspicion of what could happen in the Soviet Union, and the other was the illness of Jock Stein.

He had had a bad dose of flu. It is generally agreed that the body is more susceptible to infections when it is under pressure, or when it wants to protest at what is going on. Goodness knows, poor Jock had had enough such pressures in recent weeks, but he made it to Stirling, albeit against medical advice and looking very ill, causing some of our female supporters to became very maternal and say that another day or two in bed would not have done him any harm. Sean Fallon was very capable and could surely have handled the team for a day. But Stein did go to Annfield and chose to return to the "old guard", with the exception of Jimmy Johnstone who had, of course, been sent off last week.

There was no automatic suspension in those days, so the omission of Johnstone was simply so that "he would be in fine fettle for the trip to Russia", said Sean Fallon, unconvincingly. We all suspected that he had been dropped to teach him a lesson. But the forward line of Chalmers, Lennox, Wallace, Auld and Hughes looked a strong one.

Several totally predictable things happened at Annfield that day. We had to stand in a long queue at the inadequate turnstiles ("they moan aboot folk no gaein tae gemmes, and when they get a big crowd, thay canna handle it" said an angry man behind me), the kick-off was delayed for ten minutes to allow the crowd to get in, and Stirling Albion, who had appeared in orange jerseys on the last two Celtic trips to Annfield, did the same today. It was almost a piece of ritual that we had come to expect, but this time Celtic and their supporters were not fazed by such gamesmanship.

Celtic seemed to have decided that enough was enough, that they had to break out of their poor form and throw the Stirling Albion monkey off their back. Playing downhill in the first half, they pressed and pressed but only had one Willie Wallace goal at half-time to show for it. "We saw his monument on the way in, and that was built even before he played for Celtic," said a father to his disbelieving son. But then, in the second half, playing up the slope (it wasn't all that pronounced, in any case), Celtic added another three goals from the old left-wing guard, two from Bertie Auld and one from Bobby Lennox, as they ran out comfortable 4-0 winners.

This was, in many ways, just what the doctor ordered. Jock's health immediately improved (although it was not yet a total recovery), we all got a boost and the team now braced themselves for the trip to the Ukraine to repair the damage caused at Parkhead and to remain in the European Cup. It would be no easy task.

My holidays were coming to an end. I had enjoyed them. There is, of course, no such thing as a good holiday job but this one at the bakery was a tolerable one with loads of companionship and crack, and I was genuinely sorry to say goodbye to the friends I had made there. It was not exactly well paid, but it did help finance footballing trips and I was able to give something to my mother for my keep. I was not really a poor student, because in the 1960s we were given a grant (not a loan) from the government to see us through university, and if you came from a working-class background with a Labour government in power, you really did quite well for yourself.

But second year at St Andrews was now beckoning and I was looking forward to that again.

OCTOBER

· · · · · · ·

The game in Kiev on October 4 coincided with me doing my packing to return for the beginning of my second year at St Andrews University. I had come a long way in the past year since, nervous and terrified, I set out for the first time. On the Saturday before term started a year ago, I went to Edinburgh to see Celtic beat Hibs 5-3. It was a great performance and a great game, but I recall returning to St Andrews in a state of great depression and apprehension, willing for two pins to go home and get a job in a factory. Now I was confident, brash, looking forward to getting started with my studies, to meeting girls and to patronising the first-year students. If my team could conquer Europe, so could I.

But how sad it was that by a cruel piece of chiasmus, the European Cup won so brilliantly at the start of the holidays was surrendered on the day before I went back. How sad it was to hear my father, reconciled to what had happened and cheerful and supportive as ever, say as everything was loaded into my cousin's car the following evening: "You've got everything except the European Cup!" We had been the European champions for about 130 days – maybe not long enough, but it was a great 130 days.

The game itself was, once again, more or less totally ignored by the TV networks and BBC Radio – something that grated considering the fact that the game at Parkhead had been shown live to the millions inside the Soviet Union. But it was typical of the half-hearted approach to sport and to Scottish football in particular. Those who had a mind to spot such things saw some sort of discrimination against Celtic and Scotland, but in fact the truth was a lot more simple. The BBC and ITV were just useless. Parsimonious, penny-pinching and out of touch with the needs of their public, but basically useless. One way or another, we were dependent on the news programmes for the result and really had to wait for the next day's newspapers for any details of the game – and pretty grisly they were too.

In the long and lamentable list of Scottish heroic failures, this one must come rather high. Celtic were unlucky, the victims of a strange referee, one Signor Antonio Sbardella, of Italy. Celtic did enough to win, and on another night, certainly would have done so. In addition, there was a strange piece of self-destruction by of all people, Bobby Murdoch. The game in Kiev ended up 1-1 – a good result it would have to be said in itself. But it all boiled down to that dreadful night at Celtic Park two weeks ago. Two years ago in the European Cup Winners' Cup, the same two teams also drew 1-1 on Soviet soil. The difference was that Celtic had won 3-0 at Celtic Park.

Celtic had certainly prepared well for this game, even to the extent of taking their own food with them. The defence was on traditional lines while the forward line ran

Johnstone, Lennox, Wallace, Auld and Hughes. The crowd
in the massive Nikita Khruschev Arena (named after that
veteran of the Cold War) was 85,000 and it was claimed that
they could have sold twice that amount, such was the desire
to see the famous Glasgow Celtic from Scotland. Celtic's
supporters in that crowd could probably be counted on
the fingers of one's hands, but the Scottish press, unlike the
BBC and STV, had made some sort of attempt to cover the
game, and their opinions showed a remarkable uniformity
that Celtic were distinctly unlucky. This point was tacitly
agreed with in the Soviet press, who emphatically did not
sing the praises of Dinamo Kiev, restricting themselves to
congratulating their team for having defeated the great
Glasgow Celtic.

The position was that Celtic had to score twice. A new
law about the goals scored away from home counting
double in the event of the scores finishing level had been
introduced. Thus 1-0 for Celtic would not do, 2-1 would
lead to extra time, whereas 3-2 would win it, for more
goals would have been scored away from home. But for
Celtic, the whole exercise reminded one of the old Scots
proverb of locking the stable door after the horse had been
stolen.

About 60 minutes had gone when the first incident
occurred. The game had been level up till then, although
the game had been spoiled by some finicky and inconsistent
refereeing. Murdoch had been booked earlier for something
that seemed like a foul committed by another Celtic
defender, and it was clear that frustration was growing.
There was no clear belief that the referee was a "homer" or
that he had been in any way intimidated by the crowd or
knobbled or bribed by the Kiev officials – although you can

never make such statements with any degree of certainty. He was probably just officious and seemed, himself, to be very nervous.

Thirty minutes remained and Celtic still needed two goals. A free kick was awarded against Celtic for something not obvious to the Scottish press. Murdoch, in frustration, bounced the ball in a direction away from the play, and found himself sent to the pavilion by Signor Sbardella. It was a decision described as "laughable", but Bobby really should have known better, something he himself admitted in later years. There was nothing violent or malicious in what he did, and it could hardly have been called "time wasting", for it was Celtic who were chasing the game. But Bobby had already been booked and he really ought to have twigged that this neurotic little bird of a man was looking for a chance to earn a name for himself. However, away he went, his head covered in a green towel to the dressing room. He would later describe it as one of the worst moments of his life, leaving his team-mates to play ten versus eleven for half an hour – but the decision was harsh.

But this Celtic team were not the champions of Europe for nothing, and almost immediately, having decided in the wake of Bobby's dismissal to throw caution to the winds, scored. A free kick was taken by Bertie Auld across the penalty area and the ball came to Bobby Lennox, who managed to squeeze the ball home from an almost impossible angle. Now Dinamo began to tremble, now the small Scottish contingent began to remember what had happened in Lisbon, and then with only a few minutes remaining, John Hughes scored when the goalkeeper dropped the ball, and Hughes prodded the ball home between the goalkeeper's legs.

The crowd were stunned, for this was the difference between victory and defeat, but the delirious joy of the Celtic bench was stalled when it was seen that Signor Sbardella had awarded a free kick to Dinamo. It even took the Kiev crowd a few seconds to realise that they had been reprieved. Celtic's protests were of no avail, and to this day anyone who was at that game will state categorically that there was no contact between Hughes and the goalkeeper whatsoever. Yogi himself remains adamant. Just on time, Dinamo scored an irrelevant goal. They had won anyway.

The uproar about this incident, had it occurred in a Western country with loads of TV footage, would have been significant, but Celtic's response was dignified and almost philosophical. Maybe Scottish TV coverage might have at least highlighted the misjudgement of the referee, but the main mistake lay in expecting anything else in eastern Europe, and we had to come back to the undeniable truth that we should have done better at Celtic Park. But we were out. If there was any comfort to be gained in all this, it was that Dinamo Kiev went on record to say how impressed they were with Celtic's sporting demeanour after the game, something that perhaps hints that they themselves had a guilty conscience about it all. Dinamo's sympathy with Celtic even extended to them sending a telegram of best wishes before the Racing Club game in the World Club Championship.

But for me, it was thus a sombre trip back to university the following day. It was nice to see old friends again – some had grown beards, some had gone all hippy, no-one agreed with the Americans on Vietnam – and there was a lot to look forward to... but there was still something missing and yes, it was the European Cup.

But there are times when one has to say *sunt lacrimae rerum* in the words of Virgil, the Roman poet. A rough translation might be "life can be sad at times" or more vulgarly "shit happens". The whirligigs of time had certainly turned viciously on Celtic supporters, but all you can do is take it on the chin, dust yourself down and fight back, saying things like "let's make the best of it" or "Hitler's deid" or more appropriately in our context: "There's another game on Saturday."

Indeed there was. Jock Stein had apparently been really ill in Russia. His flu had not cleared up and the flight had caused a relapse, and his ankle injury of ten years ago had flared up again. The two were not unconnected and had a great deal to do with stress, but Jock carried on. He refused a heavy cast on his ankle when one was offered by the Victoria Hospital, insisting on a light plastic one, and kept hobbling around, telling everyone that there were still three Scottish trophies plus the World Club Championship, where they would be facing the Racing Club of Argentina.

More immediately, there was Hibs at Parkhead. Hibs were looked upon as the "nearly men" of Scottish football who never really won anything, even though they were never far away from the action. Their record at Parkhead was particularly bad. Their supporters seemed destined to perpetual frustration and misery and, even as early as 1967, people made jokes about them not having won the Scottish Cup since 1902. They had suffered dreadfully since the departure of Jock Stein to Celtic in 1965, but now under manager Bob Shankly (who had led Dundee to the Scottish League title in 1962) things were slowly, albeit partially, improving. Not today, though, for a hurting Celtic team hammered them 4-0 with Bobby Murdoch, the villain

perhaps in Kiev, making his plea for redemption with a
couple of marvellous goals from outside the box as Celtic
won easily before a large and appreciative crowd of 40,000.
Stein made no changes from the side that had lost in Kiev –
a vote of confidence – and the players repaid him by playing
some marvellous stuff. It was often said that Celtic in the
Stein era played their best football against Hibs, for Hibs
were, like Celtic, an attacking team. If this was so, this was
one of the best performances of the Stein era.

The pleasing aspect was that there was no hangover or
fallout from the Kiev game. In the past, even this season,
there had been evidence of one defeat leading to another
and before you know where you are, you are in freefall.
The team had clearly been brought back down to reality,
and they were aware that although they were now out of
the European Cup, there were still other tournaments to
be played for.

Morton now were the unfortunate victims. This was
in the Scottish League Cup semi-final at Hampden on
Wednesday, October 11, and the football played that night
was absolutely devastating. Now back in St Andrews and
living fairly impecuniously, I had to husband my resources.
One of our number now had a car, but we decided to go to
see the World Club Championship game against Racing
Club of Argentina the following week rather than the semi-
final against Morton. It was a decision that I would bitterly
regret.

I missed one of the best displays of open attacking
football that one was ever likely to see. Even by the standards
of the Stein era, this one was good and fortunately there
were some highlights shown on TV later that night, with
the goal scored by John Hughes one of his best, certainly,

and a contender for one of the best of all time. It was a goal that had even the most anti-Celtic of Englishmen singing its praise, as it was played on TV.

A crowd of 45,662 saw Celtic come out in green jerseys with white pants and white stockings, a brighter combination than the all-green that they sometimes wore. Those who arrived late missed a great treat, for by 21 minutes the score was Celtic 5 Morton 1. Celtic scored in the second and fourth minutes then after Morton had had the audacity to pull one back, Celtic hit another three in quick succession. The key word was "quick" for seldom had Hampden seen such football played at pace by a team who had now started to believe in themselves yet again. There was also an element of frustration and anger at what had happened, and a determination to fight back.

John Hughes had been in inspired form throughout, and his goal in the second half was much praised. Playing towards the King's Park end of the ground, Yogi picked up a ball in his own half, turned on the speed as he brushed the Morton defence aside and hammered home from outside the penalty box. This was the seventh goal of the night, with 7-1 being an emotive scoreline for Celtic (because of the famous event of October 1957, ten years previously). It was almost as if Celtic, out of compassion for the ex-Celts in the Morton ranks, Eric Smith and Jim Kennedy, decided that enough was enough.

It had been a devastating performance, with Murdoch and Auld orchestrating things from midfield, finding the speedy Lennox and Wallace with ease, and Johnstone and Hughes both playing marvellous individual games. It was indeed a lesson in football, but the question that we all asked the following morning was why it couldn't have come a week earlier. We all agreed that there was a difference between Greenock Morton and Dinamo Kiev, but it still rankled that Celtic had not shown the courage of their convictions that awful night at Parkhead back in September.

The world had now seen what Celtic could do. It was so frustrating to know that they could do such things, but failed to turn it on at times when it was really necessary. The memory remains of the faces of some English students watching the highlights on TV that night, lovers of Arsenal, Manchester City, Derby County and Middlesbrough, their jaws dropping in amazement at the sheer speed and skill of the Celtic forward line. Naturally, they took refuge in sneers about the quality of Morton, and asked why we hadn't done it against Kiev. It was so frustrating to have no answer.

Celtic were, however, now in the final of the Scottish League Cup to play Dundee, who had beaten St Johnstone in the other semi-final, that same night. It promised to be a great game, but it was overshadowed by other events. Racing Club of Argentina were due at Hampden on Wednesday, October 18, and the other leg was in Buenos Aires on November 1. This meant that Celtic would play the League Cup Final on Saturday, October 28, and then have to fly on the lengthy journey to Argentina that same night. Such was the price of success.

In the meantime, I had settled for my second year at St Andrews, doing Latin, Greek and a dreadful subject that everyone had to do called Moral Philosophy. In theory this sounded a good idea, for Moral Philosophy, along with Political Economy, was much studied in the 18th century by men like Adam Smith and David Hume, of what was called the Scottish Enlightenment. In practice, it was a disaster. It was taught very badly – some tutorials were even held in pubs – and lectures were at 6pm. Not surprisingly, they were badly attended, and the standard of lecturing was dispiritingly bad. Behaviour was dreadful, with students throwing paper aeroplanes at each other – in my case with uplifting messages like "7-1 and Jock Stein is the new God" at people of the other persuasion, who retaliated with stuff about King Billy and the Pope. It was all good-natured but did not disguise the fact that we should have been studying about Ethics and the Meaning of Life. Yet maybe what I was doing was the meaning of my life.

All this was in stark contrast to the high-powered stuff in the real subjects of Latin and Greek, where the teaching was excellent and the pressure high as we delved into Herodotus and Virgil's *Eclogues*. It was hard work, but enjoyable as well and a time that I look back on with a certain amount of pleasure – until the complications of a girl entered the scene.

But that was in the future. The present was a Glasgow derby visit to Partick Thistle at a windy Firhill on the Saturday immediately before the game against Racing Club. Indeed some of the Argentinians had already arrived and had their introduction to Scottish football in Maryhill at that quintessentially Scottish ground called Firhill, with its funny-shaped terracings and sometimes strange playing surface. "Firhill for thrills" was the saying, and it was a ground on which Celtic usually played well. Partick Thistle's colours were red and yellow, almost like those of a racing jockey – but that was not why they were called the Harry Wraggs. It was Glasgow rhyming slang for "Jags". Thistle were also called the "old unpredictables" because they were capable of gross disparities in performance from week to week, largely perhaps because of their inveterate tendency to sign up old men whose careers at other clubs had now come to an end.

Celtic had had deserved cause for complaining about referees in recent weeks. Here, however, they received a break when referee Mr Kellock, of East Kilbride, saw fit to send off Davie McParland, the stalwart of Partick Thistle. McParland would, in time, become assistant manager at Celtic Park, and was generally well respected in the game, involving himself in the players' union and other things. In the 30th minute, with no goals scored and, if anything, Thistle having the better of the play, McParland was tackled by Wallace. It was probably a foul to Thistle, but then the two men indulged in a little of the pushing and shoving that it is often described as "handbags" – an uncomplimentary and indeed sexist jibe about women having a cat fight at a Glasgow dance hall in the 1950s over some man, and hitting each other over the head with their handbags.

Wallace and McParland were two tough characters, but there was absolutely nothing in it, with neither man guilty of anything other than a little squaring up to each other. However, to the consternation of the crowd, even the Celtic crowd, McParland was invited to leave the proceedings. Wallace was embarrassed and even made a half-hearted attempt to intervene on McParland's behalf, but Mr Kellock was adamant and Thistle were now a man down, their misery compounded when Billy McNeill opened the scoring for Celtic just on the half-time whistle.

In the second half Bertie Auld, himself a Maryhill boy, took over and supplied Lennox and others time and time again. Lennox scored four goals and Celtic ran out 5-1 winners, a result that might have been a little less emphatic if Thistle had had 11 men. But for Celtic, it was two points, and other things were now causing concern, namely the game against the Argentinians on Wednesday night at Hampden. Senor Cuneo, the vice-president of Racing Club, was impressed and had enough of a command of the English language to say that "Celtic are terrific".

Being an idealist, I was rather disturbed that the World Club Championship game was not being held at Celtic Park. Much pious stuff came out about how it was important for Scotland's football identity for the game to be played at the National Stadium of Hampden, whereas we all knew that it was about making money. Hampden could house a crowd about half as much again as Celtic Park could. In the event, the crowd was a slightly disappointing 90,000 (although some sources say 103,000) – more than Celtic Park could have housed certainly, but a little short of the Hampden capacity. Indeed, although tickets had been printed and sold, several turnstiles were open to accept cash (ten shillings, the equivalent of 50p, and in 1967 an astonishing amount for a football match). But it was for the championship of the world.

The crowd included Harold Wilson, the Prime Minister, who was given a respectful round of applause in the solidly Labour city that Glasgow was, and a party of Rangers players led by manager Scot Symon. The BBC network radio commentary was provided by the veteran Raymond Glendenning, now technically retired but still called upon now and again and as clear an example of an English "jolly old chap" as one could have imagined with his love of sports cars, his pipe, his handlebar moustache and scarf wrapped round his neck. There was no live TV coverage, but then again, we did not expect any.

Goal aggregate did not count in this competition, which meant that a 1-0 win was as good as 6-0, and it was clear from an early stage that the Argentinians were not interested in anything other than getting a draw. They were not particularly careful how they did it, either, and some of the tackles on Jimmy Johnstone in particular were shockers. Jimmy was just about to start a 21-day suspension beginning the next day (although moves were on hand to allow him to play in the South American return) for being sent off for a third time against St Johnstone in September, but the Argentinians knew that he was the key man. He was not the only man to receive rough treatment – Lennox could not play for Scotland on Saturday as a result, and Auld and McNeill also suffered – but in the end Celtic got the win that they deserved.

Celtic started off playing towards the Rangers or Mount Florida End, which presented the strange sight of having an enclosure roof in the throes of being built. Celtic and their fans were less than happy about that for it would have meant that on a wet Scottish Cup Final sometime in the future, Rangers fans would be dry and their chants would echo and reverberate more than the encouragement from the wet Celtic fans.

Naturally hidden handshakes, the rolling up of trouser legs and invisible flutes were detected in all this, but the truth was more likely that the Rangers End was a little smaller and therefore cheaper to cover. The SFA threw their money around "like manhole covers", we used to say, in odd student imagery... and have you ever seen anyone throwing manhole covers about?

In this game, we at the crowded Celtic End saw little action in the first half for Racing seldom seemed interested in attacking, and Celtic's domination of the midfield was complete, although they were finding it difficult to get past the rough tackling of Racing. This was amazingly well tolerated by the Spanish referee, but it was not only tackling – it was punching and spitting when the ball was nowhere near. Clearly, the ethos of the South American game was totally different from that of the Scottish one. The worst tackle was, predictably, on Jimmy Johnstone by a chap called Rulli, who managed to have Jimmy more or less parallel with the ground and about two feet above it.

For a long time in the second half, it began to look as if the dirty tactics of Racing were going to triumph. It has to be admitted that there was some good Argentine defending as well, not least by a man with the unlikely name of Perfumo, called Profumo by the Celtic fans who were deliberately mixing him up with the Minister of War (sic) in the Conservative government of 1963 who had been compelled to resign after associating with the same "lady" as a Russian military attache. (Someone else with the Glasgow humour in him said, "Perfumo! He's stinking!") But Celtic kept pressing forward and about halfway through the second half they got their reward, when Billy McNeill headed home a corner taken by Bertie Auld. We got a great view of it and much was the rejoicing on the terracing behind.

Thereafter, to a certain extent at least, the play improved from the Argentinians, for they now had to chase the game and try to equalise. In fact, they had a few good players, but that had never been obvious until this point, and we began to get a little edgy, not least when Ronnie Simpson had to make a brilliant dive to save the day with only two minutes left after an Argentinian called Rodriguez had been left unguarded by the careless Celtic defence.

We did also get one brilliant piece of acting from Bertie Auld. He was headbutted by the back of someone's head, but it did not really do him a great deal of harm. Milking the moment, however, our Bertie took his time before going down in instalments like a dying swan. It was brilliant acting and earned Celtic time before, to the great relief of everyone, the referee blew for time up after one of the nastiest games of football ever seen at Hampden Park. *The Celtic View* of the following week was quite happy to use words like "fraud" to describe this game and attacks Senor Gardeazabal, of Spain, for failing to control the Argentine players.

Going down the steps of the East Terracing at Hampden was always a hazardous experience in the 1960s. This night it was more so, because it was in the dark with inadequate lighting and the crowd was huge. Separated from my friends and my feet off the ground, I was swept along and genuinely feared for my life. It did have its funny moment, though. The chap in front of me turned as well as he could and uttered the words which my friends kept taunting me with in future years: "Hey, Jum, get your knee oot o my arse!" I replied that there was little that I could do about it, such was the pressure of the crowd, or words to that effect. He then made the immortal reply: "Ye're no needin it up as far as all that!"

When we got back to the car, we were so relieved that we were still alive and had avoided being crushed to death in that crowd that my retelling of the story of my knee was greeted with gales of laughter. Various remarks which would now be described as homophobic were made about me and no-one wanted to sit beside me in the back seat. Later, once the mirth had died away, a more philosophical and indeed physiological discussion took place about "ye're no needin' it up as far as all that", as if it were a matter of degree how far one could insert a knee into someone's posterior. My reply, which spread round the University of St Andrews the following day, was redolent of Winston Churchill: "Some knee! Some arse!"

There was, of course, a more serious side to all that. When the Ibrox disaster happened in 1971, causing the deaths of 66 people, we were not really all that surprised. It might have happened a lot earlier than it did – and this was one such occasion. Football clubs and the SFA would wring their hands in horror, shed crocodile tears, come out with what can, in retrospect, be described as "crap" about how "the safety of fans is paramount", but in fact they did nothing.

On the footballing side, however, we began to worry about Celtic. If the Argentinians were prepared to act like that in Scotland – and we even began now to sympathise with Alf Ramsey's use of the word "animals" the previous year – what on earth would they be like in their own country?

The answer, of course, was that they were a million times worse, and we began to wonder whether it might be no bad idea for Celtic to cut their losses and refuse to go. Chairman Bob Kelly, apparently, also expressed at this stage some misgivings, which were shared by the press. Was the World Clubs Cup worth all that? In the end, however, Mr Kelly was convinced by his fellow directors and by Jock Stein that it would be cowardice and indeed folly not to go and to try to win the cup that would make Celtic the best team in the world.

Hindsight tells us that he was wrong and that life would have been a great deal better for all concerned if Celtic had refused to go. Indeed in comparison with El Cilindro, as it was called, Ibrox Park, Tynecastle and Pittodrie were havens of sportsmanship and gentlemanly behaviour. It would turn out to be a dreadful experience.

But in the meantime, the Scottish season continued. There was no Celtic game on Saturday, October 21 for Scotland were playing in Northern Ireland. Simpson, Gemmell, Wallace and Murdoch were in the Scottish side, with only Simpson distinguishing himself by saving a penalty and keeping the score down to 0-1 in what was a dreadful Scottish performance. Scottish fans were there in large numbers and were particularly disappointed following the great performance against England in April. Bobby Murdoch in particular kept up his tradition of failing to reproduce his Celtic form for Scotland. Jimmy Johnstone might have made some difference but he, of course, was beginning his 21-day suspension.

Murdoch had an early opportunity to make amends, at least as far as the Celtic fans were concerned, when Celtic played Motherwell at Parkhead on the following Tuesday night.

He was outstanding in the 4-2 victory, with Wallace, McNeill, Lennox and Chalmers scoring the goals, the only black spot being the careless defending which conceded two goals. Indeed this would be a feature of Celtic all throughout the glory years – that the defence was never as watertight as we would have liked. But as the forwards kept scoring the goals, no-one really identified it as a major problem.

In the meantime, steps were being taken by Celtic and the SFA to allow Jimmy Johnstone to play in the following week's game in Argentina. Some of us had a few moral and ethical objections to this one, but no-one in high places seemed to bother. For one thing, the Argentinians seemed to have no scruples about doing exactly the same thing with one of their players, and for another there was simply no structure to this semi-unofficial competition, and Jimmy was going to play, said Jock Stein. He was still suspended for the domestic games, however, including Saturday's League Cup Final against Dundee.

It was an odd feeling in the days leading up to that League Cup Final. It was almost as if it didn't really matter, for the team would be flying to South America, apparently, that very evening. Life would go on whether we won the League Cup Final or lost it. Yet I recalled the League Cup Final of three years earlier, which was approached by all supporters as if it were a matter of life and death. It was death as it turned out for Rangers won 2-1 in an absolute nightmare of a game, where we were well on top but couldn't score, then Rangers took advantage of it. It was the catalyst that led to the virtual collapse of Celtic until Jock Stein arrived in March 1965. The League Cup finals of 1965/66 and 1966/67 (both wins for Celtic over Rangers) were similarly much talked about and anticipated beforehand and dissected afterwards. This one did not seem to matter all that much.

Dundee were now managed by Bobby Ancell, the same Bobby Ancell who had failed to turn out for Dundee in the vital game in 1948 in which Celtic saved themselves from relegation by a 3-2 win. (Yes, 19 years previously, Celtic were battling to avoid relegation. Now they were playing to be champions of the world.) Ancell was "injured", but the story went that he did not want to take part in this game because he was being asked to do something underhand. You see, Celtic were going to win this game anyway, if you get my meaning. It made no sense for Dundee to relegate the goose that laid a very large golden egg, and I often feel that the stories from Celtic sources that went around about "Dundee on a huge bonus to win" or "hysterical support in the rest of Scottish football for Dundee" were simply put about to hide this truth, which was quite obvious to those who were bright enough to spot it. Anyhow, Ancell had wanted no part in the charade, and did not play.

Full marks to the man, and he had a football brain as well. Although hampered at Dundee by a board of directors who, apparently, wanted to sell their star men rather than have a good football team, Ancell had nevertheless built up a fair side. There were two McLeans, George, who used to play for Rangers, and Jim, who would in future years make a name for himself across the road at Tannadice, a Stewart, a Stuart and a survivor of the team who had had that great run in the European Cup in 1963 in Bobby Cox. They had a tradition of playing good football, were well organised at the back and quite skilful at the front, but infuriatingly inconsistent in the view of their fans.

George McLean had a point to prove to Rangers and indeed the world. He had been signed in 1962 from St Mirren. As used to happen a great deal in the past, if one had a good game against Rangers, one often found oneself the subject of transfer speculation and then a move to Rangers followed. In this case, the good game against them was the Scottish Cup Final of 1962. McLean fitted in well at Ibrox. A natty dresser, good-looking and doing nothing to discourage the nickname of "Dandy", he associated with and married a beautiful model called Liz Cleland, and McLean in many ways symbolised the slickness and success of Rangers in the early 1960s.

But Berwick had changed all that. McLean and Forrest were held to blame for the missed chances at Shielfield Park and McLean never played again. This was, of course, to Rangers' detriment for McLean was surely good enough to have helped them win the Cup Winners' Cup, but by now he had found his way to the less rarefied atmosphere of Dens Park.

Dundee had a good pedigree in the League Cup. They were the first team to win the trophy two years in a row when they had defeated Rangers and Kilmarnock in 1951/52 and 1952/53, and that was at a time when Celtic had never won it at all. Now Celtic were bidding for their third Scottish League Cup in a row, and if they managed that, they would be the first team ever to achieve a hat-trick of League Cup wins. The two teams had never met in the final of the Scottish League Cup, but they had met in the final of the Scottish Cup and that was, of course, the famous occasion of Patsy Gallagher's goal and Jimmy McGrory's diving header in 1925. The old-timers, like my father, who had seen that one, glowed and went all misty-eyed at the recollection.

Those who saw Dundee win the Scottish League in 1962 retain a soft spot for them. That was a fine side, so fine in fact that the Dundee directors decided to sell the best players in a move which showed, at the very least, a decided lack of ambition. Other phrases like "asset-stripping", "pocket-lining" and "cashing in" were also heard, but by 1967 they had definitely downsized. Using the smokescreen of "small clubs need to sell" – a piece of nonsense which even seemed to persuade the very powerful local press – they would be quite happy to see their teams suffer, and of course they would pay the penalty for that in full several times before the end of the century, as their crowds simply disappeared. Bankruptcy and administration were no strangers to Dens Park. But in 1967, they were still a respectable side, and would certainly give Celtic a good game.

The crowd was given as 66,660 – possibly a tad disappointing, but then again Celtic fans had been at Hampden ten days earlier and were maybe suffering from a little "turnstile fatigue" while Dundee fans were perhaps pessimistic about their team. In the absence of the suspended Jimmy Johnstone, Steve Chalmers played on the right wing and the other forwards were Lennox, Wallace, Auld and Hughes. The defence was as per Lisbon. It was a crisp enough autumn day with intermittent sunshine – possibly a bit cold, but it was not yet winter.

Recollections of this game are confused. This is not because of too much drink but more because there was simply so much going on. The forwards all played well, but the defending on both sides was woeful. Yet it was an amazing spectacle, particularly in the latter stages, when Dundee simply would not give up. The 5-3 scoreline meant that Celtic had won the Scottish League Cup for the third year in a row, but questions were asked about Billy McNeill and Ronnie Simpson. As the forwards had won the game, however, they stayed as nothing more than questions.

Playing towards the Mount Florida End, Celtic started well. Steve Chalmers scored first through a header, then John Hughes scored with one of his individualist goals. All this within the first ten minutes and some supporters, delayed at the inadequate turnstiles at the distant King's Park End, arrived to find that the score was 2-0. Before half-time, however, George McLean pulled one back – a somewhat fortuitous deflection which ricocheted off McNeill into the net, past a bewildered Simpson. This was enough to bring Dundee back into the game and set up a second half which had us all a little punch drunk by the five goals scored in such a short time. It was like watching a basketball game.

The first 25 minutes of the second half yielded no goals, but reflected a great deal of credit on Dundee, who passed the ball around with confidence and on several occasions tested Ronnie Simpson. In the 73rd minute, however, the game seemed to be over when Stevie Chalmers scored his second goal as he rounded the goalkeeper, having been released by a visionary pass from Bobby Murdoch. That made it 3-1, but scarcely had we begun to sing "We Shall Not Be Moved" when we saw John Clark having to head clear off his line and then Jim McLean put the ball past Ronnie. This quietened us for a while, but then Lennox scored a goal out of nothing, finding a loose ball, manoeuvring himself into a good position and hitting home past an unprepared Dundee defence.

That was 4-2, and as we were now within the last ten minutes, the fun seemed over. But there was another goal for each side to come yet when George McLean scored a good goal before Willie Wallace finally killed it all. It had been fun while it lasted, but it was another major trophy for Celtic. Remarkably, the Celtic crowd cheered Dundee to the echo as they collected their losers' medals, with even George McLean getting a magnanimous clap. (After all, he now hated Rangers more than we did!) The presentation of the League Cup to Celtic, on the other hand – in 1967 the winners received their medals first – had lacked the usual euphoria and hysteria. Celtic fans, like the Celtic players themselves, had other things on their minds – and, of course, there was no lap of honour allowed, following the attempt by Rangers supporters to injure Celtic players two years ago.

Recalling the trauma of the previous midweek coming down those same inadequate steps, I was particularly careful to allow most of the crowd to get away before I ventured downwards from the East Terracing. It was the first time that I began to appreciate the English word "ochlophobia", meaning the fear of a crowd. It often is used in the context of what a crowd can do when led by a mischievous rabble rouser, but in my case it was fear of being crushed to death. Fifty years later, that residual fear is still with me.

Nevertheless, it had been a good game of football and it is always a nice feeling to get one trophy under one's belt, as it were. The journey home passed with the sort of glow that we had become familiar with. The Scottish League Cup and Celtic had had a funny relationship. Celtic traditionally started the season badly and were frequently out of the League Cup before we knew where we were, but we had now won it three years in a row and five times in all, only once behind Rangers. It was the fourth major honour this calendar year, and we looked forward to hearing good news from Argentina on Wednesday night.

We spared a thought for our heroes now high above the Atlantic on their 20-hour journey to South America, a continent that very few people had any experience of. They would be celebrating too, but none too energetically for they had the stern eye of Jock Stein keeping watch on them.

In any case, there are limits to how far one can celebrate on an aeroplane. Pubs in St Andrews, however, did not have such limitations. My ochlophobia had now gone, and there was the thought of the Scottish League Cup draped in green and white ribbons.

Sunday, Monday and Tuesday saw a quiet end to the month of October. In the midst of other things, no-one made a great deal of fuss about the fact that Rangers had failed to beat Dunfermline at Ibrox, earning only a goalless draw. Although this result obeyed the Old Firm dynamic that when one member has a very good day, winning in this case a trophy, the other member cannot cope with it and drops a point or two, it was hardly a total disaster for Rangers against a more than competent team in Dunfermline, and they were still top of the league. But this result would have major implications for them, as we shall see.

NOVEMBER

· · · · · · ·

Seldom can so much have happened in one day as occurred on Wednesday, November 1, 1967. Certainly in the history of Scottish football, such a day can only have occurred rarely. It was often said of Jock Stein that he was brilliant at getting Rangers off the back pages of newspapers by leaking a story to the press of more apparent value than whatever Rangers were doing. Here, we joked, Rangers were getting their own back on him. When Celtic were playing in a really big game – literally for the championship of the world in faraway Argentina – Rangers released an even bigger story. Indeed it was rather drastic. They sacked their long-term manager Scot Symon.

But even that story did not make the headlines. The main story was a very tragic one – that a Dundee teacher was shot dead at St John's Secondary School by a gunman wearing an army uniform. She was teaching needlework when the man walked in. Another teacher was injured but the pupils, although traumatised, were unharmed. The fact that the man was wearing an army uniform and the school was Roman Catholic might have raised a few eyebrows, but there didn't seem to be any deeper significance. The man was eventually overpowered by police dogs. It was one of those isolated incidents which happens very seldom, as in Dunblane in March 1996.

The Rangers story also had to compete for the headlines with the Foreign Secretary George Brown, who unleashed an impassioned outburst at Lord Thomson of Fleet over the way his journalists were reporting news. Brown, a loveable character, enjoyed the support of the Labour movement for this and for other things, but the Tory press was asking Harold Wilson when he was going to sack his Foreign Secretary. They did not seem to like a Foreign Secretary who spoke his mind.

But in Glasgow, the talk was undeniably of the sacking of Scot Symon. There had been a few rumours for a day or two after the painful 0-0 draw against Dunfermline and apparently he had been sacked on the Tuesday night. A businessman, working on behalf of the Rangers board had, the story went, gone to his house and told him. Symon did not appear at Ibrox on November 1, but the first the players knew about it was when they finished training at lunchtime. They were then told that he had resigned, *not* been sacked. Not that it mattered, really. He was away and the new manager was David White, one-time boss of Clyde but assistant to Symon since the summer.

When this news reached Argentina, the first reaction was incredulity. Back in St Andrews, I was told it at lunch by a Rangers supporter who was close to tears, and it all seemed surreal and absurd. Symon had been their manager since 1954 and had won them six Scottish League titles, five Scottish Cups and four Scottish League Cups. He had made them a reasonable (although not total) success in Europe, having reached two European Cup Winners' Cup finals, and they were currently top of the league.

Aye, but there was a rub, my Rangers friend and I agreed. Symon had *not* won a European trophy, whereas Celtic now had. His only failing was that he was not Jock Stein. Yet on Wednesday, November 1, Rangers were ahead of Celtic. Even with their disappointing draw against Dunfermline, they were undeniably and mathematically at the top of the Scottish League. Basically, one cannot help saying with the considerable help of retrospect, it was a Rangers own goal. Celtic in Argentina should have been happy.

Symon had been a remarkable character, beginning his footballing career with Dundee, then Portsmouth, then he had come to Rangers as war approached in 1938. He also, being a Perthshire man, won a cap for Scotland at cricket as well as football – a rare distinction indeed. We always joked that his game for Scotland at football was against Hungary and this was recorded in the *Wee Red Book* as 1 HUN. Yes indeed, we said, he was 1 Hun!

But if his playing career was good, his managerial career was outstanding. Twice he won the Scottish League Cup as manager of East Fife (a hard school to cut one's teeth, and what an achievement!) and then, when he moved to Preston North End, he took them to the FA Cup Final in 1954. While still with East Fife, he had lost a Scottish Cup Final in 1950 to Rangers, who had kept their eye on him, and when Struth retired, Symon was approached to take over.

Symon had always been well dressed and dignified. He never lost the place with newspaper reporters or with his players, at least not in public, and brought success to Rangers. His benign and polite, if somewhat cold, demeanour, however, masked the undeniable fact that he was the front man for an organisation which practised religious discrimination and stood for most things which modern thinking was gradually coming to despise. Nevertheless, he deserved a great deal of credit for his handling of difficult men like Sammy Baird, Willie Woodburn and Jim Baxter. But his recent signings in the summer of 1966 and 1967 – one got the impression that he had been pressurised or panicked into buying some of them – had been no great success and now he was having to carry the can for the failures of Berwick and Nuremberg, although we all knew that the man who had really sacked him was the man at that moment preparing his team for the World Club Championship in Argentina.

Symon was still only 56 and indeed would become manager of Partick Thistle in a few years' time. A fellow student of mine who studied 19th-century British History cited a parallel. It was that of the great British Foreign Secretary, Palmerston, who ruled the roost brilliantly until Bismarck came along in Prussia. Symon was the same with Rangers, until Stein came along at Celtic.

The whole business brought Rangers into even more disrepute, however. It was generally agreed by Rangers and Celtic supporters alike that this was no way to treat a man who had contributed so much to their cause. What made things worse was that they now pushed David White – "the boy David", as he was unkindly called – into the big job where frankly, for public relations and everything else, Jock Stein would wipe the floor with him. White might have been good if he had been given more time to learn the trade under Symon.

As it was, he reminded one of Tacitus's assessment of the Roman Emperor Galba… "in everyone's opinion, he would have been capable of being Emperor… if he hadn't become the Emperor."

All this meant that if Celtic players were nervous before the World Club Championship, they had much to talk about in the dressing room, for such a decision cannot but have had some beneficial effect on Celtic's chances of winning the league. But would they be world champions as well?

Thus the day of Wednesday, November 1 was a strange one. I went to lectures, did my studying and everyone would have thought that things were normal. And indeed things were a great deal more normal than they had been on May 25, the day of the European Cup Final. There was an air of unreality about it, leaving aside the Rangers business. For one thing, I was aware that we could not *lose* the actual championship in Buenos Aires. Worst-case scenario, even a 0-6 thumping would only mean a play-off in neutral Uruguay. A draw or a win would mean that Celtic were the champions of the world.

But this was not the circumstances that one associated with cup finals and championships. This was Scotland in early November, when the weather was what is generally described as "dreich". Knee-deep in yellow leaves, heavy skies, occasionally drizzling but not particularly cold. In addition, the university was in full flow with people talking about lecturers, tutorials, essays, proses and whether university was the real place for someone, after all. It was difficult to think about football in Argentina.

Argentina was a long way away in every sense. Countries like Australia and New Zealand were further away, but they spoke English and we had a reasonable idea of what happened there. The USA and South Africa, as well, although we disapproved of Vietnam and apartheid, were basically our people, but Argentina was a place beyond our experience with military coups, a dictator called Peron, whom they had now got rid of (although they brought him back a few years later), imprisonments without trial, and people who disappeared if they disapproved of the government. In 1967, I had lived about 20 years on the planet and had yet to meet anyone who had ever been there. Mind you, they had crossed swords with England in the World Cup.

Allied to this was the almost total lack of media coverage of the game. It probably would have been impossible for the game to be shown live on television because of the lack of satellites and things like that, but no live radio coverage had been scheduled either. The best chance would appear to be the news and football results on the radio at 9.30pm. There was even some doubt about when the kick-off would be. "Our Special Correspondent in Buenos Aires" (always an indication that a newspaper had not even sent a reporter and they were just going to live like vultures and jackals picking up what everyone else had said) would tell us that it would be an afternoon kick-off in Argentina, which meant evening here. In fact, we discovered later that it was 7.30pm GMT – except that it wasn't quite that, for reasons we would discover later.

So there was little I could do until that radio news bulletin. I did something in the meantime that I had been steeling myself to do for some time. I needed a partner for the residence ball on November 17. There was a girl I knew slightly and rather liked, so I picked up the phone (no mobiles in 1967) and invited her. I had been terrified to ask her straight out in case she said no and I would not have been able to cope with the humiliation. But my courage was rewarded when she said, "Are you kidding? Thank you very much. Of course." I recall the actual words, and from now on this girl entered my life.

For the rest of 1967, things went well on that front and the romance prospered. It would totter in early 1968 and eventually collapse on the day that we won the league in April, but for the moment things were going well. I had a spring in my step – but would my team be the world champions later that night?

I have but vague recollections of the way that the news was given on the radio. A poor line, some bits of the report barely comprehensible from a man with a heavy Spanish accent, but the salient reports were that Celtic had lost 2-1, with Tommy Gemmell scoring a penalty. Something had happened to Ronnie Simpson and John Fallon had been in the goal, but there was now a game in Montevideo, Uruguay on Saturday. So Celtic were not, or not yet, the world champions.

It would be the following day before we would hear all the details, but although disappointed, we were not broken-hearted. There was something rather predictable about it all, and all it really meant was that we were still in it. We put off the radio and started to talk about Scot Symon, with the opinions of the two Rangers sympathisers among us sharply divided.

One thought that he had been harshly treated and that Rangers had made the wrong decision, the other thought that Rangers were now so far behind Celtic that something had to be done about it. But they weren't all that far behind. They had beaten Celtic in September and were currently top of the league.

The Rangers argument continued, and the general feeling about Celtic was that, although it was a pity, we would do it on Saturday, because Uruguay, although South Americans, were no friends of Argentina and their crowd would back Celtic. I went to bed reasonably philosophical about things. It was when we read the details of the game in the newspapers of the following day that we found out what had really happened. We changed our minds rather quickly.

The game had been tough but anyone who saw the Argentinians at Hampden would not have been surprised at that. The real horror of the night was the felling of Ronnie Simpson by a missile. This was even before the game started. The game had to be delayed so that John Fallon could take over in the goal. John told me years later the circumstances in which he was asked to take over: "…and then I saw Jock Stein hobbling up to me with his characteristic limp, which always seemed worse when he was angry or under pressure and gesticulating, as he shouted, 'Don't just stand there! Get on the park! You're f***in' playing!' It was as brutal as that."

The Argentinian newspapers, to their credit, condemned the missile attack and injury to Ronnie Simpson, but no-one ever seemed to conduct any kind of investigation into how it occurred. Given the fact that there was a fence between the crowd and the playing area to stop such things from happening, there was even the possibility that the crime had been committed by one of the Racing players or one of the ball boys.

If that was what Argentinian football was all about, then we should come home. Many newspapers thought so as well and apparently Bob Kelly, who had expressed reservations in the first place, now intensified his opposition, but was again outvoted by the other directors. Jock Stein was as unhappy as anyone, but thought, reluctantly, that Celtic must honour their commitments and play the third game in neutral Uruguay. It would have been a great deal better for all concerned if Celtic had indeed simply called it quits, allowed Racing Club to have the cup, and flown home. But the decision to play the game was taken, and what a catalogue of infamy now has to be recorded.

The whole thing reminded me of the Athenian expedition to Sicily in 415–413 BC. Not everyone was in favour of this crazy outing in the first place, and after an initial lack of success, the opportunity presented itself to withdraw with dignity. Granted there would have been a certain loss of face, but the army and reputation would have been intact. They were all set to do just that, but then an eclipse of the moon gave the Athenians the impression that the gods wanted them to stay there. They stayed and received what, in football terms, would be called a "severe pumping". There was no eclipse of the moon in Argentina, but the decision to stay was an equally tragic one.

I found myself now in the odd position of not caring too much. If my hero Ronnie Simpson (whom I had loved since his Newcastle United days in 1955) could be hit by a brick, or a stone or whatever, and with the suggestion that the missile may have been hurled by someone on the playing area *before* the game started, just what was the point of playing football against this mob?

Those who wanted Celtic to come home were right. Yes, they would have been accused of cowardice, and yes, they would have lost money but a point would have been made about Argentinian football, and Celtic's name would not have been entirely tarnished.

Some members of the Scottish press urged them to do just that. Mind you, such is the versatility of the journalism profession that those who were advising them to come home would have been the first to jump on the "cowardice" bandwagon once Celtic had decided to do so. And there is also the point that had Celtic cut their losses, there would always have been the niggling question of whether that was the right thing to do. We would never have known whether they were good enough to become world champions. Celtic, in fact, and their supporters would have "died wondering".

In addition, Uruguay was a different country. A friend who was studying Spanish assured me that they were all peaceful there and that Uruguay was called "the Switzerland of South America". Montevideo was a lovely city, and there would be a different referee. My only experience of Uruguay was a bad one – I was not yet six years old when I had an early experience of TV, watching Uruguay beat Scotland 7-0 in the 1954 World Cup. It was a traumatic childhood experience.

The game would be on Saturday, November 4 with once again an evening kick-off GMT. Coverage would still be more or less non-existent, so I took my new girlfriend to the pictures that night to see *Dr Zhivago* (as I recall) and came back to be told what had happened. Once again, all that we really knew on the Saturday night was that we had lost, and that there had been several sendings-off and unsavoury incidents. It was the Sunday before the real horrors became apparent and a couple of days later before we saw on TV the dreadful things that had happened.

One would have to be naïve to say that Celtic were the injured innocents. One of the reasons why this game should not have been played was that players were carrying grievances from the last two games and vendettas were the order of the day. The tackle on Jimmy Johnstone was unbelievably bad, but so too were the actions of John Hughes and Tommy Gemmell – the Gemmell one replayed by the BBC – and it remains a mystery why the blameless Bobby Lennox was sent off, but sent off he was, accompanied by a policeman with a sword.

Basically, Celtic lost it in several senses. They lost their discipline and, in so doing, lost the goodwill that they had earned in the summer from their brilliant play in the European Cup. It was a shameful, shameful time for the club, and the directors thought so as well for every player was fined £250. That was stupid as well, for it included John Fallon, the reserve goalkeeper who had never fouled anyone and had played brilliantly in both games, having been called on to do so at short notice after the number one goalkeeper had been seriously injured by a thug.

The Celtic View of the Wednesday after the game was upset and mystified. Written before the players came home, and relying, like everyone else, on the secondary sources of what little coverage there had been in the press, it could not understand why Bobby Lennox was sent off, but by implication seemed to admit that the other sendings-off were not entirely unjustified. And it summed up the feelings of most supporters when it said: "What can be said, without fear of contradiction, is that the vast majority of Celtic supporters are dismayed, not so much because Celtic did not win the glamorous title of World Club Championship as because they appeared to have lost the reputation which all concerned with the club, intimately or not, valued greatly – the reputation of being a disciplined team."

It was, all in all, an experience I preferred to forget about and to relegate to the back of my mind. The team flew back to face the flak of the press, but to their credit, they took it on the chin and set about picking up the pieces. The foreign trips of this autumn had ended in disaster, with a touch of Scottish self-destruction about the pair of them, but there was still a Scottish season to be played for. In case anyone had forgotten, the Scottish League Cup had been retained, and there was still the Scottish League and, in January, the Scottish Cup was due to begin.

It was clear, however, that Celtic were going to require a major effort if they were to recover. It had been a chastening autumn, and now as winter approached, they would have to regroup and quite simply, start winning games. The first one was at Airdrie.

Not everyone liked Airdrie, but there remained something very quaint about their odd strips with tiny numbers inside the V at the back, and the old pavilion in the corner. It was not dissimilar to the old Celtic Park one destroyed by fire in 1929, and very reminiscent of quite a few cricket pavilions. But this was not cricket weather, or anything like it.

There was something very Scottish about this day, with heavy rain and a huge Celtic crowd packing the inadequate enclosure at Broomfield. This was Scotland in November. The contrast between that and where they were a week earlier could not have been greater. The incessant rain made quite a few of us wonder about a postponement, something that would not have been the greatest disaster in the world for Celtic, but the weather had up to this point been quite dry and the pitch stood up to it very well. The pitch was heavy but if you are going to play football in Scotland, particularly the west of Scotland, that is something that you simply have to get used to.

Another thing that one has to get used to is the hardness of Scottish football. Granted, there was none of the spitting that the Argentinians indulged in, but there was no gentle treatment, as evidenced by the booking of an Airdrie player by referee JRP Gordon in the first minute for fouling John Hughes. Welcome back, Celtic.

Craig was ill, Lennox was injured and Johnstone was still suspended, so Celtic reverted to the Gemmell and O'Neill full-back combination, which had prevailed until last Hogmanay. Bobby Murdoch was moved to the forward line again, and the increasingly impressive Jim Brogan was given a game at right-half. Indeed it was Brogan who scored the first goal, and Murdoch the second. It was the boost that Celtic and their fans needed and I recall the impressive scarf-raising and flag-waving to show that we were all in this together. There was something very Scottish and very Celtic about all this, and a further boost to the team was given when Joe McBride came on in the second half to make his first meaningful appearance since the previous Christmas Eve, a day which now seemed half a lifetime ago, given all that had happened in this tumultuous year of 1967.

Two home games followed against Kilmarnock on the Wednesday and Falkirk on the Saturday. Both were 3-0 victories. On the Wednesday night, 30,000 (a very impressive crowd for a dismal Wednesday in November) turned up to show solidarity with the team on their first home game after South America, and this game also saw the return of Jimmy Johnstone after his suspension. Playing in all green, the team turned on a great performance. Johnstone was absolutely brilliant and virtually unplayable, the wonder being that Celtic did not score more goals against an under-strength and quite clearly overwhelmed Kilmarnock side. Gemmell missed a penalty, a Chalmers goal was mysteriously disallowed but eventually Auld, Hughes and Chalmers scored the goals which beat Kilmarnock.

Falkirk were next to appear. It was the sort of dull November day on which, in my view, league titles are won. The 33,000 cheered when they saw Joe McBride return for his first full game – or so we thought. Within two minutes, the luckless Joe was led off with a head wound, and Willie Wallace had to take his place. For a while, the play was stopped by a dog which ran on to the field – no-one seemed to know who it belonged to or how it got in – but then Steve Chalmers scored a remarkable goal which John Hughes might have had reason to be unhappy about. John shot for goal from about ten yards, and the ball looked as if it might be going in anyway, but Chalmers got his head on to this fierce drive and diverted it into the net. Chalmers scored again before half-time and a somewhat pedestrian and mundane second half was livened up only by a Hughes goal at the death.

Celtic had thus completed their first three games since South America with three victories. Rangers had been winning as well, however, and were three points ahead of Celtic (although we had a game in hand), but the important thing was that Celtic had returned to winning ways. We had two advantages over Rangers. One was that we had no more European distractions that year, and the other was the more basic one that, undeniably, we had a better team than Rangers. We had had our misfortunes, most of them self-inflicted in the autumn, but we were still there.

That night of our victory over Falkirk, however, saw an event which seemed to shake society to its roots and prove once and for all that there was a class born to rule and that socialism was the work of the devil! All this was according to the right-wing press and the Conservative Party, and it was all because the Labour government decided to devalue the pound from $2.80 to $2.40! The effect of this on most people was absolutely negligible, and if anything it was beneficial in that it made it easier to sell British goods abroad, but you would not have thought so from the hysterical reaction of "the British people", as *The Daily Express* loved to call the middle classes.

Words like "humiliation", "catastrophe" and "disaster" were bandied about and Prime Minister Harold Wilson was called the greatest traitor of all time, with suggestions that he was doing all this to deliberately weaken Great Britain in her dealings with the Soviet Union. Calls were made for his resignation on almost a daily basis in the House of Commons and elsewhere, and you would have thought that economic ruin was just round the corner. In fact, most people were still doing rather well out of the amiable man from Yorkshire with the Gannex raincoat and the pipe, and who still retained my respect and even my love for keeping us out of that horrendous Vietnam war, which seemed to be getting more pointless and more bloody every time you read about it.

Wilson said "the pound in your pocket has not been devalued" and was much pilloried for it, but what he said was substantially true. His Chancellor of the Exchequer, James Callaghan, (who would himself became Prime Minister a decade later) was unhappy about devaluation and offered to resign but was eventually bought off by a swap of jobs, becoming Home Secretary – and an able one he was as well. But it was a time when we had to face the righteous indignation of the well-heeled middle classes who were suffering such terrible deprivations as not being allowed to take any more than £50 out of the country when they went on holiday. Aw, dear! And they had to pay income tax as well!

My life continued pleasantly as a student. I enjoyed my Classics, reading Herodotus and Virgil's *Eclogues*, had loads of friends and was getting increasingly fond of the new lady. She studied French and German, was a bit middle class and would tend to side with the Conservatives in any argument, but she had a social conscience as well.

She could be a bit neurotic from time to time about her work, but she could be cheerful and happy sometimes as well. Ah yes, happy days.

Three Celtic players, Craig, Johnstone and Lennox, played for Scotland on November 22. It was a win, albeit a rather unsatisfactory 3-2 win over Wales, on a foggy night (there had been some doubt over the game a few hours before kick-off) before an unpleasant and unsupportive Scottish crowd. We had toyed with the idea of going but couldn't really afford it, and contented ourselves by listening to the game on the radio.

It was just as well that I didn't because I would have been very angry, not so much at the Scotland players as at the Scotland crowd, or rather the Rangers faction of it, who booed the Celtic players when they got the ball, particularly Jimmy Johnstone, who was subjected to fatuous chants of "Henderson! Henderson!", something that, apparently, embarrassed Willie Henderson himself. Eventually to the horror of the press who this time did not cover it up, they started chanting "Rangers! Rangers!" rather than "Scotland! Scotland!" It was appalling.

It was not, of course, the first time that this had happened, but it was no less dispiriting and, in my view, a major cause of Scotland's under-performing at Hampden. One thought, for example, of the World Cup game against Poland in 1965, when we lost two late goals, effectively making life very difficult for us if we wanted to qualify for the 1966 World Cup. That game was riddled with partisan, sectarian chanting from the Mount Florida End.

Scotland had in the 1960s a good coterie of players. There was no reason why they could not have done a great deal better than they did. They had their great moments, as at Wembley in April 1967, but too often failed to perform as well as they should have at Hampden. To a large extent, this was due to the voluble Rangers faction in the crowd, who turned on Celtic players and any Anglo whom they suspected of having some connection, however tenuous, with the Roman Catholic Church (or even worse, keeping a Rangers player out of the team) when things were going badly and even when things were going well. It was very dispiriting. Celtic supporters were often accused of being half-hearted in their support of Scotland. That was the reason.

It may have been a minority, but it was a noisy one. Many decent Rangers supporters were embarrassed at this, but it had gone on for a long time. Historically, it went back to the 1920s, when the Church of Scotland, to its shame, used to pass motions (pun certainly intended) at its General Assembly deploring Irish immigration as some sort of threat to the Scottish race. There was no such thing as the Scottish race, of course, and it remained a major source of puzzlement how educated people could associate themselves with this sort of balderdash, which was by no means dissimilar to what even more dangerous people were saying in Germany at the same time.

Rangers supporters at that time, in the years between the wars, sang songs like "The Bonnie Bonnie Banks of Loch Lomond" and "The Wells o Wearie" (a favourite, apparently, of no less a person that Willie Struth himself), with a few unpleasant add-on words about the Pope and Papists, and the general impression was that they were claiming Scotland for themselves. Rangers tried to distance themselves from the excesses of this, but there seemed little doubt that they had lit the torch for it with their wicked sectarian policies, which attracted all sorts of "head cases" to their cause. Once again, the parallel in Germany was a disturbing one.

But this was now the 1960s, and we would have hoped to see more progress made. The Labour Party in Scotland said nothing, terrified of losing votes, the Church of Scotland was gradually mellowing but still did not denounce sectarianism loudly enough, and one did get tired of reading in *The Glasgow Herald* obituaries of Church of Scotland ministers who, among other things, were great Robert Burns fans and could recite or sing "A Man's A Man For A' That" – but were still season ticket holders at Ibrox!

So much for that. I used to rant brilliantly about such things as a student with the unbridled passion that certainty and conviction of one's cause brings, but the main thing was that Celtic still had to win games. The next one was almost a home game for St Andrews University students – it was at Stark's Park, Kirkcaldy, the home of Raith Rovers. It was a fine opportunity to persuade some English students to come along and see the great Glasgow Celtic that I talked about endlessly.

Stark's Park had housed some great crowds in the old days when Raith Rovers had a good team (as they did in the 1920s and the 1950s), but on this occasion it really struggled to contain the huge Celtic support which swamped the turnstiles. The pushing and jostling to get into the ground was getting dangerous and the game had to be delayed for more than ten minutes. The weather was dry, at least, although a little on the cold side, but the pitch looked firm. Stark's Park now had two shelters behind each goal and what they called the "railway enclosure" on the opposite side of the field from the stand, that funny L-shaped structure. It had been opened on December 30, 1922 when Celtic, with men like Joe Cassidy and Andy McAtee on board, came to call.

It was the railway enclosure we found ourselves in. Underfoot were cinders, it was dark, there were holes in the roof (just like home, someone said, for the Jungle had holes too) and the whole structure creaked and shook disconcertingly whenever a train went past on the line immediately behind the enclosure.

But there was an atmosphere, and even a good atmosphere between the two sets of supporters, who exchanged banter and abuse with each other. The Raith supporters had adapted "The Wild Rover" song, so popular at the time, to

"... and its no, nay, never, no nay never no more!

Will you beat the Raith Rovers nay never, no more!"

Meanwhile, the Celtic fans were still off to Dublin in the green so that the bayonets could slash the Orange sash to the rattle of the Thomson gun!

Raith had just been promoted and played the game with a passion which unsettled Celtic. Indeed for the first half, one would have to say that the Rovers were the better side. Two things surprised me. One was that it was a game in which no-one had numbers on their backs. Celtic, of course, had theirs on their pants as they did in those days, and Raith Rovers had opted not to wear any at all, whether to "throw" their Celtic opponents or from the sheer eccentricity of manager Tommy Walker, one time of Hearts, no-one knew. This was permitted in 1967. The other thing that surprised us was the vitriol hurled at Willie Wallace, who had, of course, played for Raith Rovers at one time. But mercifully, there was nothing sectarian about it. Their objection seemed to be that he had abandoned Kirkcaldy for the large metropolis of Edinburgh to play for Hearts, then compounding the crime by moving to Glasgow.

It was a game from which Raith Rovers took a great deal of credit, not least from Jock Stein himself, who was full of praise for Tommy Walker's approach to the game. Tommy had been manager of Hearts when they were good with attacking players like Alfie Conn Sr, Willie Bauld, Jimmy Wardhaugh and Alec Young, and he clearly was trying to do the same with Raith Rovers. Sadly, he did not quite have the players at Kirkcaldy to back up this admirable attacking philosophy, but did at least make an effort to entertain the public. They gave the European champions as good as they got.

Eventually, Celtic broke the deadlock from the penalty spot after goalkeeper Bobby Reid had brought down John Hughes. Tommy Gemmell took it – we worried about that because he had missed a few of late – and scored off the bar. Still Raith fought and Ronnie Simpson, now apparently dropped from the Scotland international side, was called upon to save the day on several occasions, but Willie Wallace scored a second with a long-range shot and Celtic now took charge, even missing another penalty.

It was a hard-fought victory, however, and my English friends were very impressed by what they had seen. When we got back to St Andrews, we heard that Rangers had beaten Hibs – which was depressing – but the main talking point of that game was that both centre-forwards had been sent off for kicking lumps out of one another. In view of future events, it is worth noting who they were – the Rangers one was a chap called Alex Ferguson, and the Hibs one was a guy called Colin Stein (no relation to Jock), who would in a year's time jump ship and join Rangers.

The devaluation hoo-ha had now died down, and the farming community was in a state about foot and mouth disease. Fortunately, there was no wholesale slaughtering of sheep and cows, like there would be in 2001, but horse racing in the UK was cancelled for a while, and farmers kept threatening us with even higher prices for their produce.

The month of November finished on a quiet note for Celtic, forced to watch from the sidelines as other Scottish teams, Rangers and Hibs, progressed in Europe. All our competitive football that season would have to be played in Scotland. It remained a sore, sore point that the team had decided to play so badly on that awful night of September 20.

DECEMBER

· · · · · · ·

December brought cold weather, as it often does. November is not normally a desperately cold month with its rain, wind and fog, and ice and snow tend not to appear until December. This is what happened in 1967. There was a fall of snow (although, in truth, not very much) and it certainly was cold. At university, exams were approaching as well, but so too was the thought of the approaching Christmas and New Year holidays. My last exam was going to be Wednesday, December 13, and I would go home that night.

Never a great Christmas fan then (and certainly not now), I always found myself disappointed when it came, considering all the talk about it for weeks in advance. In 1967, Christmas was still a bit behind New Year in importance in Scotland, but it was slowly beginning to win the battle. For a long time in Scotland, several hundred years in fact, Christmas had actually been banned, such was the Presbyterian horror of people actually enjoying themselves!

In the 20th century it was celebrated – I always got something from Santa Claus and we had a Christmas dinner – but nothing like on the scale that it would be in England, or indeed in future years in Scotland. Christmas had only been a public holiday in Scotland since 1958, and the celebrations were distinctly low key. The cliché "Christmas is too commercialised" was beginning to be heard in 1967, but it was not as true as it was about to become.

We had long arguments about this, but I argued that the commercialisation of Christmas was a good thing in that, although it led to much profit for the capitalists, it nevertheless showed that the working classes since 1945 had gained for themselves enough money to make it possible for Christmas to *become* commercialised. But my family celebrated Christmas only to a limited extent and I always thought that Christmas was a huge anti-climax. It was a time for children, of course, so I felt that it would be churlish of me to say that I didn't enjoy Christmas. I was also aware, as I am now, that Christmas could be a horror story for so many people.

New Year was different. Wild Bacchanalian celebrations were the order of the day throughout Scotland. Drink was in plentiful supply and it really was something I enjoyed, going round people's houses and having a good time. There was the downside to it as well in the shape of hangovers and wakening up to the realisation that I had done or said things I should not have (particularly as far as young ladies were concerned) and which were to cause much embarrassment in the future. But everyone was the same.

Football certainly takes a dip in December. Crowds drop because the weather is worse and everyone has to do Christmas shopping. It also seems such an effort to go out to a game in the wind and the rain and the cold. The New Year fixtures almost come as a relief as they signal the year is on the turn and Christmas is past.

But back to early December 1967, and Celtic's first game of the last month of that eventful year was against Dundee United at Parkhead. Dundee United had, of course, given Celtic more than a little bother in 1966/67, beating us twice, and they were notorious for defending in depth on their visits to Glasgow. An additional source of interest was, of course, the presence of Davie Wilson, an ex-Rangers player, in the Dundee United ranks and a decent crowd of about 34,000 turned up to see the encounter.

For the neutral, it was a very good game indeed, but for us it was intensely frustrating. Celtic were playing in all green, for in those days the home team changed in the event of a colour clash, and Dundee United's strip of all white was considered to be too similar to the green and white hoops. Strange to relate and contrary to what we expected, Dundee United actually took the game to Celtic and what made it worse for us all was that Davie Wilson played brilliantly, leading us to wonder whether Rangers had made yet another of their many mistakes in letting him go prematurely. Ronnie Simpson was called upon several times to keep the visitors from scoring, but it would be a mistake to suggest that it was all one-sided, for John Hughes had several good runs for Celtic, without achieving the breakthrough. Half-time came with the game goalless, but it was in the second half that the fun really started.

Dundee United were playing with no particular strain on them, for they were under no real pressure in that even if they lost at Parkhead, it was not likely to be considered a disaster. The manager of a provincial club will not, after all, get the sack if he fails to win at Celtic Park. United started the second half looking as if they were about to sweep Celtic off the park, and put Ronnie Simpson under sustained pressure for some time. Ronnie was beaten on one occasion and needed Tommy Gemmell to clear the ball off the line.

It was getting too much for Willie Wallace. He had had some hard luck early in the game, and his frustration was seen when he bundled Tommy Miller (brother of Rangers' Jimmy Miller) out of play at one point, for which he was given a long talking-to by the referee, a Mr Greenlees of Lochgelly, in Fife, and a booking. (A "booking" meant one's name going into the referee's notebook, for this was before the days of yellow and red cards). Then Andy Rolland of United was booked for a vicious tackle on Gemmell, and while this was going on, some people on the terracings got frustrated as well for a few bottles and cans began to appear on the running track, and police were seen to dive into the crowd.

Hooliganism, we thought, we had eradicated – and at Celtic Park, too. It was, in fact, extremely rare to see it at home, and the hope was expressed that the miscreants would be severely dealt with. Contrary to the myth that Celtic supporters and the police do not like one another, the "polis" were actually cheered when they dragged out a few culprits.

After Wallace missed another chance, putting the ball past the post, Dundee United went ahead and it was Davie Wilson who scored with a fierce drive from outside the penalty box. Any depression was dispelled within a minute, when Bobby Murdoch was on hand to level things for Celtic. He shot, the goalkeeper parried it to Chalmers, the goalkeeper parried it again and, third time lucky, Murdoch scored. But the game continued at its frantic pace, and in a desperate effort to win the game, Stein brought on Joe

McBride in place of right-back Chris Shevlane, and put Wallace back to the right-back position.

This had the unfortunate effect of making Willie Wallace, famously adaptable and versatile, the direct opponent of Davie Wilson, who frankly, was too good for Willie in that position. Davie, clearly enjoying riling the Parkhead crowd, was not slow in giving the verbals to Willie either, and the powder keg eventually exploded when Davie was seen lying on the ground with Wallace in the vicinity. Very few people saw what actually happened, but those who did admit unanimously that Willie "laid one on him" or, as they say in Glasgow, "gave him a dull one". The referee, Mr Greenlees, was one of those who saw nothing but the linesman in front of the Jungle did, and after a long consultation, Wallace was summoned and the referee pointed to the pavilion.

Wallace himself claimed years later, in his book *Heart Of A Lion,* that he never touched him. "I threw a punch at him and Davie, the football super diver, was on the deck before I was halfway to his chin…," Wallace wrote. He also claims that he heard Jock Stein say that he (Wallace) deserved to get sent off because he missed Wilson! Nevertheless, by admitting that he threw a punch, Willie incriminated himself, for the actual throwing of the punch meant that Willie deserved a suspension.

Parkhead was in an uproar and one or two more supporters were removed, as more bottles and cans were hurled from behind the Railway End goal. Considering the low number of Dundee United supporters there – about 200 at most – there would have been no point in attacking them, but such was the mentality of the culprits that cans were thrown anyway at no-one at all, or even at Celtic supporters.

But there had been no injustice, however much Wilson, the man who once claimed that he had Rangers engraved on his heart, provoked and exaggerated the incident.

More importantly, very little time now remained and Celtic had to settle for a draw. It had been a very interesting and exciting game of football in spite of the unsavoury incidents at the end, but the bad news was that Rangers had scored a late winner against Airdrie and were thus now four points ahead of Celtic, admittedly with a game in hand.

December 2, 1967 was exactly the sort of day that Celtic did not need. Struggling to regain respectability and even credibility after the South American adventure, Celtic were once again portrayed as hooligans by the press, who enjoyed it all, however much their leader columns deplored the actions of a "mindless minority" and urged Celtic to take strong action against them. Strong action was certainly taken by the SFA against Willie Wallace for, after the following two games, he was banned on December 18 until January 5, ruling him out of the New Year game against Rangers. Effectively, he did not play again until January 20.

The Celtic View the following Wednesday had an odd piece by "Kerrydale" about newspapers giving accounts of football matches as if they were boxing matches, ending up with a "game played not so many miles from the centre of Glasgow" where a "player" was reprimanded by the referee but continued with "sly" attacks on the opposition, the goalkeeper in particular, and then was felled by an opponent, but "the fly fellow ended the game in as sprightly a fashion as he had begun it without even a caution to sully his fair name". Ah-ha! The key word is "fair", as in fair hair. Could this possibly be Davie Wilson referred to here?

Jock Stein, in the same edition, was angrier, condemning the trouble among spectators at the ground, and again, without mentioning a name, having a go at Willie Wallace for getting his marching orders when the team needed him. "Players who are ordered off cannot in any sense contribute to the goals-for total," Stein said. All in all, not a good day for Celtic, yet it was not the major sporting talking point in Scotland that night. That centred on another ordering off, this time an All Black called Colin Meads. His team were comfortably beating Scotland at Murrayfield but he saw fit to tackle a Scottish player using his feet rather than his hands, and he thus became the first rugby player to be sent off in an international since 1924. Such things did not happen at all often in rugby.

Celtic had a better day on December 9. Snow had fallen throughout Scotland, particularly in the east, enough to postpone Rangers' game at Dundee United and to give Celtic a chance to halve the points differential. Celtic managed to keep their game on by the deployment of some straw mats which kept the snow from reaching the pitch, and also kept the frost away. The opponents were Hearts who, it is fair to say, were having an up-and-down sort of season, but who could always be guaranteed to put up a good performance against Celtic. A good crowd of 36,000 appeared to see a Celtic team which included the welcome return of Jim Craig and Bobby Lennox, who had not featured since South America, even though, incongruously, they had both played for Scotland.

This time, the crowd saw a better Celtic performance, which was a little short of top-notch but satisfactory nevertheless. Hearts were in pre-Christmas mode and giving away early goals. George Fleming managed to head past his goalkeeper early in the game, then a few minutes later their centre-half Alan Anderson, who had impressed this season and was mentioned in the context of playing for Scotland, was caught in two minds and allowed Chalmers to run on and score.

Celtic were thus two up early on, and then the happy singing crowd saw a brilliant goal from Bobby Lennox. It was manufactured by his pal Jimmy Johnstone – the Likely Lads, as we called them, after the name of a sit-com of the time – whose understanding with Lennox was sometimes uncanny. Normally, we associated Lennox's goals with fast running on to a through ball, or a tap-in in a crowded penalty area, but not here. Johnstone beat a couple of men then cut one back to Lennox on the edge of the box. Lennox fired a tremendous shot in, giving Jim Cruickshank no chance.

Celtic were now three goals up and well on top. But Hearts pulled one back before half-time through Jim Fleming when Celtic took their foot off the pedal. This set up an excellent second half in which both teams came close on many occasions, but there was no further scoring. It was a great game, but on reflection, possibly one of the coldest that many of us have ever encountered. Nevertheless, the gap was now two points, and we reckoned that if Celtic could win their last three games in 1967, then beat Clyde on New Year's Day, January 2, when Rangers appeared, would give us an excellent opportunity to level things.

Celtic received due praise for the deployment of their straw mats, which were put back down again almost immediately after the last player left the pitch. This would protect the pitch for future games. Jock Stein, to his credit, always had a thing about playing the game whenever possible for he hated the idea of a fixture pile-up. Still more did he hate the idea of fans travelling to a game to find it off, as had happened the previous New Year, for example, at Ibrox, and his obsessions in this regard were much appreciated by fans like myself, who had to travel some considerable distance to see a game. On one famous occasion a few years later, when a Celtic game at Dens Park, Dundee was called off, Stein himself took up his position on the M80 just outside Glasgow to wave to supporters' buses and tell them to turn back.

One has to bear in mind that this was 1967, an era well before the instant communication of the internet or mobile phones, and normally when someone was on a train or a bus or in a car, they were incommunicado with the outside world until they arrived at their destination. Radio stations did occasionally give news, but they couldn't be relied upon and not everyone was within easy reach of a radio. It was not even unknown for radio stations to give false news if some prankster phoned in to say that a game was off or on.

Jock Stein, for all his faults, was very much a fans' man. "Football without fans in nothing" he would always say, and, of course, he was a fan himself, suddenly appearing unannounced to see Queen's Park v Alloa on a Tuesday night, for example, or driving long distances to see a game in England. Bertie Auld would always tell how Jock would open the dressing room window before a game to allow the players to hear the fans arriving – for they were the important people, the "life's blood of the game" (another of his favourite phrases).

The downside of all that, of course, was that he tended to have very little to talk about other than football. The wife of one of the players at that time used the word "boor" to describe him. That was hard, I felt, but unless you talked about football, it was often difficult to get him to talk about anything else, and it all came down to the fact that he was a football fan himself. He may have upset a few players in his time, but seldom did he deliberately upset the fans.

And the fans saw another great game next Saturday, this time at Dens Park, Dundee. By now, I was back home having completed the first term of my second year at St Andrews University. My folks were naturally delighted to see me and I had forgotten just how much my father talked about Celtic, past and present. But then again, so did I! It was nice to see old friends again and to catch up with local gossip – the usual stories about pregnancies, embezzlements, sackings and fights, and a cracker this time about an old school associate of mine, a Rangers man, being arrested at Ibrox for obscene singing, in particular the three add-on words at the end of "The Sash My Father Wore"!

He was actually not a bad guy, believe it or not, and when I met him he told me and the rest of the pub about how he had been a "guest" from the Saturday until the Monday morning when he was fined £5. The bed and breakfast was not great, however, for the policeman in charge of the food was a Celtic supporter who deliberately let their food get cold before he gave it to them. Another policeman also kept making weak jokes to them about "lodgings" and "lodgers" and how this wasn't the Orange or the Masonic Lodge! My friend, whom I actually sympathised with, warned me not to get caught singing any Irish songs, or else I might get similar treatment. As if I would!

He felt particularly bitter about "agents provocateurs". These were the policemen who had been working in plain clothes, if you can call wearing Rangers scarves and

the bunnets that they wore in the 1960s "plain clothes".
They had infiltrated the Den, as it was called, in the old
Ibrox enclosure where the Govan Stand is now and sang
along with the fans, until they came to the bad words, and
suddenly a few fans were grabbed and "taken away". This
was "pour encourager les autres", as the French would say.
So much for the police and the legal system co-operating
with Rangers fans.

However, I was becoming slowly more aware that my
home was now less and less my home, and that my real
domain was the university where I continued to love my
Latin and Greek, and where, of course, I now had a lady
friend who had not yet turned sour on me. She would duly
do so after she told her parents about me. They could just
about cope with me supporting the Celtic, but, hang it all,
I voted Labour as well. I even wanted the Americans out of
Vietnam, white supremacy stopped in Rhodesia and South
Africa and an end to nuclear bombs. No point in bringing
your daughter up as well as they had when she associated
with chaps like that, was there? How could they face the
church on Sunday? Mind you, that was just my side of the
story. The other side was that I was fanatical, paranoid,
obsessive and socially inept – just like most Celtic fans, I
suppose!

The day after I came home was BBC *Sportsview*'s Review
of the Year. Part of the show was in Glasgow and it involved
David Coleman giving Celtic the Team Award of the Year.
It was a fitting occasion, I felt, although maybe a little
spoiled by Coleman making Jock Stein rub shoulders with
Matt Busby, the manager of Manchester United, in the
hope (justified as it turned out) that Manchester United
would win the trophy in 1968 now that Celtic had started

something. Matt, a real Celtic fan, must have been a little embarrassed by all that. Once again, however, we felt a pang of regret about the events of September 20, and possibly more about the transfer of Pat Crerand in 1963 – something that remains an open wound.

All this was of little immediate concern, however. Far more important was the winning of two points at Dens Park on December 16. Celtic and Dundee had contested, as you will recall, the Scottish League Cup Final, a matter of seven weeks ago. Given all that happened in the meantime, it seemed more like a lifetime. The League Cup Final was a game in which the supporters of both sides were almost punch-drunk by the amount of goals scored. This one was the same – for both Celtic and Dundee were attacking teams, and the defending was shocking – but the result was even closer than the League Cup Final.

The weather was cold, but 23,000 were at Dens Park – something which pushed its capacity – with long queues to get in. The queues were caused by the incompetence of Dundee FC and their reluctance to open all their turnstiles rather than anything else. Those who were late missed Billy McNeill scoring the first goal, then after George McLean had pulled one back, Celtic scored three through Lennox, Johnstone and Wallace, all in such quick succession that it was difficult to recall in which order the goals were scored. Jocky Scott then pulled one back for Dundee, but the 4-2 scoreline in favour of Celtic at half-time was a fair reflection on the play, as the thunderous reception given by the Celtic fans clearly indicated.

When Willie Wallace (this was his last game before his suspension) scored again early in the second half, that seemed to be that. Celtic were far ahead, but made the potentially fatal mistake of pushing forward for even more goals. Possibly they were running out of steam, possibly the Dundee defence had learned how to cope with Lennox and Johnstone, but no more goals came, at least not at that end. Fifteen minutes remained when Irish international Billy Campbell scored for Dundee, and then Dundee, having acquired a second wind, took over. Four minutes remained when Sam Wilson scored a fourth goal, and the final few minutes were spent in severe anxiety, recalling to many fans like myself another occasion nearly six years earlier across the road at Tannadice when a 5-1 lead became 5-4.

When referee Mr Patterson of Bothwell blew for full time, there was a huge sigh of relief followed by a genuine and spontaneous burst of applause for a great game of football, with even a few handshakes exchanged by supporters of each side. Celtic supporters, having won, were able to be magnanimous and Dundee supporters were genuinely pleased by the performance of their own side. As one of them said to me: "We only play well against Celtic." It was indeed true. Dundee had inflicted some horrors on their fans this season, and were uncomfortably near the bottom of the table.

Mind you, it must be said that Celtic supporters can be a miserable bunch sometimes. They are also incredibly fickle. When they were ahead, there were songs and cheers about "champions of Europe", but when the late goals went in, men like Gemmell and McNeill were booed and jeered. "This'll never dae, Cellic," was now the cry. There is, of course, and always has been among Celtic supporters, a group who are never happy unless they are unhappy. How that group of people coped with Lisbon, I'll never know, but surely part of following a team lies in sticking with them and being faithful through and through. I was only half-joking when I said that, on the plane coming home from Lisbon, there would have been some Celtic supporters who said "that Jimmy Johnstone will never make it", "Billy McNeill? I don't know what they see in him!" and "Jock Stein simply hasn't got a clue".

So we walked back to the bus station, and I, at least, was lifted by the performance of the team, but the edge was taken away from it with the news from Ibrox. Rangers had actually succeeded in putting ten goals past the hapless Raith Rovers, who had nevertheless notched two themselves. This was bad news, for having played Raith Rovers three weeks earlier, they didn't seem all that bad, and the goal margin, allied to the fact that we had shipped four ourselves, meant that Rangers were now not only two points ahead but had a better goal average. Such things could upset us geeks and pedants, even though there were still 20 league games to go.

December in 1967 was often a sort of close season, as it were, with little midweek football being played and the Saturday games attracting smaller attendances than might have been the case otherwise. This was because of the imminence of Christmas and other factors. European football certainly had to stop because so many countries in central Europe suffered real winter, being so far from the sea. But there was no close season at St Andrews University, some of whose departments had the idea of giving you class exams when you got back in January. I was almost glad about that, for it gave me something to do. Otherwise Christmas could have been a boring time, especially the run-in to Christmas.

The hit song at the moment was a strange one from the Beatles called "Hello, Goodbye". It had a nice harmony to it, I suppose, but didn't really say very much. Had it been anyone other than the Beatles, it would never have been heard of. Cruel people likened it to Celtic and the European Cup, which they had said Hello to in May and then Goodbye to in October. My favourite that December (although I was much jeered at for saying so) was a song by Des O'Connor called "Careless Hands", but then again my taste in pop music was unorthodox to say the least. And even that song was likened to Celtic, who let the European Cup slip from their hands after having an all-too-brief hold on it.

On December 21, Davie McLean died. Davie, you will remember, was the ex-Celt whom I had met, all too briefly, in the summer, and his passing was much mourned at Forfar Athletic's game against St Mirren, where there was a well-observed minute's silence for a man whose career had been quite remarkable. How I now bitterly regretted not cultivating him a little more when I had the opportunity. Following the death of Jimmy "Napoleon" McMenemy in 1965, he was virtually the only man of that great era left, and I'm sure I could have learned a great deal from the genial Davie. He certainly never lost his love for "the Celtic", as he kept calling them, and only a few days before his death, he had been at Dens Park to see Dundee v Celtic. (He had, of course, played with distinction for both teams.) It was so appropriate that his last football match had been such a great game and a victory for Celtic. His younger brother, George, had also been a professional football player who had played mainly for Bradford, and in his latter days ran a chip shop in Forfar.

Celtic were at Cappielow on December 23 to play Greenock Morton. The pitch was rain-soaked and heavy (this was Greenock, remember), and Jock Stein, having had a good look at the pitch first, made the decision to bring in Joe McBride, in danger of becoming "the forgotten man" of Celtic Park since his injury at Aberdeen exactly a year earlier, to play the difficult team that was Morton. A tough game was expected and that was what happened. Although the score was 4-0 in favour of Celtic at the end, with Joe McBride scoring a hat-trick, the scoreline is, in fact, slightly misleading for three of Celtic's goals came in the last 15 minutes, when Morton began to tire. McBride scored early on, but then Morton fought back and it was an anxious second half until Celtic broke away and put the game out of sight.

Rangers beat Kilmarnock 4-1 at Ibrox that day, so it was still Rangers ahead by two points, and thus we spent Christmas. It was becoming clear that the game on Tuesday, January 2, 1968 at Celtic Park was to be a vital one, but also that Celtic were slowly becoming favourites for that match. We had expected that Rangers might suffer a mini collapse under new manager David White, but that had not happened yet. Indeed everything was upbeat down Ibrox way, their supporters were chirpy and they were playing competently. They had perhaps, on the surface at least, recovered from their trauma of 1967. Or had they? 1968 would prove to be quite a year.

Thirty-six thousand were at Celtic Park to see the last game of 1967 against Dunfermline. Dunfermline were the team most likely to be the third force in Scotland, but they had never quite broken through as yet, with only their triumph in the 1961 Scottish Cup to show for what they had achieved, although they had also lost to Celtic in the 1965 Scottish Cup Final. For a provincial outfit, they were doing very well and, frankly, deserved a bigger support than they got. A good game was expected, and indeed Celtic turned on their best form. The final score was 3-2 but that was only because Dunfermline scored with a penalty kick in the last minute to make the scoreline more respectable.

Celtic were again without Lennox, who had come home from South America with various complaints, but his replacement was Steve Chalmers and it was Chalmers who scored two of Celtic's goals, the other one coming from McNeill. While the score was still 3-1, Dunfermline had their centre-half Roy Barry sent off after a clash with Bertie Auld. Bertie was by no means innocent, but needed attention from the trainer before he could resume.

And so ended Celtic playing in 1967. A great cheer greeted the final whistle. A lot of it was relief at the gaining of another two points, but there was also an element of thank you to the club and the players for what they had done in the past year. It had been a remarkable 12 months, without a shadow of a doubt the most momentous year in the 80-year history of the club.

Leaving aside the fact that all the Scottish domestic trophies were in our possession, May 25 was indeed, in the words of the song, the best day of our lives. But then there was Real Madrid as well, as if to prove that it was no fluke. The autumn was less good, and one would like to know exactly what the problem was with that "seven days from Hell" in September, particularly the uncharacteristic blow-up on September 20 against Dinamo Kiev. Complacency? Taking the Ukrainians too easily? Just too many players having a bad day? Yet what was undeniable was that they had experienced really bad luck in Kiev, with questionable refereeing (not that that is an unusual problem abroad), and then there had been that tournament in South America which, in retrospect, we would have been better off having nothing to do with. But then, following the trauma of that experience, there had been a comeback, with the team not playing at their absolute best but nevertheless well enough to make one feel reasonably optimistic about 1968.

Jock Stein had made sure that he was indeed immortal, as Bill Shankly had famously said to him at Lisbon, and the players were now well known all over the world. Maybe a few got too big for their boots on the field, (hence, perhaps, the Dinamo Kiev horror), but they all remained humble off it. They were just really a bunch of young Scotsmen, all born within a few miles of Glasgow. Padraig Pearse said of the patriots after the Easter Rising: "They have redeemed Dublin from many shames and made her name splendid among the names of nations." The Lisbon Lions did exactly the same for Glasgow and Scotland.

Hogmanay was a Sunday. It was good to reflect on how much had happened in the past 12 months. We had all moved on in our lives, some forwards, some regrettably backwards, but there can be little doubt that we had all been given a huge boost and lift by the events of May 25. How great it was to see every TV programme reviewing the events of 1967 include the Lisbon experience, and I have lost count of the amount of times I saw the Gemmell and Chalmers goals. The pedants and the detractors could say that Gemmell's goal was technically offside because of several Celtic forwards being ahead of the defence, but only the most finicky of officials could say that anyone could "interfere with play" with a shot of that speed hurtling past them.

And then Stevie Chalmers. As we sipped my dram on Hogmanay, we toasted Stevie in particular, my father and I reminiscing about that awful day in 1963 at Tannadice Park, when he was subjected to the worst filth I would ever want to hear. He was having a bad day, he was out of position on the left wing, nothing would happen for him, and a pack of cretins and louts gave him hell – and these were meant to be Celtic supporters. I recall my tears of frustration that day for one of the game's great gentlemen, but now I was shedding tears of a different sort for that charming and unpretentious man. I wonder if those responsible ever regretted their behaviour that day. After all, not many players score a winning goal in a European Cup Final. He can't have been all that bad a player.

The bells came, Andy Stewart sang on the TV to welcome in 1968. 1967 was at an end and we would never see anything like it again.